HAMMOND®

Family Reference

WORLD ATLAS

DOUBLEDAY & COMPANY, INC.

GARDEN CITY   NEW YORK

Contents

GAZETTEER-INDEX OF THE WORLD

ABBREVIATIONS

Aust.	—Australian	I.	—Island	Rep.	—Republic	U.K.	—United Kingdom
Br.	—British	Is.	—Islands	S.	—South	U.S.A.	—United States of
Cond.	—Condominium	It.	—Italian or Italy	S. Afr.	—South Africa		America
Den.	—Danish or Denmark	N.	—North	Sp.	—Spain or Spanish	U.S.S.R.	—Union of Soviet
E.	—East	Neth.	—Netherlands	sq. mi.	—square miles		Socialist Republics
Eq. Guin.	—Equatorial Guinea	N.Z.	—New Zealand	S.S.R.	—Soviet Socialist Republic	W.	—West
Fr.	—France or French	pen.	—peninsula	Terr.	—Territory		
Fr. Poly.	—French Polynesia	Port.	—Portugal or Portuguese	Trust.	—Trust Territory		

Country	Area (Square Miles)	Population	Index Ref.	Plate No.
Afghanistan	250,775	19,280,000	A 2	48
Africa	11,707,000	431,900,000		62–65
Alabama, U.S.A.	51,609	3,665,000		104–105
Alaska, U.S.A.	586,412	382,000		106–107
Albania	11,100	2,482,000	E 5	35
Alberta, Canada	255,285	1,838,037		96–97
Algeria	919,591	16,776,000	G 5	62
American Samoa	76	30,000	K 7	56
Andorra	188	26,558	G 1	27
Angola	481,351	6,761,000	K14	64
Antarctica	5,500,000			11
Antigua and Dependencies (Br.)	171	73,000	G 3	77
Argentina	1,072,070	23,983,000		70
Arizona, U.S.A.	113,909	2,270,000		108–109
Arkansas, U.S.A.	53,104	2,109,000		110–111
Armenian S.S.R., U.S.S.R.	11,506	2,491,900	F 6	37
Ascension I., St. Helena	34	1,146	D13	64
Asia	17,128,500	2,535,333,000		42–43
Australia	2,967,909	13,684,900		58–59
Australian Capital Terr.	939	204,200	H 7	59
Austria	32,375	7,540,000	B 3	32
Azerbaidzhan S.S.R., U.S.S.R.	33,436	5,117,100	G 6	37
Azores, Portugal	902	275,900	B 4	62
Bahamas	5,382	197,000	C 1	76
Bahrain	240	300,000	F 4	44
Balearic Islands, Spain	1,936	558,287	H 3	27
Bangladesh	55,126	82,900,000	G 4	48
Barbados	166	253,620	G 4	77
Belgium	11,781	9,813,000	C 6	20
Belize	8,867	122,000	B 1	78
Benin	43,483	3,200,000	G10	62
Bermuda (Br.)	21	52,000	G 2	77
Bhutan	18,147	1,200,000	G 3	48
Bismarck Arch., Papua New Guinea	18,976	209,051	E 6	56
Bolivia	424,163	4,804,000	G 7	68
Bophuthatswana, S. Africa	15,571	1,174,200	M17	65
Botswana	224,764	700,000	L16	65
Brazil	3,284,426	90,840,000		69,71
British Columbia, Canada	366,255	2,466,608		98–99
British Indian Ocean Terr.	29	600	L10	43
Brunei	2,226	155,000	E 4	54
Bulgaria	42,823.	8,800,000	G 4	34
Burma	261,789	31,240,000	A 2	53
Burundi	10,747	4,100,000	N12	65
California, U.S.A.	158,693	21,520,000		112–113
Cambodia	69,898	8,110,000	D 4	53
Cameroon	183,568	6,600,000	J10	62
Canada	3,851,809	22,992,604		84–85
Canal Zone (U.S.A.)	647	44,650	E 3	79
Canary Islands, Spain	2,808	1,170,224	B 4	26
Cape of Good Hope, South Africa	261,705	2,794,873	L18	65

Country	Area (Square Miles)	Population	Index Ref.	Plate No.
Cape Verde	1,557	302,000	N 5	9
Caroline Is., Terr. of the Pacific Islands	463	54,563	E 5	56
Cayman Is. (Br.)	100	10,652	B 3	76
Celebes, Indonesia	72,986	7,665,000	G 6	55
Central African Empire	236,293	1,800,000	K10	63
Central America	197,575	19,800,000		78–79
Ceylon (Sri Lanka)	25,332	14,000,000	E 7	49
Chad	495,752	4,178,000	K 8	63
Channel Is. (Br.)	74	128,000	E 6	17
Chatham Is., N. Z.	372	716	J10	56
Chile	292,257	8,834,820		70
China (mainland)	3,691,000	853,000,000		50–51
China (Taiwan)	13,971	16,426,386	K 7	51
Christmas I., Aust.	52	3,032	O11	43
Cocos Is., Aust.	5.4	604	N11	43
Colombia	439,513	21,117,000	F 3	68
Colorado, U.S.A.	104,247	2,583,000		114–115
Comoros	719	266,000	P14	65
Congo	132,046	1,400,000	J12	64
Connecticut, U.S.A.	5,009	3,117,000		116–117
Cook Is. (N.Z.)	91	17,046	K 7	56
Corsica, France	3,352	269,831	A 6	25
Costa Rica	19,575	1,800,000	E 5	79
Crete, Greece	3,218	483,075	G 8	35
Cuba	44,206	8,589,000	B 2	76
Curaçao, Netherlands Antilles	182	196,170	E 4	77
Cyprus	3,473	640,000	E 5	46
Czechoslovakia	49,373	14,900,000	D 2	32
Daito Is., Japan	17	2,359	M 6	51
Delaware, U.S.A.	2,057	582,000		139
Denmark	16,629	5,065,313	E 9	19
District of Columbia, U.S.A.	67	702,000	B 5	138
Djibouti	8,880	250,000	P 9	63
Dominica	290	70,302	G 4	77
Dominican Republic	18,704	4,188,000	D 3	77
Ecuador	109,483	6,194,000	E 4	68
Egypt	386,659	37,900,000	M 6	63
El Salvador	8,260	3,480,000	C 4	78
England, U.K.	50,516	46,417,600		17
Equatorial Guinea	10,831	320,000	H11	62,64
Estonian S.S.R., U.S.S.R.	17,413	1,357,000	C 3	36
Ethiopia	471,776	27,946,000	O 9	63
Europe	4,057,000	666,116,000		14–15
Faerøe Is., Den.	540	39,000	D 2	14
Falkland Is. & Dependencies (Br.)	6,198	1,905	H14	71
Fiji	7,055	569,468	H 7	56
Finland	130,128	4,729,000	O 5	18
Florida, U.S.A.	58,560	8,421,000		118–119
France	210,038	53,300,000		24–25
French Guiana	35,135	51,000	K 3	69
French Polynesia	1,544	135,000	M 7	56

4

Country	Area (Square Miles)	Population	Index Ref.	Plate No.
Gabon	103,346	526,000	J12	64
Gambia	4,127	524,000	C 9	62
Georgia, U.S.A.	58,876	4,970,000		120–121
Georgian S.S.R., U.S.S.R.	26,911	4,688,000	F 6	37
Germany, East (German Democratic Republic)	41,768	16,850,000		22–23
Germany, West (Federal Republic of)	95,985	61,846,000		22–23
Ghana	92,099	9,900,000	F10	62
Gibraltar (Br.)	2	30,000	D 4	26
Gilbert Islands (Br.)	354	47,711	H 6	56
Great Britain & Northern Ireland (United Kingdom)	94,399	56,076,000		16–17
Greece	50,944	9,046,000	F 6	35
Greenland (Den.)	840,000	54,000	B12	10
Grenada	133	96,000	G 6	77
Guadeloupe and Dependencies (Fr.)	687	332,000	F 3	77
Guam (U.S.A.)	212	111,000	E 4	56
Guatemala	42,042	5,348,000	B 3	78
Guinea	94,925	4,500,000	D 9	62
Guinea-Bissau	13,948	517,000	C 9	62
Guyana	83,000	763,000	J 2	69
Haiti	10,694	4,969,000	D 3	76
Hawaii, U.S.A.	6,450	887,000		122
Holland (Netherlands)	15,892	13,800,000	E 4	20
Honduras	43,277	2,751,000	D 3	78
Hong Kong (Br.)	403	4,400,000	J 7	51
Hungary	35,919	10,590,000	E 3	33
Iceland	39,768	220,000	C 2	14
Idaho, U.S.A.	83,557	831,000		123
Illinois, U.S.A.	56,400	11,229,000		124–125
India	1,269,339	605,614,000		48–49
Indiana, U.S.A.	36,291	5,302,000		126–127
Indonesia	788,430	131,255,000		54–55
Iowa, U.S.A.	56,290	2,870,000		128–129
Iran	636,293	32,900,000	F 3	45
Iraq	172,476	11,400,000	D 3	44
Ireland	27,136	3,109,000	B 4	17
Israel	7,847	3,459,000		47
Italy	116,303	56,110,000		28–29
Ivory Coast	127,520	6,673,013	E10	62
Jamaica	4,411	1,989,000	C 3	76
Japan	145,730	112,200,000		52
Java, Indonesia	48,842	69,323,000	K 2	55
Jordan	37,737	2,700,000		47
Kalâtdlit-Nunât (Greenland)	840,000	54,000	B12	10
Kampuchea (Cambodia)	69,898	8,110,000	D 4	53
Kansas, U.S.A.	82,264	2,310,000		130–131
Kazakh S.S.R., U.S.S.R.	1,048,300	14,185,000	G 5	38
Kentucky, U.S.A.	40,395	3,428,000		132–133
Kenya	224,960	13,300,000	O11	65
Kirgiz S.S.R., U.S.S.R.	76,641	2,933,000	H 5	38
Korea, North	46,540	17,000,000	C 2	52
Korea, South	38,175	34,688,079	C 3	52
Kuwait	6,532	1,100,000	E 4	44
Laos	91,428	3,500,000	D 3	53
Latvian S.S.R., U.S.S.R.	24,595	2,365,000	B 3	36
Lebanon	4,015	3,207,000	F 6	46
Lesotho	11,720	1,100,000	M17	65
Liberia	43,000	1,600,000	E10	62
Libya	679,358	2,500,000	K 6	62–63
Liechtenstein	61	25,000	J 3	31
Lithuanian S.S.R., U.S.S.R.	25,174	3,129,000	B 3	36
Louisiana, U.S.A.	48,523	3,841,000		134–135
Luxembourg	999	358,000	H 8	20
Macao (Port.)	6.2	300,000	H 7	51
Madagascar	226,657	7,700,000	R15	65
Madeira Is., Portugal	307	249,300	A 2	26
Maine, U.S.A.	33,215	1,070,000		136–137
Malawi	45,747	5,100,000	N14	65
Malaya, Malaysia	50,806	9,000,000	C 7	53
Malaysia	128,308	12,368,000	C–F 4	54
Maldives	115	136,000	L 9	43
Mali	464,873	5,800,000	E 9	62
Malta	122	319,000	E 7	29
Man, Isle of (Br.)	227	59,000	D 3	17
Manitoba, Canada	251,000	1,021,506		92–93
Mariana Is., Terr. of the Pacific Islands	182	11,827	E 4	56
Marquesas Is., Fr. Poly.	492	5,174	N 6	56
Marshall Is., Terr. Pac. Is.	69	19,328	H 4	56
Martinique (Fr.)	425	341,000	G 4	77
Maryland, U.S.A.	10,577	4,144,000		138–139
Massachusetts, U.S.A.	8,257	5,809,000		140–141
Mauritania	452,702	1,318,000	D 8	62
Mauritius	790	899,000	S19	65
Mayotte (Fr.)	144	40,000	P14	65
Mexico	761,601	50,900,000		80–81
Michigan, U.S.A.	58,216	9,104,000		142–143
Midway Is. (U.S.A.)	2	2,220	H 3	56
Minnesota, U.S.A.	84,068	3,965,000		144–145
Mississippi, U.S.A.	47,716	2,354,000		146–147
Missouri, U.S.A.	69,686	4,778,000		148–149
Moldavian S.S.R., U.S.S.R.	13,012	3,823,000	C 5	37
Monaco	368 acres	23,610	G 6	25
Mongolia	606,163	1,500,000	E–H 2	50–51
Montana, U.S.A.	147,138	753,000		150–151
Montserrat (Br.)	40	12,302	G 3	77
Morocco	241,224	18,000,000	E 5	62
Mozambique	308,641	9,300,000	O15	65
Namibia (South-West Africa, S. Afr.	317,827	883,000	K16	64–65
Natal, S. Afr.	33,578	4,315,847	N17	65
Nauru	7.7	8,000	G 6	56
Nebraska, U.S.A.	77,227	1,553,000		152–153
Nepal	54,663	12,900,000	E–F 3	49
Netherlands	15,892	13,800,000	E 4	20
Netherlands Antilles	390	223,558	E 4	77
Nevada, U.S.A.	110,540	610,000		154
New Britain, Papua New Guinea	14,098	138,689	F 6	56
New Brunswick, Canada	28,354	677,250	C 3	86
New Caledonia & Dependencies (Fr.)	7,335	136,000	G 8	56
Newfoundland, Canada	156,185	557,725	J 4	86
New Hampshire, U.S.A.	9,304	822,000		155
New Hebrides (Br.-Fr. Cond.)	5,700	97,468	G 7	56
New Jersey, U.S.A.	7,836	7,336,000		156–157
New Mexico, U.S.A.	121,666	1,168,000		158–159
New South Wales, Aust.	309,433	4,847,800	H 6	59
New York, U.S.A.	49,576	18,084,000		160–161
New Zealand	103,736	3,121,904	M 7	59
Nicaragua	45,698	1,984,000	E 4	78
Niger	489,189	4,634,000	H 8	62
Nigeria	379,628	83,800,000	H10	62
Niue (N. Z.)	100	2,992	K 7	56
Norfolk I., Aust.	13.3	1,870	G 8	56
North America	9,363,000	314,000,000		74–75
North Carolina, U.S.A.	52,586	5,469,000		162–163
North Dakota, U.S.A.	70,665	643,000		164–165
Northern Ireland, U.K.	5,452	1,537,200	G 3	17
Northern Territory, Aust.	520,280	98,400	E 3	58
Northwest Territories, Canada	1,304,903	42,609	E–J 3	84–85
Norway	125,053	4,027,000	F 6	18
Nova Scotia, Canada	21,425	828,571		86–87
Oceania	3,292,000	21,500,000		56
Ohio, U.S.A.	41,222	10,690,000		166–167
Oklahoma, U.S.A.	69,919	2,766,000		168–169
Oman	120,000	800,000	G 5	45
Ontario, Canada	412,582	8,264,465		90–91
Orange Free State, S. Afr.	49,866	1,744,798	M17	65
Oregon, U.S.A.	96,981	2,329,000		170–171
Orkney Is., Scotland	376	17,675	E 1	16
Pacific Is., Terr. of the (U.S. Trust)	707	120,000	D–G 5	56
Pakistan	310,403	72,370,000	B 3	48
Palau Is., Terr. Pac. Is.	184	12,291	D 5	56
Panama	29,209	1,444,000	G 6	79
Papua New Guinea	183,540	2,800,000	B 7	54
Paraguay	157,047	2,340,000	J 8	69,71
Pennsylvania, U.S.A.	45,333	11,862,000		172–173
Persia (Iran)	636,293	32,900,000	F 3	45
Peru	496,222	13,586,30	E 5	68
Philippines	115,707	43,751,000	H 4	55
Pitcairn Is. (Br.)	18	67	O 8	56
Poland	120,725	34,364,000		21
Portugal	35,549	8,825,000	B 3	26
Prince Edward I., Canada	2,184	118,229	F 3	87
Puerto Rico	3,435	2,712,033	G 2	77

5

Country	Area (Square Miles)	Population	Index Ref.	Plate No.
Qatar	4,247	150,000	F 4	45
Québec, Canada	594,860	6,234,445		88–89
Queensland, Aust.	666,991	2,015,300	G 4	59
Réunion (Fr.)	969	475,700	R20	65
Rhode Island, U.S.A.	1,214	927,000		141
Rhodesia (Zimbabwe Rhodesia)	150,803	6,600,000	M15	65
Rumania	91,699	21,500,000	G 3	34
Russian S.F.S.R., U.S.S.R.	6,592,812	133,913,000	D–R 4	38–39
Rwanda	10,169	4,241,000	N12	65
Sabah, Malaysia	28,460	633,000	F 4–5	54–55
St. Christopher-Nevis-Anguilla (Br.)	138	62,000	F 3	77
St. Helena & Dependencies (Br.)	162	6,438	E15	64
St. Lucia	238	101,100	G 4	77
St-Pierre & Miquelon (Fr.)	93.5	6,000	H 6	87
St. Vincent & Dependencies (Br.)	150	89,129	G 4	77
Sakhalin, U.S.S.R.	29,500	600,000	P 4	39
San Marino	23.4	19,000	D 2	28
São Tomé e Príncipe	372	80,000	H11	64
Sarawak, Malaysia	48,050	950,000	E 5	54
Sardinia, Italy	9,301	1,473,800	B 4	29
Saskatchewan, Canada	251,700	921,323		94–95
Saudi Arabia	829,995	7,200,000	D 4	44
Scotland, U.K.	30,414	5,261,000	D 2	16
Senegal	75,954	5,085,388	D 9	62
Seychelles	145	60,000	T 6	9
Shetland Is., Scotland	552	18,494	G 1	16
Siam (Thailand)	198,455	42,700,000	C 3	53
Sicily, Italy	9,926	4,680,715	D 6	29
Sierra Leone	27,925	3,100,000	D10	62
Singapore	226	2,300,000	E 6	53
Society Is., Fr. Poly.	677	81,487	L 7	56
Solomon Is.	11,500	196,708	G 6	56
Somalia	246,200	3,170,000	R11	63,65
South Africa	458,179	24,400,000	L18	65
South America	6,875,000	186,000,000		68–71
South Australia, Aust.	380,070	1,247,100	E 5	58
South Carolina, U.S.A.	31,055	2,848,000		174–175
South Dakota, U.S.A.	77,047	686,000		176–177
South-West Africa	317,827	883,000	K16	64–65
Spain	194,881	36,000,000		26–27
Sri Lanka	25,332	14,000,000	E 7	49
Sudan	967,494	18,347,000	M 9	63
Sumatra, Indonesia	164,000	17,345,000	C 6	54
Suriname	55,144	389,000	J 3	69
Svalbard, Norway	23,957	2,808	C 2	18
Swaziland	6,705	500,000	N17	65
Sweden	173,665	8,236,461	J 6	19
Switzerland	15,943	6,489,000		30–31
Syria	71,498	7,585,000	G 5	46
Tadzhik S.S.R., U.S.S.R.	55,251	2,900,000	G 6	38
Tahiti, Fr. Poly.	402	61,519	M 7	56
Tanzania	363,708	15,506,000	N13	65
Tasmania, Aust.	26,383	410,800	J 8	59
Tennessee, U.S.A.	42,244	4,214,000		178–179
Texas, U.S.A.	267,339	12,487,000		180–181

Country	Area (Square Miles)	Population	Index Ref.	Plate No.
Thailand	198,455	42,700,000	C 3	53
Tibet, China	471,660	1,270,000	C 5	50
Togo	21,622	2,300,000	G10	62
Tokelau (N.Z.)	3.9	1,603	J 6	56
Tonga	270	102,000	J 7	56
Transvaal, S. Afr.	109,621	10,971,521	N17	65
Trinidad & Tobago	1,980	1,040,000	G 5	77
Tristan da Cunha, St. Helena	38	292	O 7	9
Tuamotu Arch., French Polynesia	341	6,148	M 7	56
Tunisia	63,170	5,776,000	H 5	62
Turkey	300,946	40,284,000		46
Turkmen S.S.R., U.S.S.R.	188,455	2,158,000	F 6	38
Turks & Caicos Is, (Br.)	166	6,000	D 2	76
Tuvalu	10	5,887	H 6	56
Uganda	91,076	11,400,000	N11	65
Ukrainian S.S.R., U.S.S.R.	233,089	49,438,000	D 5	37
Union of Soviet Socialist Republics	8,649,490	258,402,000		36–39
United Arab Emirates	32,278	240,000	F 5	45
United Kingdom	94,399	56,076,000		16–17
United States of America land	3,536,855			
land and water	3,615,123	216,237,000		102–103
Upper Volta	105,869	6,144,013	F 9	62
Uruguay	72,172	2,909,000	J10	71
Utah, U.S.A.	84,916	1,228,000		182
Uzbek S.S.R., U.S.S.R.	173,591	11,963,000	G 5	38
Vatican City	116 acres	704	B 6	29
Venezuela	352,143	10,572,000	G 2	68
Vermont, U.S.A.	9,609	476,000		183
Victoria, Aust.	87,884	3,713,200	G 7	59
Vietnam	128,405	46,600,000	D 3	53
Virginia, U.S.A.	40,817	5,032,000		184–185
Virgin Is. (Br.)	59	10,484	H 1	77
Virgin Is. (U.S.A.)	133	62,468	H 1	77
Wake I. (U.S.A.)	2.5	437	G 4	56
Wales, U.K.	8,017	2,778,000	E 4	17
Wallis & Futuna (Fr.)	106	9,000	H–J 7	56
Washington, U.S.A.	68,192	3,612,000		186–187
Western Australia, Aust.	975,920	1,148,100	C 4	58
Western Samoa	1,133	159,000	J 7	56
West Virginia, U.S.A.	24,181	1,821,000		188–189
White Russian S.S.R., U.S.S.R.	80,154	9,522,000	C 4	37
Wisconsin, U.S.A.	56,154	4,609,000		190–191
World	57,970,000	4,240,700,000		8–9
Wyoming, U.S.A.	97,914	390,000		192
Yemen Arab Republic	77,220	5,600,000	D 7	44
Yemen, Peoples Democratic Republic of	111,101	1,700,000	E 7	44
Yugoslavia	98,766	21,520,000	C 3	34
Yukon Territory, Canada	207,076	21,836	C 3	84
Zaire	918,962	25,600,000	L12	65
Zambia	290,586	4,936,000	M14	65
Zimbabwe Rhodesia	150,803	6,600,000	M15	65

THE SOLAR SYSTEM

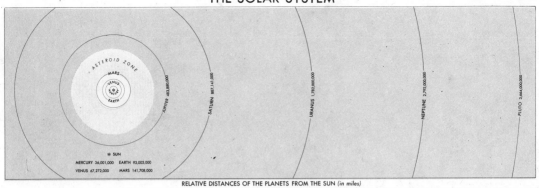

RELATIVE DISTANCES OF THE PLANETS FROM THE SUN (in miles)

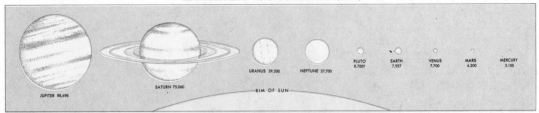

RELATIVE DIAMETERS OF THE PLANETS (in miles)

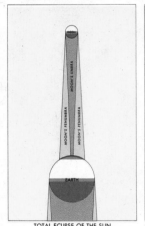

TOTAL ECLIPSE OF THE SUN

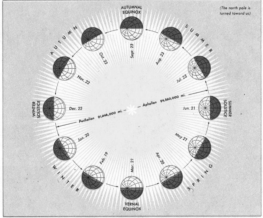

MONTHLY ILLUMINATION OF THE EARTH

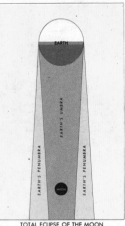

TOTAL ECLIPSE OF THE MOON

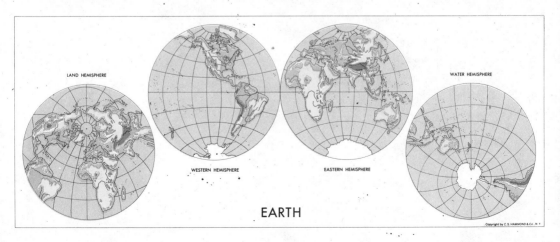

EARTH

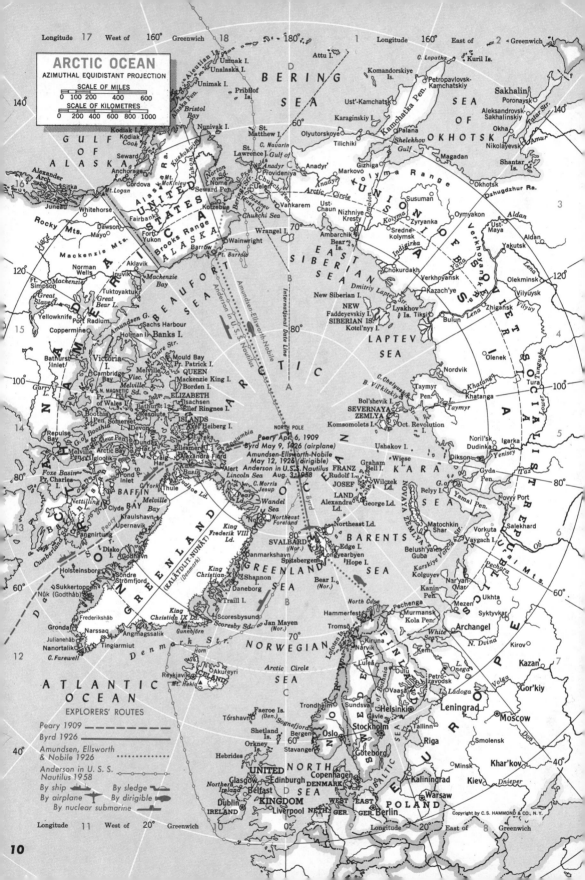

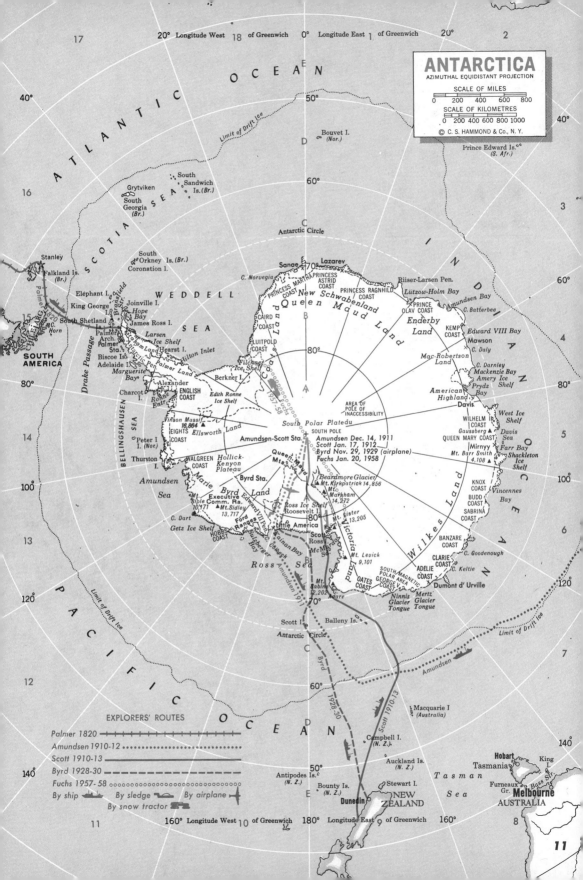

Map of
EUROPE
SCALE OF MILES

| 0 | 100 | 200 | 300 | 400 |

☆ Capitals of Countries
● Cities
━━━ Boundaries of Countries
┅┅┅ Other Boundaries
▲ Mountain Peaks

Mountains Highlands Lowlands Depression Water

Copyright by C. S. Hammond & Co., N.Y.

NORWEGIAN SEA

Reykjavik
ICELAND

Faeroe Islands
(Danish)

Shetland Islands
(British)

Orkney Islands

Trondheim

Bergen

Oslo

Göteborg

Hebrides

Scotland

Northern Ireland

Glasgow

GREAT

Skagerrak

Kattegat

NORTH SEA

DENMARK
Copenhagen

British Isles

IRELAND

Dublin

IRISH SEA

Liverpool

BRITAIN
England

London

Greenwich

Hamburg

NETHER-LANDS

The Hague

Amsterdam

EAST
Berlin

Oder

WEST
GERMANY

Brussels

BELGIUM

Bonn

English Channel

Le Havre

LUXEM-BOURG

Nantes

Seine R.

Paris

Loire River

Frankfurt

GERMANY

Prague

CZECHO-

Rhine R.

Danube

Munich

LIECHT.

Vienna

ATLANTIC OCEAN

Bay of
Biscay

FRANCE

SWITZER-LAND

Bern

AUSTRIA

Lyon R.

Bilbao

Bordeaux

Mt. Blanc

Milan

Trieste

Zagreb

Oporto

PYRENEES

Rhône

Genoa

Po River

Venice

YUG

Lisbon

Iberian

Madrid

SPAIN

Marseille

MONACO

ADRIATIC

PORTUGAL

Cape St. Vincent

Peninsula

ANDORRA

Barcelona

Corsica
(French)

Rome

SAN MARINO

ITALY

Valencia

Balearic Islands
(Spanish)

VATICAN CITY

Seville

Sardinia
(Italian)

Naples

GIBRALTAR (British)
Strait of
Tangier Gibraltar
Ceuta (Spanish)

Algiers

Palermo

Rabat

Melilla
(Spanish)

Tunis

Sicily
(Italian)

MOROCCO

AFRICA

ALGERIA

TUNISIA

MEDITERRANE

MALTA

Longitude West of Greenwich

12

EUROPE
LAMBERT AZIMUTHAL EQUAL AREA PROJECTION
SCALE OF MILES
0 100 200 300 400 500
SCALE OF KILOMETERS
0 100 200 300 400 500
Capitals of Countries
International Boundaries
Canals
© Copyright HAMMOND INCORPORATED, Maplewood, N. J.
BARENTS SEA
White Sea
Kolguyev I.
KANIN PEN.
KOLA PEN.
Murmansk
Archangel
Vorkuta
Salekhard
Nar'yan-Mar
Pechora
Mezen'
Ust-Tsil'ma
Northern Dvina
Onega
Kotlas
Syktyvkar
Nyandoma
Velikiy Ustyug
Petrozavodsk
L. Onega
L. Ladoga
Helsinki
(Helsingfors)
Vyborg
LENINGRAD
Gulf of Finland
Tallinn
ESTONIAN S.S.R.
Narva
L. Peipus
Riga
LATVIAN S.S.R.
LITHUANIAN S.S.R.
Kaunas
Vilna
Kaliningrad
Minsk
WHITE RUSSIAN S. S. R.
Pinsk
Brest
WARSAW
Vitebsk
Smolensk
Vologda
Rybinsk Res.
Cherepovets
Yaroslavl
Kostroma
Ivanovo
Kalinin
(Tver)
MOSCOW
(Moskva)
Gor'kiy
(Nizhniy Novgorod)
Dzerzhinsk
Balakhna
Kazan'
Kirov
(Vyatka)
Kotel'nich
Perm'
(Molotov)
Izhevsk
Sarapul
Berezniki
Kama
Sverdlovsk
Nizhniy Tagil
Chelyabinsk
Magnitogorsk
Zlatoust
Ufa
Kuybyshev
(Samara)
Ul'yanovsk
Orenburg
(Chkalov)
Aktyubinsk
Ural'sk
Saratov
Engel's
Penza
Tambov
Tula
Kaluga
Orel
Bryansk
Kursk
Voronezh
Michurinsk
Volgograd
(Stalingrad)
Tsimlyansk Res.
Astrakhan'
Gur'yev
Fort Shevchenko
Elista
Rostov
Taganrog
Zhdanov
Donetsk
Makeyevka
Kharkov
Kiev
Dnepropetrovsk
Zaporozh'ye
Krivoy Rog
Nikolayev
Kherson
Odessa
Kishinev
L'vov
UKRAINIAN S. S. R.
UNION OF SOVIET SOCIALIST REPUBLICS
RUSSIAN SOVIET FEDERATED SOCIALIST REPUBLIC
Sea of Azov
CRIMEA
Simferopol'
Sevastopol'
Yalta
Krasnodar
Novorossiysk
Maykop
Armavir
Pyatigorsk
Groznyy
Makhachkala
El'brus 18,481
Ordzhonikidze
Caucasus
Sochi
Sukhumi
Batumi
Tbilisi
GEORGIAN S.S.R.
ARMENIAN S.S.R.
AZERBAIDZHAN S.S.R.
Baku
Erivan
Leninakan
Nakhichevan'
CASPIAN SEA
G. of Kara Bogaz
Krasnovodsk
BLACK SEA
RUMANIA
Bucharest
Constanța
Galați
Brăila
Ploiești
Brașov
Cluj
Iași
BULGARIA
Sofia
Varna
Burgas
Plovdiv
ISTANBUL (Constantinople)
Bosporus
Sea of Marmara
Dardanelles
TURKEY
Ankara
(Angora)
Bursa
Eskişehir
İzmir
(Smyrna)
Konya
Adana
Kayseri
Sivas
Samsun
Sinop
Trabzon
Erzurum
IRAN
SYRIA
Aleppo
Latakia
CYPRUS
Nicosia
Larnaca
Athens
Crete
Rhodes
AEGEAN SEA
GREECE
Thessaloniki
FINLAND
L. Inari
Oulu
L. Oulu
Tampere
Turku
Vaasa
Kuopio
Tornio
Gulf of Bothnia
North Cape
Vadsö
Pechenga
(Petsamo)
Kandalaksha
Kirovsk
Kem'
Tobol'sk
Tyumen'
Kurgan
Troitsk
Kustanay
Ob'
Irtysh
Khanty-Mansiysk
Surgut
Berezovo
Ural
Emba
Temir
Chelkar
Volga
Don
Oka
Dnieper
Dnestr
Danube

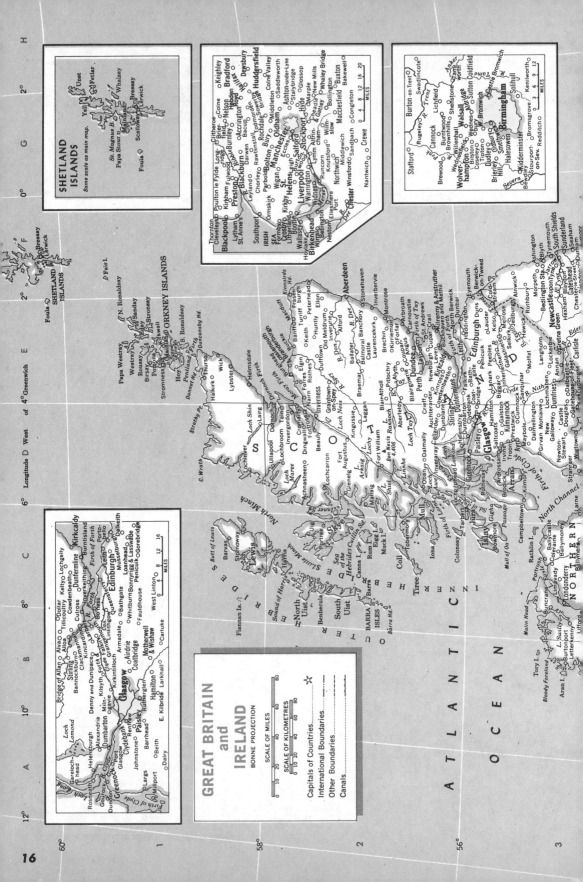

Copyright by C.S. HAMMOND & CO., N.Y.

17

NORWAY, SWEDEN, FINLAND and DENMARK

CONIC PROJECTION

SCALE OF MILES

SCALE OF KILOMETERS

Capitals of Countries .... ★
Administrative Centers .... ⊙
International Boundaries ....
Internal Boundaries ....
Canals ....

SUBDIVISIONS
Indicated by Numbers
Fylker in NORWAY
1 Akershus .... G 6
2 Vestfold .... G 7
3 Østfold .... G 7
4 Oslo .... G 7
5 Bergen .... D 6

Oslo is the administrative
center for Akershus and
Oslo Fylker; Bergen for
Hordaland and Bergen
Fylker.

Län in SWEDEN
6 Göteborg och
Bohus .... G 7
7 Västmanland ... K 7
8 Södermanland . K 7
9 Östergötland .... J 7
10 Malmöhus .... H 9
11 Kristianstad .... J 8

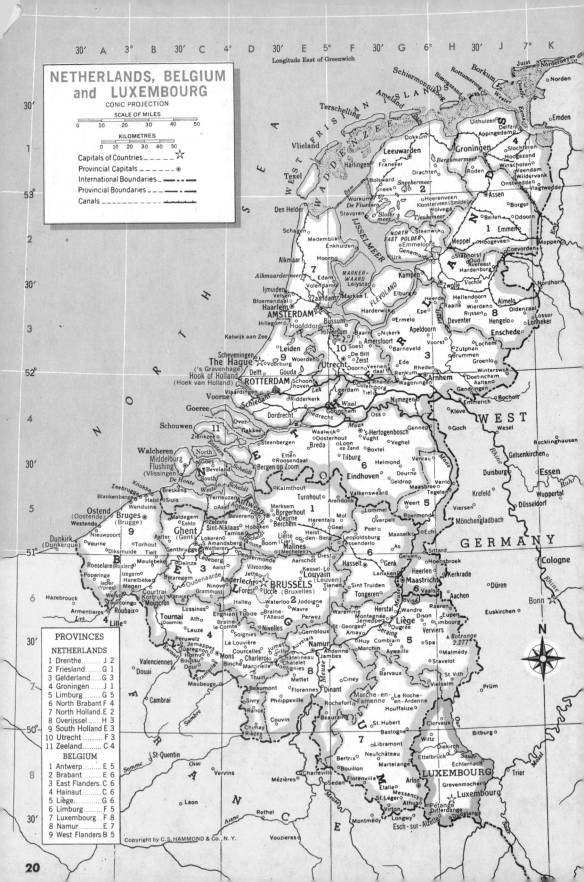

NETHERLANDS, BELGIUM and LUXEMBOURG

CONIC PROJECTION

SCALE OF MILES

0 10 20 30 40 50

KILOMETRES

0 10 20 30 40 50

Capitals of Countries .... ☆

Provincial Capitals .... ⊙

International Boundaries ....

Provincial Boundaries ....

Canals ....

PROVINCES

NETHERLANDS
1 Drenthe......... J 2
2 Friesland....... G 1
3 Gelderland...... G 3
4 Groningen....... J 1
5 Limburg......... G 5
6 North Brabant F 4
7 North Holland. E 2
8 Overijssel..... H 3
9 South Holland E 3
10 Utrecht .... F 3
11 Zeeland........ C 4

BELGIUM
1 Antwerp........ E 5
2 Brabant........ D 6
3 East Flanders.. C 6
4 Hainaut........ C 6
5 Liège.......... F 6
6 Limburg........ F 6
7 Luxembourg..... E 7
8 Namur.......... E 7
9 West Flanders B 5

20

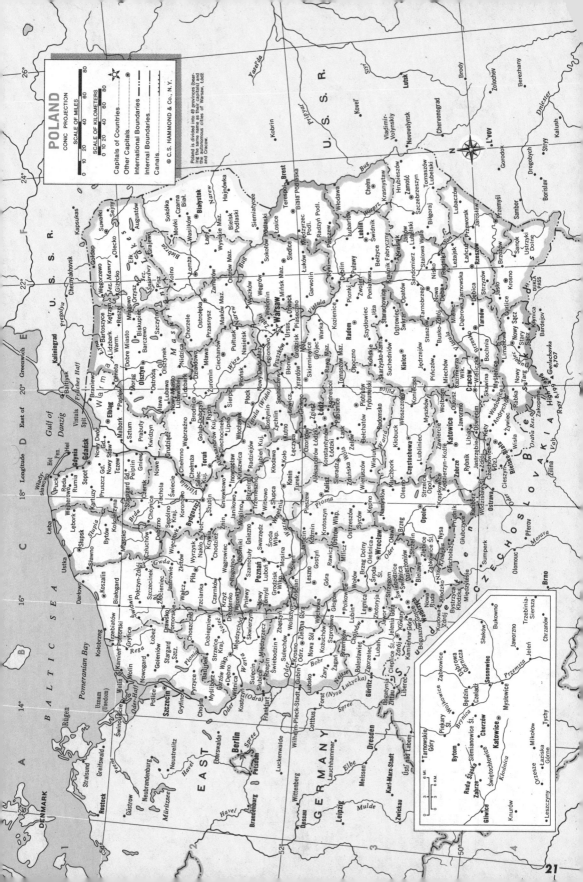

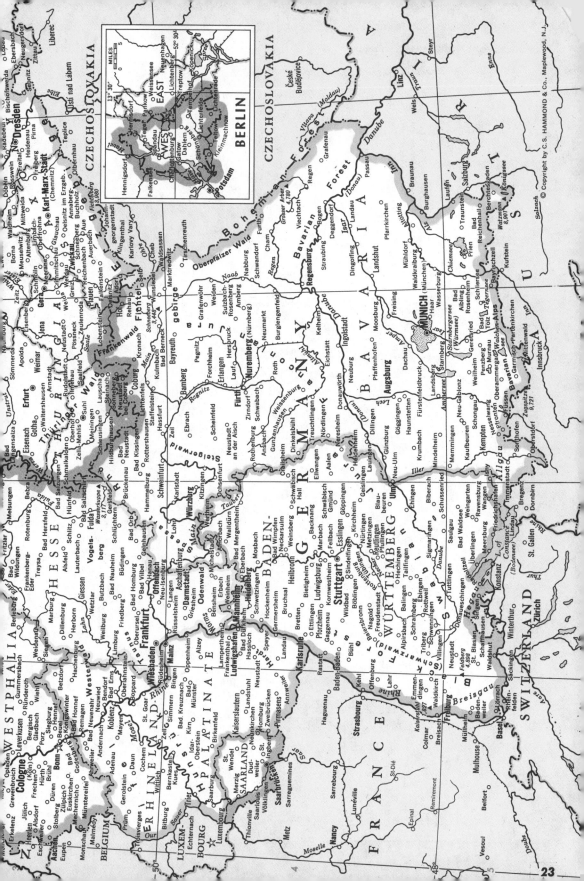

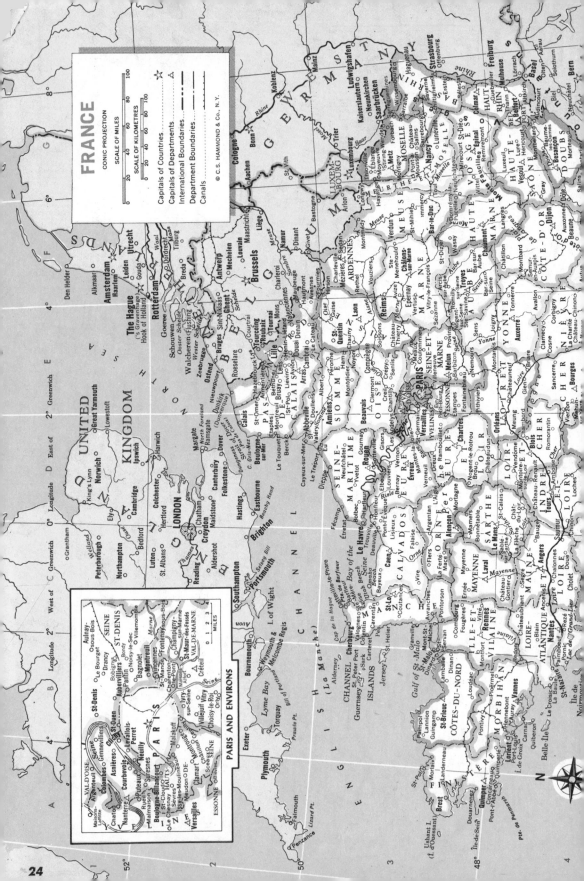

FRANCE

CONIC PROJECTION

SCALE OF MILES

SCALE OF KILOMETRES

Capitals of Countries	★
Capitals of Departments	△
International Boundaries	
Department Boundaries	
Canals	

© C. S. HAMMOND & CO., N.Y.

PARIS AND ENVIRONS

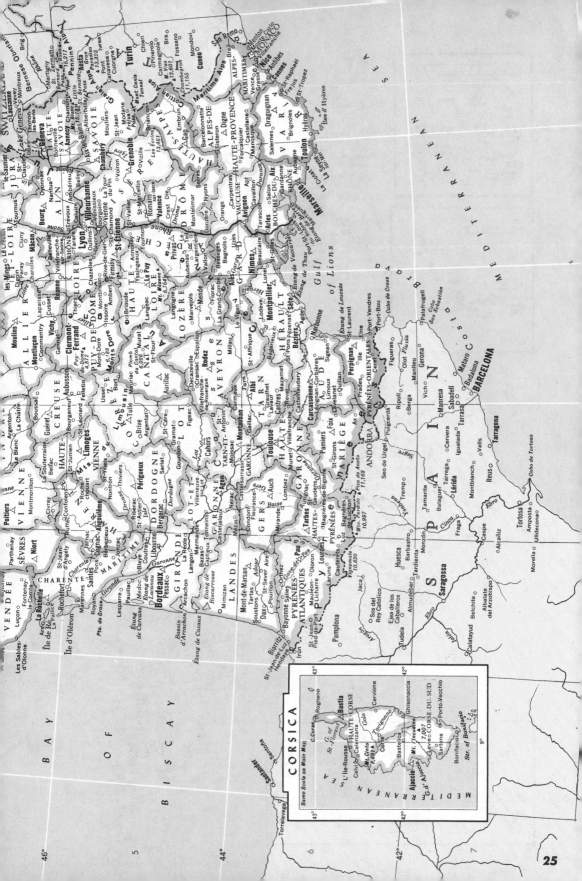

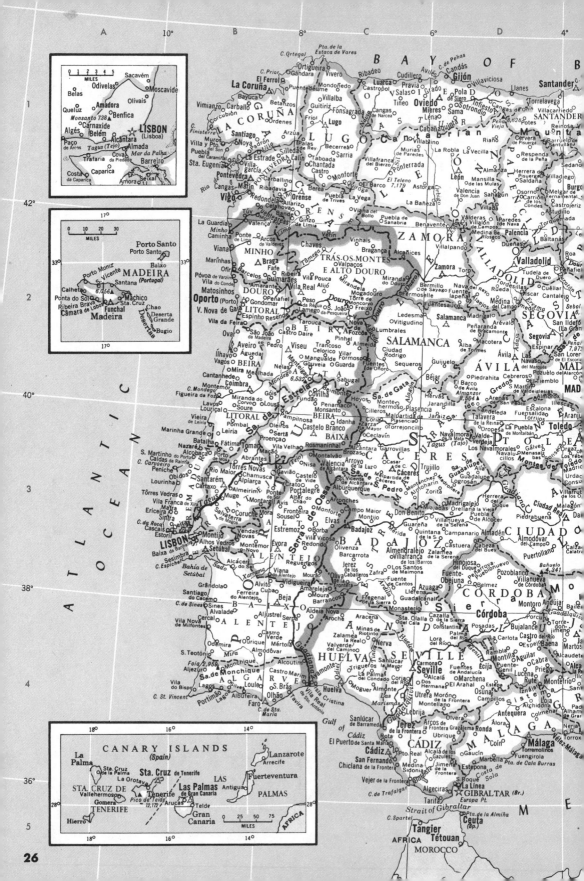

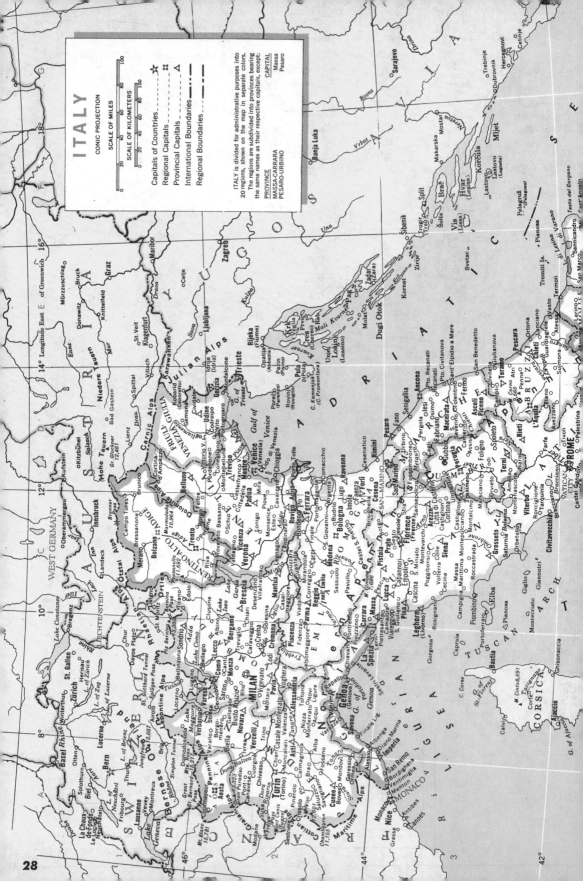

ITALY

CONIC PROJECTION

SCALE OF MILES

SCALE OF KILOMETERS

Capitals of Countries	⍟
Regional Capitals	⊠
Provincial Capitals	△
International Boundaries	▬▬▬
Regional Boundaries	▬ ▪▪▪ ▬

ITALY is divided for administrative purposes into 20 regions, shown on the map in separate colors. The regions are subdivided into provinces bearing the same names as their respective capitals, except:

PROVINCE	CAPITAL
MASSA-CARRARA	Massa
PESARO-URBINO	Pesaro

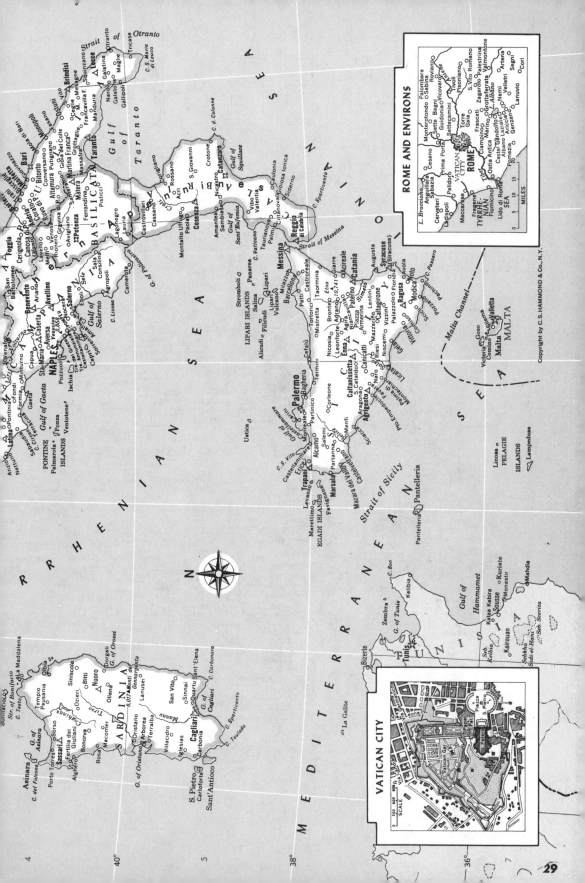

SWITZERLAND and LIECHTENSTEIN

CONIC PROJECTION

SCALE OF MILES

0   5   10   20   30

SCALE OF KILOMETRES

0 5 10   20   30   40   50

Capitals of Countries .... ☆
Capitals of Cantons .... ◎
International Boundaries .... ▬ ▪ ▬ ▪ ▬
Canals .... ▬▬▬▬

® Copyright HAMMOND INCORPORATED, Maplewood, N. J.

31

AUSTRIA
CZECHOSLOVAKIA
and HUNGARY

CONIC PROJECTION

SCALE OF MILES

0 10 20   40   60   80

SCALE OF KILOMETRES

0 10 20   40   60   80

Capitals of Countries..........☆   International Boundaries._____
Republic Capital..........◉   Internal Boundaries._____
Administrative Centers..........△   Canals._____

Czechoslovakia is divided into two socialist republics, Czech (capital-Prague) and Slovak
(capital-Bratislava), ten regions (Kraj) and the independent cities of Prague and Bratislava.

Copyright by C. S. HAMMOND & CO., N.Y.

33

THE BALKAN STATES

CONIC PROJECTION

SCALE OF MILES

0 25 50 75 100 125 150 175

SCALE OF KILOMETRES

0 25 50 75 100 125 150 175

Capitals of Countries ⋆

Administrative Centers △

International Boundaries

Major Internal Boundaries

Minor Internal Boundaries

Canals

BULGARIA and GREECE are divided into counties and departments, respectively. Because of the scale no attempt has been made to delimit and name these subdivisions, their administrative centers have, however, been designated.

The larger divisions named in Greece are well-known geographical regions, without administrative function.

RUMANIA consists of thirty-nine counties and three cities of regional status, Bucharest, Constanța and Petroșeni. Scale does not permit delimiting these counties.

ALBANIA is divided into twenty-seven districts. Scale does not permit the delimitation of these divisions.

YUGOSLAVIA is a federation of six republics. The Serbian republic includes an autonomous province (Voyvodina), and an autonomous region (Kosovo-Mitohiyan).

© C. S. HAMMOND & Co., N. Y.

Administrative Divisions bear same
names as their respective Capitals
or Centers, except:

Abkhaz A.S.S.R.	F6
Adygey Aut. Oblast	F6
Adzhar A.S.S.R.	F6
Bashkir A.S.S.R.	J4
Chechen-Ingush A.S.S.R.	G6
Chuvash A.S.S.R.	G3
Crimean Oblast	D6
Dagestan A.S.S.R.	G6
Kabardin-Balkar A.S.S.R.	F6
Kalmuck A.S.S.R.	F5
Karachay-Cherkess Aut. Obl.	F6
Karelian A.S.S.R.	D2
Komi A.S.S.R.	H2
Komi-Permyak Nat'l Okrug	H3
Mari A.S.S.R.	G3
Mordvinian A.S.S.R.	G4
Nagorno-Karabakh Aut. Obl.	G7
Nenets Nat'l Okrug	H1
North Ossetian A.S.S.R.	F6
South Ossetian Aut. Obl.	F6
Tatar A.S.S.R.	G3
Trans-Carpathian Oblast	B5
Udmurt A.S.S.R.	H3
Volyn Oblast	C4

Sukhumi	F6
Maykop	F6
Batumi	F6
Ufa	J4
Groznyy	G6
Cheboksary	G3
Simferopol'	D6
Makhachkala	G6
Nal'chik	F6
Elista	F5
Cherkessk	F6
Petrozavodsk	D2
Syktyvkar	H2
Kudymkar	H3
Yoshkar-Ola	G3
Saransk	G4
Stepanakert	G7
Nar'yan-Mar	H1
Ordzhonikidze	F6
Tskhinvali	F6
Kazan'	G3
Uzhgorod	B5
Izhevsk	H3
Lutsk	C4

37

© C. S. HAMMOND & CO., Maplewood, N.J.

ADMINISTRATIVE DIVISIONS NOT NAMED ON MAP

Division	Ref.
1. Abkhaz A.S.S.R.	E5
2. Adygey Aut. Oblast	D5
3. Adzhar A.S.S.R.	E5
4. Aginsk-Buryat Nat'l Okrug	M4
5. Chechen-Ingush A.S.S.R.	E5
6. Chuvash A.S.S.R.	E4
7. Gorno-Altay Aut. Oblast	J4
8. Gorno-Badakhshan Aut. Oblast	H6
9. Jewish Aut. Oblast	O5
10. Kabardin-Balkar A.S.S.R.	E5
11. Karachay-Cherkess Aut. Oblast	E5
12. Karakalpak A.S.S.R.	G5
13. Khakass Aut. Oblast	J4
14. Komi-Permyak Nat'l Okrug	F4
15. Mari A.S.S.R.	E4
16. Mordivian A.S.S.R.	E4
17. Nagorno-Karabakh Aut. Oblast	E5
18. Nakhichevan' A.S.S.R.	E6
19. North Ossetian A.S.S.R.	E5
20. South Ossetian Aut. Oblast	E5
21. Tatar A.S.S.R.	F4
22. Tuvinian A.S.S.R.	K4
23. Udmurt A.S.S.R.	F4
24. Ust'-Ordynsk-Buryat Nat'l Okrug	L4

Map of
ASIA
SCALE OF MILES
0   200   400   600   800   1000

★ Capitals of Countries
● Cities
▬▬ Boundaries of Countries
▬▬ Other Boundaries
▲ Mountain Peaks
╌╌╌ Canals

Water
Lowlands
Depression
Highlands
Mountains

Copyright by C. S. Hammond & Co., N.Y.

Longitude   East of   Greenwich

PHILIPPINES

Molucca Is.
CELEBES SEA
BANDA SEA
Moluccas
Timor
Celebes
Flores
AUSTRALIA

Taipei (Taiwan)
Taiwan (Formosa)
Luzon
Mindanao
Manila
I   N   D   O   N   E   S   I   A
Sumbawa
Sumba
Bali
Java
JAVA SEA

HONG KONG (British)
Canton
Hainan
Sabah
(British)
BRUNEI
(British)
Borneo
S A R A W A K
M A L A Y S I A
Sarawak
Djakarta
SOUTH CHINA SEA

Kunming
Yangtze
Mekong R.
Hanoi
Ho Chi Minh City
CHINA
VIETNAM
CAMBODIA
THAILAND
Bangkok
Gulf of Siam
Kuala Lumpur
MALAYA
Singapore
Sumatra
Medan

BURMA
Salween River
Irrawaddy
Rangoon
ANDAMAN SEA

Ganges
Calcutta
BANG.
Mt. Everest
NEPAL
Kathmandu
Brahmaputra

Andaman Is.
(Indian)

BAY
OF
BENGAL

Nicobar Is.
(Indian)

I   N   D   I   A   N

New Delhi
Ahmadabad
INDIA
DECCAN
PLATEAU
Hyderabad
Madras

SRI LANKA
(CEYLON)
Dondra
Head
Colombo
Cape Comorin

Equator

O   C   E   A   N

BRITISH INDIAN
OCEAN TERR.

PAKISTAN
Indus
Tropic of Cancer
Karachi
Bombay

Laccadive Is.
(Indian)

MALDIVES

Tropic of Capricorn

ARABIAN
SEA

OMAN
Rub' al Khali
Desert
Socotra
(P.D.R. Yemen)

SEYCHELLES

MAURITIUS

Réunion
(French)

A R A B I A
Mecca
SEA
YEMEN
ARAB
REP.
San'a
PEOPLE'S DEM.
REP. YEMEN
Aden   Gulf of Aden
DJIBOUTI
SOMALIA
ETHIOPIA

MADAGASCAR

BAHRAIN
QATAR
UNITED ARAB
EMIR.
AFRICA

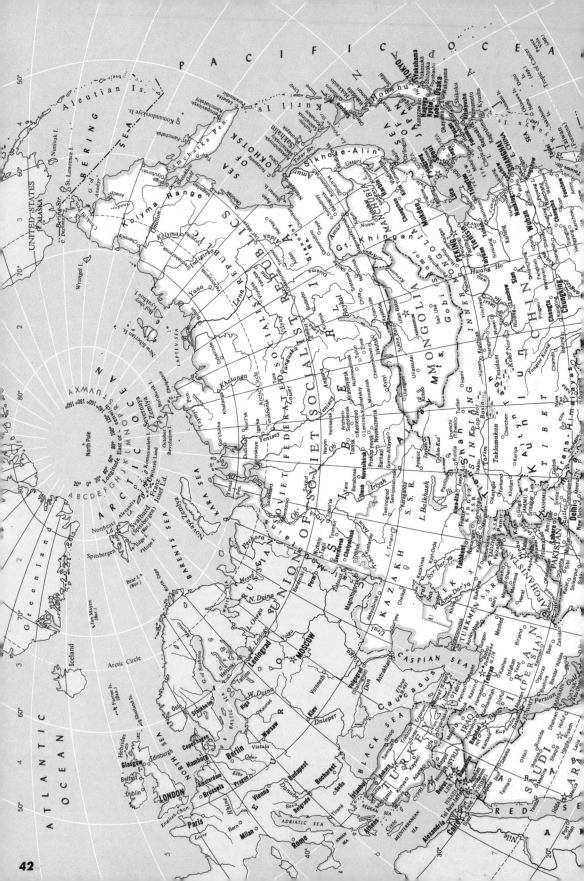

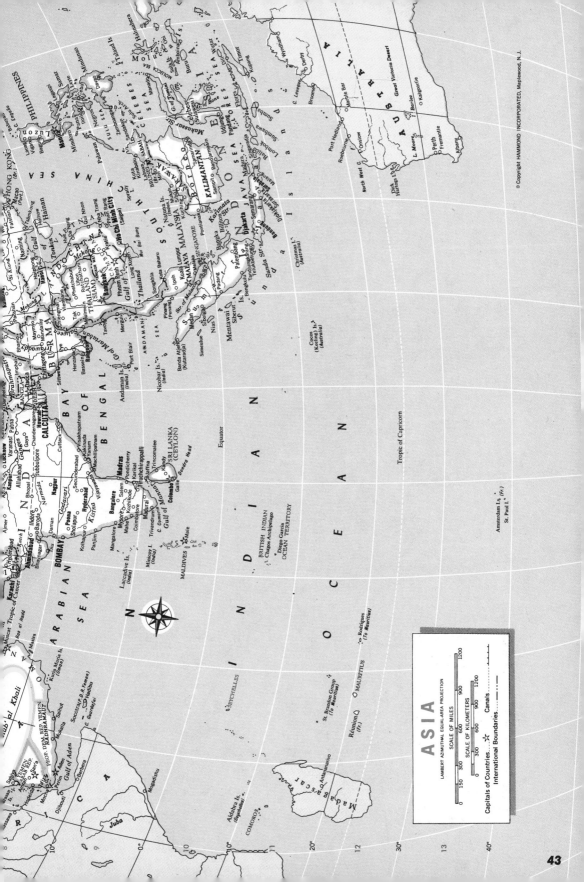

PHILIPPINES

HONG KONG

SOUTH CHINA SEA

Hainan

CELEBES SEA

MOLUCCA SEA

FLORES SEA

BANDA SEA

I N D O N E S I A

KALIMANTAN

SARAWAK

BRUNEI

SABAH

A U S T R A L I A

Great Victoria Desert

Perth
Fremantle
Albany

JAVA SEA

Djakarta

MALAYA

MALAYSIA

SINGAPORE

Kuala Lumpur

Sumatra

Palembang

BURMA

THAILAND
(SIAM)

Bangkok

Phnom Penh

Ho Chi Minh City
(Saigon)

Mekong

Gulf of
Thailand

INDOCHINA

Hanoi

Gulf of
Tonkin

CALCUTTA

BAY

OF

BENGAL

Brahmaputra

Ganges

ANDAMAN
SEA

Andaman Is.
(India)

Nicobar Is.
(India)

Equator

I N D I A

Godavari

Krishna

Madras

Bangalore

Hyderabad

SRI LANKA
(CEYLON)

Colombo

Gulf of Mannar

BOMBAY

ARABIAN
SEA

Laccadive Is.
(India)

Minicoy I.
(India)

MALDIVES

Tropic of Cancer

Karachi

Muscat

PEOP. DEM. REP. YEMEN
HADHRAMAUT

YEMEN

Aden

Gulf of Aden

A F R I C A

Mogadishu

I N D I A N

O C E A N

Tropic of Capricorn

Amsterdam I.▲ (Fr.)
St. Paul I.

Cocos
(Keeling) Is.²
(Australia)

Christmas I.
(Australia)

BRITISH INDIAN
OCEAN TERRITORY
Chagos Archipelago

Diego Garcia

Rodrigues
(To Mauritius)

MAURITIUS

Réunion △
(Fr.)

St. Brandon Group
(To Mauritius)

SEYCHELLES

MADAGASCAR

Antananarivo

COMOROS

Aldabra Is.
(Seychelles)

Juba

0°

10°

20°

30°

40°

6

7

8

9

10

11

12

13

44

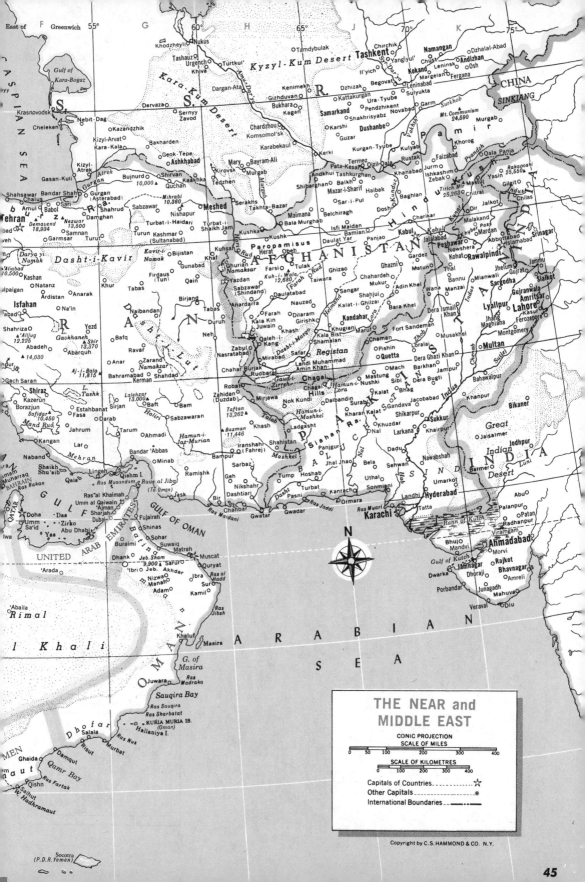

THE NEAR and MIDDLE EAST

CONIC PROJECTION
SCALE OF MILES

SCALE OF KILOMETRES

Capitals of Countries............... ☆
Other Capitals............... ⊛
International Boundaries ___.___.___

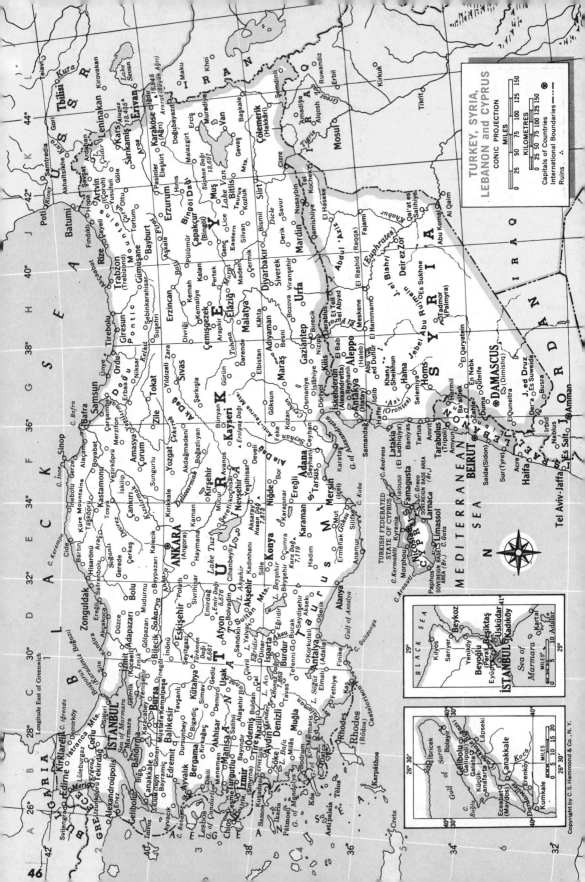

TURKEY, SYRIA,
LEBANON and CYPRUS

CONIC PROJECTION

MILES
0   25   50   75   100   125   150

KILOMETRES
0 25 50 75 100 125 150

Capitals of Countries ⊛
International Boundaries ----
Ruins ∴

Copyright by C.S. Hammond & Co., N.Y.

ISRAEL and JORDAN

CYLINDRICAL PROJECTION

Copyright by C.S. HAMMOND & CO., N.Y.

SCALE OF MILES

SCALE OF KILOMETRES

Capitals of Countries ⭐

Other Capitals ◉

International Boundaries

Internal Boundaries

Demilitarized Zone Boundaries

Neutral Zone Boundaries

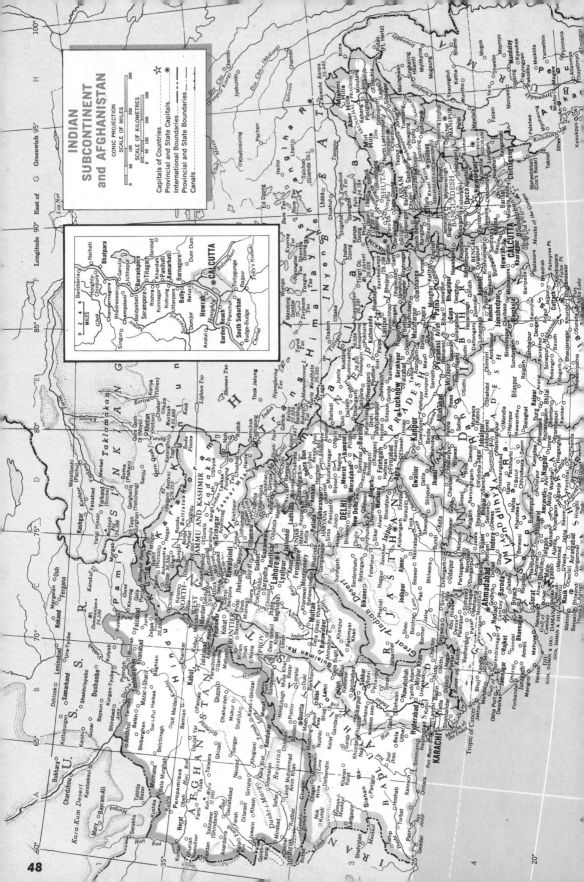

*Wuhan municipality consists of
Hankow, Hanyang and Wuchang

PHILIPPINES   Luzon

51

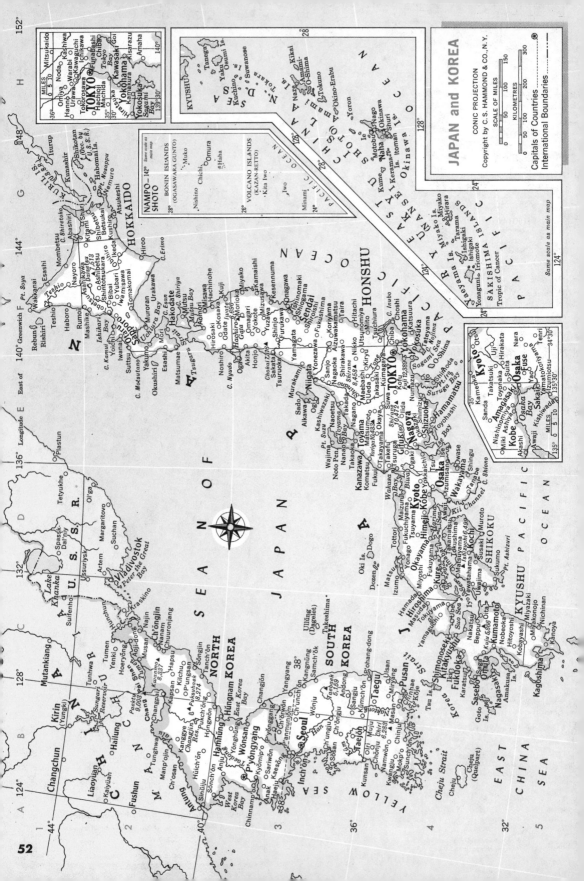

BURMA, THAILAND,
INDOCHINA and MALAYA
CONIC PROJECTION
SCALE OF MILES
0 50 100   200   300
SCALE OF KILOMETRES
0 50 100   200   300
Capitals of Countries.............⊛
Capitals of States...............⊙
International Boundaries.....▄▄▄▄

© C. S. HAMMOND & Co., Maplewood, N. J.

EASTERN NEW GUINEA

MILES
0   50   100   200

INDIAN OCEAN

54

PACIFIC OCEAN

LAMBERT AZIMUTHAL EQUAL-AREA PROJECTION

NAUTICAL MILES

STATUTE MILES

KILOMETRES

Capitals of Countries

Other Capitals

56

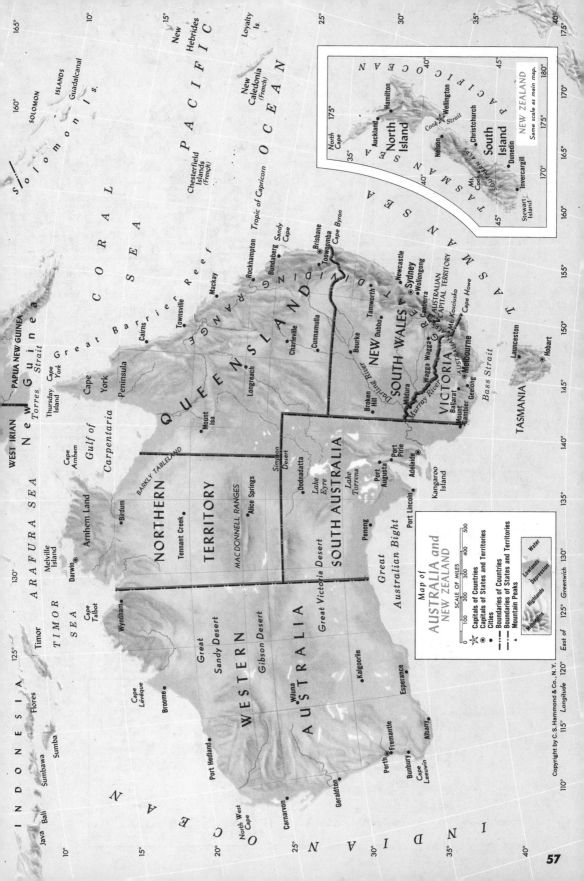

Map of
AUSTRALIA and
NEW ZEALAND

SCALE OF MILES

100 200 300 400 500

● Capitals of Countries
◉ Capitals of States and Territories
● Cities
···· Boundaries of Countries
─── Boundaries of States and Territories
▲ Mountain Peaks

Water
Lowlands Depression
Highlands
Mountains

NEW ZEALAND
Same scale as main map.

57

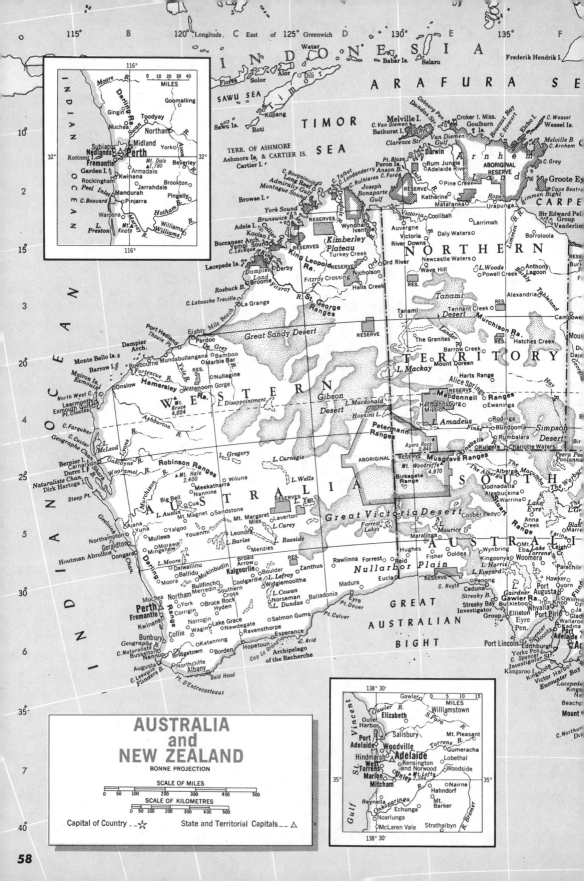

Inset — Perth region

INDIAN OCEAN

116°
Moore
Darling Ra.
Gingin
Muchea
Moore R.
Goomalling
Toodyay
Northam
Yorko
Midland
Subiaco
Nedlands
Perth
Fremantle
Garden I.
Rottnest I.
Armadale
Kwinana
Rockingham
Peel Inlet
Mandurah
Jarrahdale
Brookton
Pingelly
Pinjarra
Warpona
L. Preston
Mt. Dale ▲ 1,780
Beverley
Avon R.
C. Bouvard
Murray R.
Hotham R.
Williams
Williams R.
Mt. Keats

0 10 20 30 40
MILES

32°

Main map

INDONESIA

Longitude   East of   Greenwich

Wetar
Frederik Hendrik I.

ARAFURA SEA

Flores   Solor   Alor   Dili   Babar Is.   Selaru
SAWU SEA   Kupang
Sawu Is.   Roti   TIMOR   SEA

TERR. OF ASHMORE
Ashmore Is. &
Cartier I.   & CARTIER IS.

Browse I.

Melville I.
C. Van Diemen   Bathurst I.   Croker I. Miss.   Goulburn   C. Wessel
Clarence Str.   RESERVE   Is.   Boucaut Bay   Wessel Is.
Van Diemen   C. Stewart   Echo I.   Melville B.
P. Blaze   Gulf   C. Arnhem
Peron Is.   Anson B.   Darwin   A r n h e m   C. Grey
Rum Jungle   Katherine   ABORIGINAL   Groote E.
Pine Creek   RESERVE   Cape Arnhem
Adelaide River   L a n d   Rope   Limmen Bight
Matarancka   Urapunga   CARPE

Bonaparte
Joseph   Gulf
Bougainville   Long Reef   C. Talbot   C. Londonderry   C. Forde
Admiralty Gulf   C. Rulhieres
Montague Sound   C. Bougainville
York Sound
Brunswick B.   Drysdale R.
Adele I.   Wyndham   Victoria   Coolibah   Larrimah
Koolan I.   Ivanhoe   Auvergne   Daly Waters   Borroloola
Buccaneer Arch.   RESERVES   Victoria   Sir Edward Pel.
Yampi Sound   Kimberley   River Downs   N O R T H E R N   Group
King Leopold Ra.   Plateau   Ord R.   Newcastle Waters   Vanderlin
Lacepede Is.   Turkey Creek   Nicholson   L. Woods   Anthony
Dampier   Derby   Ord River   Wave Hill   Powell Creek   Lagoon
Land   Fitzroy   Halls Creek   RES.   Alexandria   Tableland
Broome   Fitzroy Crossing   Tanami   Camooweal
Roebuck B.   R. St. George   Tennant Creek   Mou
C. Latouche Treville   Ranges   T a n a m i   Du
La Grange   D e s e r t   Tanami   Barrow Creek   RES.   Hatches Creek   Da
Eighty Mile Beach   The Granites   Dajo
Port Hedland   Pardoo   Mount Doreen   T E R R I T O R Y
Thouin Pt.   Great Sandy Desert   L. Mackay   Harts Range
Dampier Arch.   De Grey   RESERVE   Alice Springs
Monte Bello Is.   Roebourne   Marble Bar   Macdonnell Ranges   Ewaninga
Barrow I.   Mundabullangana   Nullagine   Macdonnell Ranges
Muiron Is.   Fortescue R.   RES.   Gibson   Hermannsburg   Rodinga
Exmouth   Onslow   Wittenoom Gorge   Desert   L. Macdonald   Mission   Bundooma   Simpson
North West C.   Hamersley   Hopkins L.   L. Amadeus   Finke   Rumbalara   D e s e r t
Learmonth   W E S T E R N   Mt.   L. Disappointment   Ayers Rock ▲   Charlotte Waters
Exmouth Gulf   Bruce   L. Macdonald   Petermann   2,845   Peera Pee
Pt. Cloates   Ashburton R.   4,024   Ranges   Kulgera   Foolanna
C. Farquhar   L. Gregory   Musgrave Ranges   The Alberga   Macumb
C. Cuvier   R.   ABORIGINAL   RESERVE   Mt. Woodroffe   Oodnadatta   The Warbu
Bernier I.   Gascoyne R.   L. Carnegie   Birksgate   4,970   Algebuckina   The
Dorre I.   McLeod   Robinson Ranges   S O U T H   Warrina   Lake
Carnarvon   Mt. Hale   Range   Coober Pedy   L. G
Naturaliste Chan.   Wooramel   ▲ 2,400   L. Wells   Great Victoria Desert   Gr
Dirk Hartog I.   Murchison R.   Wiluna   Forrest   Anna Creek   Bla
Steep Pt.   Meekatharra   Lakes   Maralinga   Mt.   Marre
Nannine   L. Yeo   L. Maurice   Coober Pedy   Eyre   Farina
A U S T R A L I A   Big Bell   RESERVES   Oodnadatta   Stuart
Ajana   Cue   L. Austin   Sandstone   Hughes   Oldea   Kingoonya   Range   Port
Lyona   Mt. Magnet   Nullarbor   Fisher   Parachil
Northampton   Yalgoo   Mt. Margaret   Leonora   Laverton   Rawlinna   Forrest   Reid   Woomera
Geraldton   Mullewa   Miss.   L. Carey   Plain   Penong   L. Everard   Hawker
Dongara   Morawa   L. Barlee   L. Raeside   Great   Reserve   Ceduna   Port
Houtman Abrolhos   Mingenew   Menzies   Eucla   C. Nuyts   Streaky B.   Pirie
L. Moore   Broad   Madura   Penong   Gawler Ra.   Quorn
Dalwallinu   Arrow   Investigator   Whyalla   Wilmi
Moora   Mukinbudin   Zanthus   Streaky Bay   Group   Eyre   Port Pirie   Glad
Bullfinch   Kalgoorlie   Boulder   Eliston   Peninsula   Kadina   Wallaroo
Muchea   Southern   Coolgardie   L. Lefroy   A U S T R A L I   Wallaroo   Gla
Northam   Merredin   Cross   Wiggiemooltha   Port Lincoln   Spencer
Perth   Bruce Rock   L. Cowan   G R E A T   Edithburgh   Gulf   **Adelaide**
Fremantle   Corrigin   Norseman   Yorke Pen.   C. Spencer
Kwinana   Hyden   L. Dundas   Balladonia   A U S T R A L I A N   Investigator Str.   Kangaroo I.   Victor Harbor
Narrogin   Eyre   Pt. Dover   Kingscote   Encounter Bay
Collie   Wagin   Lake Grace   Pt. Culver   Kings
Bunbury   Newdegate   B I G H T   Lacepede
Geographe B.   Katanning   Ravensthorpe   Beach
C. Naturaliste   Kojonup   Salmon Gums   Mount
Busselton   Hopetoun   Cap Le Grand   C. Northum
Nannup   Bridgetown   Borden   Esperance
Augusta   Northcliffe   Cap Le Grand   C. Arid
C. Leeuwin   Albany   Archipelago
Flinders B.   Bald Head   of the Recherche
Pt. D'Entrecasteaux

Inset — legend box

AUSTRALIA
and
NEW ZEALAND
BONNE PROJECTION

SCALE OF MILES
0   50   100   200   300   400   500

SCALE OF KILOMETRES
0 50 100   200   300   400   500

Capital of Country ___ ☆   State and Territorial Capitals ___ △

Inset — Adelaide region

138° 30'
Gawler
Gawler R.   Williamstown
Outer   Elizabeth   S. Para R.
Harbor   Mt. Pleasant
Salisbury
Port   Torrens R.   Gumeracha
Adelaide   Woodville   Lobethal
Hindmarsh   **Adelaide**   Woodside
West   Kensington
Torrens   and Norwood
St.   Unley   Mt. Lofty   Nairne
Marion   Mitcham   ▲ 2,384   Hahndorf
Gulf   Reynella   Mt.
Onkaparinga   Echunga   Barker
Noarlunga   Strathalbyn
McLaren Vale   R. Bremer

0   5   10   15
MILES

138° 30'

35°

Map of
AFRICA

SCALE OF MILES

0   200   400   600   800

- Capitals of Countries
• Cities
━━ Boundaries of Countries
┅┅ Other Boundaries
▲ Mountain Peaks
〜 Canals
〜 Falls

Water
Lowlands
Depression
Highlands
Mountains

Copyright by C. S. Hammond & Co., N.Y.

MAP CONTINUED ON

62

AFRICA
NORTHERN PART

LAMBERT AZIMUTHAL EQUAL-AREA PROJECTION

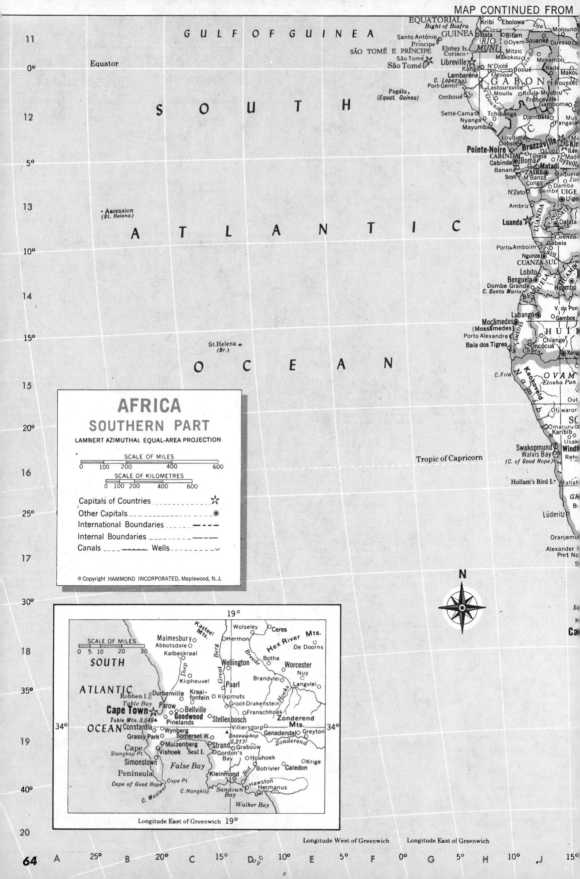

GULF OF GUINEA

EQUATORIAL
Bight of Biafra
GUINEA

Kribi Ebolowa
Dja Moloundo
Santo António Bata Bitam Souanké Ouesso
Príncipe RIO Oyem
São Tomé MUNI Mitzic Makokou
SÃO TOMÉ E PRÍNCIPE Elobey Is. Mekambo
Corisco Makou
São Tomé Libreville N'Djolé Kelle
Kango Booué Ft-Rousset
Lambaréné GABON Makou
C. Lopez Lastoursville Mus
Port-Gentil Mouila Koula-Moutou Pangala
Omboué Franceville Gamboma
Pagalu Settè-Cama Tchibanga Djambala
(Equat. Guinea) Nyanga Mayumba

Equator

S O U T H

Loudima C
Dolisie Kir
Pointe-Noire Brazzaville Lé
CABINDA Tshela Madi
Cabinda Boma Thysvil
Banana Matadi
Soyo M'Banza Maguela
Congo Zor
N'Zeto Damba
Bembe UIGE
Ambriz Uige
N'ZETO Dalata

Luanda LUANDA

Ascension
(St. Helena)

A T L A N T I C

Cuanza
Porto Amboim Gabela
Nganza CUANZA-SUL
Lobito
Benguela Huambo
Dombe Grande
C. Santa Maria
Lubango V. da Pon
Gambos
Moçâmedes HUI
(Mossâmedes) Chiange
Porto Alexandre Oncócua Xan
Baía dos Tigres

St.Helena
(Br.)

O C E A N

C. Fria OVAM
Etosha Pan
Otjiwaror S
Out

Tropic of Capricorn

Omaruru
Karibib Usak
Swakopmund Windh
Walvis Bay Reho
(C. of Good Hope)

Hollam's Bird I. Malta
GR
B
Lüderitz

Oranjemu
Alexander
Port No
S

N

19°

Kasteel
Mts.
Wolseley Ceres
Malmesbury Hermon Hex River Mts.
Abbotsdale De Doorns
Kalbaskraal Wellington Botha
SOUTH Klipheuvel Breede Worcester
Nuy
ATLANTIC Paarl Langvlei
Robben I. Durbanville Kraai- Brandvlei Hoek
Table Bay Parow fontein Klapmuts
Cape Town Bellville Groot-Drakenstein Zonderend
Table Mtn. 3,549 Goodwood Franschhoek Mts.
OCEAN Constantia Pinelands Stellenbosch Genadenda Greyton
Wynberg Villiersdorp Zonderend
Grassy Park Somerset W. Sneeuwkop Grabouw
Cape Muizenberg 5,217 Houhoek
Slangkop Pt. Vishoek Strand Gordon's Krige
Simonstown Seal I. Bay Botrivier Caledon
Peninsula False Bay Kleinmond
Cape of Good Hope Cape Pt. Sandown Hawston
C. Maclear C. Hangklip Bay Hermanus
Walker Bay

SCALE OF MILES
0 5. 10 20 30

34° 34°

Longitude East of Greenwich 19°

Longitude West of Greenwich Longitude East of Greenwich

INDIAN

OCEAN

INDIAN OCEAN

Tropic of Capricorn

ZAIRE

KENYA

Equator

UGANDA

L. Victoria

Nairobi

RWANDA

BURUNDI

Bujumbura

TANZANIA

Lake Tanganyika

Dodoma

Dar es Salaam

Zanzibar

KATANGA

Lubumbashi (Elisabethville)

ZAMBIA

Lusaka

Kilwa Kivinje

Mombasa

Pemba

Aldabra Is.
Cosmoledo Is.
Providence I.
St. Pierre

Assumption

(Seychelles)

Astove I.
Farquhar Is.

Grand Comoro
COMOROS

Moroni
Glorioso Is. (Réunion)
C. Amber

Mohéli
Anjouan

Mayotte (Fr.)

Diégo-Suarez

Nossi-Bé
Hell-Ville

Ambilobe
Vohémar

Ambanja

Analalava
Sambava

Antalaha

Maroantsetra

Majunga

Masoala Pen.
Ste-Marie I.

CABO DELGADO

Pemba

NIASSA

NAMPULA

Nacala

Nampula

Moçambique

Angoche I.

TETE

Blantyre

Quelimane

SOFALA

Beira

ZAMBÈZIA

MADAGASCAR

Antananarivo

Antsirabe

Tamatave

Fianarantsoa

ZIMBABWE

Salisbury

Bulawayo

RHODESIA

BOTSWANA

Kalahari

Desert

MOZAMBIQUE

INHAMBANE

GAZA

TRANSVAAL

Johannesburg

Pretoria

Maputo (Lourenço Marques)

SWAZILAND

Tuléar

Fort-Dauphin

ORANGE FREE STATE

Kimberley

Bloemfontein

LESOTHO

Maseru

Pietermaritzburg

Durban

CAPE OF GOOD HOPE

TRANSKEI

East London

Port Elizabeth

INDIAN OCEAN

SCALE OF MILES

0   25   50   100

Serpent I.
Flat I.
Round I.

Poudre d'Or
Poste de Flacq

Port Louis

Quatre Bornes
Curepipe

Piton de la
Petite Rivière Noire
Pte. Sud Ouest 2,711

Mahébourg

Souillac

MAURITIUS

St-Denis

Ste-Marie

Le Port
St-André

St-Paul
St-Benoît

Piton des Neiges 10,069

RÉUNION (Fr.)

Étang-Salé
Le Tampon

St-Louis
St-Pierre
St-Philippe

St-Joseph

Mascarene Islands

Longitude 56° East of Greenwich 57°

65

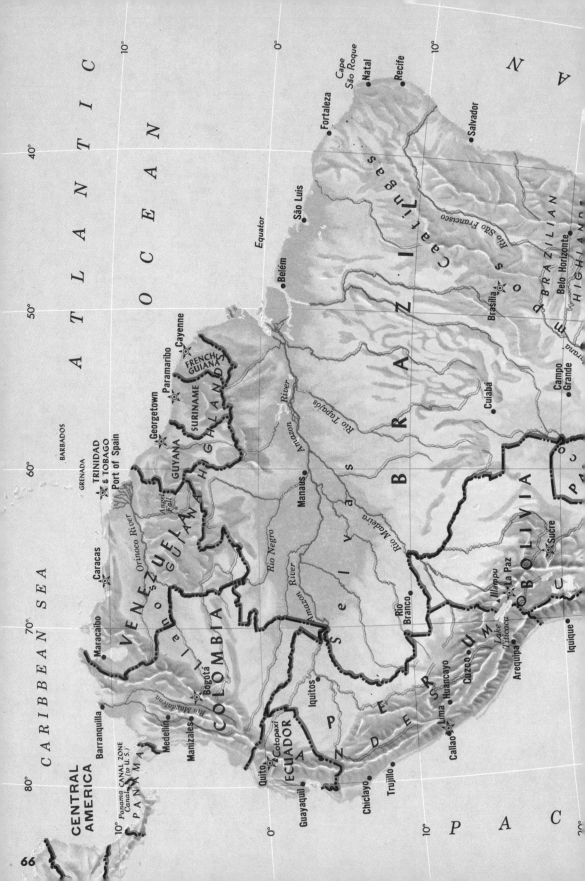

CENTRAL
AMERICA

CARIBBEAN SEA

ATLANTIC OCEAN

N

Cape
São Roque
Natal
Recife

Fortaleza

Salvador

Equator

São Luis

Belém

BRAZILIAN HIGHLAND

Belo Horizonte

Brasília

Rio São Francisco

Caatingas

Campo
Grande

Cuiabá

BRAZIL

Paraná

Rio Tapajós

Rio Tapajós

Amazon River

Rio Negro

Manaus

Selvas

Rio Madeira

Amazon River

BARBADOS
GRENADA
TRINIDAD & TOBAGO
Port of Spain

Cayenne
Paramaribo
FRENCH
GUIANA
SURINAME
Georgetown
GUYANA
GUIANA HIGHLAND

VENEZUELA

Angel Fall

Orinoco River

Llanos

Caracas

Maracaibo

Barranquilla

Medellín
Manizales
Bogotá

Rio Magdalena

COLOMBIA

Iquitos

Cotopaxi
ECUADOR
Quito

Guayaquil

Chiclayo

Trujillo

PERU

ANDES

Rio Branco

Rio Branco

Lima
Callao
Huancayo

Cuzco

Lake Titicaca
Arequipa
Illampu
La Paz

BOLIVIA

Sucre

P

Iquique

Panama CANAL ZONE
Canal (to U.S.)
PANAMA

PACI

66

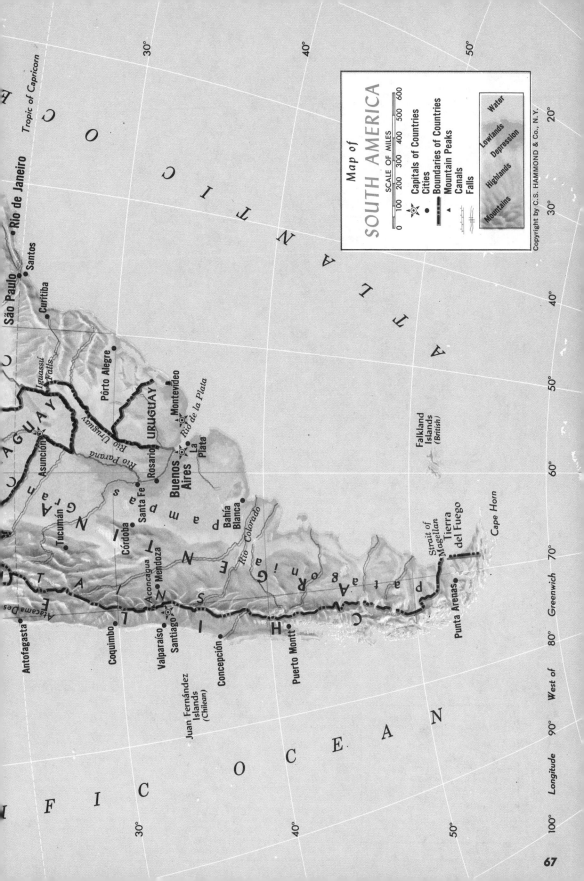

Map of
SOUTH AMERICA

SCALE OF MILES

0 100 200 300 400 500 600

☆ Capitals of Countries
● Cities
▬▬ Boundaries of Countries
▲ Mountain Peaks
▬▬ Canals
▬▬ Falls

Water
Lowlands
Depression
Highlands
Mountains

Copyright by C. S. HAMMOND & CO., N. Y.

Tropic of Capricorn

Rio de Janeiro

Santos

São Paulo

Curitiba

Pôrto Alegre

Iguassú Falls

P A R A G U A Y

Asunción

Rio Paraná

Rio Uruguay

URUGUAY

Montevideo

Rio de la Plata

Rosario

Santa Fe

Buenos Aires

La Plata

Tucumán

Córdoba

Mendoza

Aconcagua

A R G E N T I N A

Bahía Blanca

Rio Colorado

P a t a g o n i a

Atacama Des.

Antofagasta

Coquimbo

Valparaíso

Santiago

Concepción

C H I L E

Puerto Montt

Juan Fernández Islands
(Chilean)

Strait of Magellan

Tierra del Fuego

Punta Arenas

Cape Horn

Falkland Islands
(British)

A T L A N T I C   O C E A N

P A C I F I C   O C E A N

Tropic of Capricorn

30°
40°
50°

20°

30°

40°

50°

60°

70°

80° Greenwich

West of

90°

100°

Longitude

30°
40°
50°

67

MAP CONTINUED ON

SOUTH AMERICA
NORTHERN PART
LAMBERT AZIMUTHAL EQUAL-AREA PROJECTION

SCALE OF MILES
0 100 200 300 400 500

SCALE OF KILOMETRES
0 100 200 300 400 500

Capitals of Countries _____ ☆
Other Capitals _____ △
International Boundaries ____ —·—·—
Other Boundaries _____ —··—··—

ATLANTIC OCEAN

Equator

N

BARBADOS
Bridgetown

TRINIDAD
TOBAGO

Charity
Georgetown
Mahaica
New Amsterdam
Nieuw Nickerie
Springlands
Rockstone
Orealla
Groningen
Albina
St-Laurent-du-Maroni
Paramaribo
Moengo
Mana
Cayenne
Sinnamary
Devil's I.

SURINAME
FRENCH GUIANA

Guisambourg
St. Georges
Clevelândia do Norte

Amapá
I. de Maracá

AMAPÁ
Macapá
Pto. Santana
Caviana
I. Mexiana
Canal do Sul
Canal do Norte

Amazonas
Óbidos
Santarém
Belém
Bragança
Capanema

MARANHÃO
Fortaleza (Ceará)
Teresina

RIO GRANDE DO NORTE
Natal
C. de São Roque

PARAÍBA
João Pessoa (Paraíba)
Campina Grande
Olinda
Caruaru
Recife (Pernambuco)

PERNAMBUCO
ALAGOAS
Maceió

SERGIPE
Aracaju

BAHIA
Salvador (Bahia)
B. de Todos-os-Santos

MATO GROSSO
MATO GROSSO DO SUL

GOIÁS
DISTRITO FEDERAL
Brasília
Goiânia
Anápolis

MINAS GERAIS
Belo Horizonte
Ouro Prêto 9,492

ESPÍRITO SANTO
Vitória

SÃO PAULO
RIO DE JANEIRO
C. de São Tomé

Tropic of Capricorn

8
25°
9
30°
10
35°
11
40°
12
45°
13
14
55°
15

95°   90°   85°   80°   75°   70° Longitude   65° West of

A   B   C   D   E   F

P A C I F I C

O C E A N

I. de San Félix   I. San Ambrosio
(Chile)   (Chile)

JUAN FERNÁNDEZ IS.
(Chile)
I. Alejandro   I. Robinson
Selkirk   Crusoe
I. Santa Clara

Mejillones
Antofagasta
Aguas Blancas
Vol. Llullaillaco 22,057
Taltal
Chañaral
Pueblo Hundido
Caldera
Copiapó
Huasco
Vallenar
Cabo Bascuñán
Cruz Grande
La Serena
Coquimbo
Tongoy
Ovalle
Illapel
Los Vilos
Bermejo
Aconcagua 22,831
Viña del Mar
Valparaíso
Santiago
Rancagua
Pichilemu
San Fernando
Curepto
Constitución
Talca
Cauquenes
Quirihue
Talcahuano
Concepción
Arauco
Lebu
Cañete
Mulchén
Traiguén
Temuco
Nueva Imperial
Villarrica
Valdivia
Corral
La Unión
Osorno
Puerto Varas
G. de Maullín
los Coronados
Ancud
Castro
Isla de Chiloé
Cabo Quilán
G. Corcovado
ARCHIPIÉLAGO
de los
CHONOS
Pen. Taitao
C. Tres Montes
G. de Penas
I. Campana
I. Wellington
I. Madre de Dios
I. Hanover
Estrecho Nelson
ARCHIPIÉLAGO
REINA ADELAIDA
Strait of Magellan
I. Desolación
I. Sta. Inés
I. Clarence
I. Stewart
I. Londonderry
I. Hoste
Is. Wollaston
Is. Hermite
Cape Horn
Is. Diego Ramírez

Embarcación
El Chorro
San Antonio
de los Cobres
Jujuy
Rivadavia
Salta
Las Lomitas
Quebrachal
Salar de Arizaro
Alemania
Rosario de la Frontera
Tucumán
Campo Gallo
Andalgalá
Concepción
Las Termas
Santiago del Estero
Quimili
Catamarca
SANTIAGO DEL ESTERO
Añatuya
Reco
Chilecito
La Rioja
Patquia
Dean Funes
Cristo
Salinas Grandes
Serrezuela
Mar Chiquita
Cruz del Eje
Rafaela
Francisco
Santa Fe
SAN JUAN
San Juan
Villa Dolores
Córdoba
CÓRDOBA
Alta Gracia
Villa María
Cañada de Góm
Mendoza
Godoy Cruz
SAN LUIS
Bell Ville
San Luis
Río Cuarto
BUEN
Tunuyán
S. Carlos
Mercedes
Venado Tuerto
Ros
Maipo 17,464
MENDOZA
San Rafael
Rufino
Laboulaye
Lincoln
Ch
Atuel
Gral. Alvear
Ing. Luiggi
Pehuajó
Gen. Pico
Victorica
Trenque Lauquen
Telén
Sta. Rosa
LA PAMPA
BUEN
Grande
Cereales
Cor.
Gen. Acha
Doblas
Bernasconi
Cor. Pringles
Colorado
NEUQUEN
Salado
Médanos
Bahía Blanca
Pl. Huincul
Gen. Roca
Choele Choel
Zapala
Picún-Leufú
Neuquén
Colorado
L. Tri
Temuco
RÍO NEGRO
Negro
Junín de los Andes
El Cuy
Sierra Colorada
Viedma
Nahuel Huapi
San Carlos de Bariloche
San Antonio Oeste
Carmen de Patago
Pta. Bermeja
Golfo San Matías
Pta. Norte
Sierra Grande
Norquinco
Maquinchao
Pen. Valdés
Ptb. Pirámides
Pta. Delgada
Leleque
Gastre
Telsen
Puerto Madryn
Esquel
Las Plumas
Trelew
Gaimán
Rawson
CHUBUT
Chubut
Camarones
B. Camarones
C. Dos Bahías
ARCHIPIÉLAGO
Colhué Huapi
Pto. Aisén
Colonia Sarmiento
Comodoro Rivadavia
Golfo San Jorge
Colonia Las Heras
L. Buenos Aires
Deseado
Cabo Tres Puntas
Puerto Deseado
I. Higgins
L. San Martín
L. Cardiel
SANTA CRUZ
Chico
San Julián
L. Viedma
Santa Cruz
FALKL
L. Argentino
Pto. Coyle
Bahía Grande
Jason Is.
West Falkl
Weddell I.
Río Gallegos
Pto. Natales
Pta. Dungeness
Strait of Magellan
Cerro Manantiales
Falk
Porvenir
TIERRA DEL FUEGO
ANTÁRTICO
Punta Arenas
Tierra Grande del Fuego
San Diego
ATLÁNTICO
SUR
Le Maire
Ushuaia
I. de los Es
(Staten I.
Navarino
B. Nassau
Puerto Williams

D R A K E   P A S

70

SOUTH AMERICA
SOUTHERN PART
LAMBERT AZIMUTHAL EQUAL-AREA PROJECTION

SCALE OF MILES
0   100   200   300   400   500

SCALE OF KILOMETRES
0   100   200   300   400   500

Capitals of Countries _____ ☆
Other Capitals _____ △
International Boundaries _____
Other Boundaries _____

© Copyright HAMMOND INCORPORATED, Maplewood, N.J.

PARANÁ

SÃO PAULO

RIO DE JANEIRO

SANTA CATARINA

RIO GRANDE DO SUL

URUGUAY

CORRIENTES

ENTRE RÍOS

Asunción
Concepción
Horqueta
Amambaí
Londrina
Jacarezinho
Botucatu
Campinas
Volta Redonda
Petrópolis
Niterói
Tropic of Capricorn

Ponta Grossa
Curitiba
Porto Alegre
Montevideo
La Plata
Mar del Plata
Gen. Alvarado (Miramar)
Necochea
Quequén

Tropic of Capricorn

Chile inset

Petorca
Papudo
La Ligua
La Calera
Quillota
Viña del Mar
Pta. Curaumilla
Valparaíso
Santiago
Algarrobo
San Antonio
Cartagena
Melipilla
Curacaví
San Bernardo
Paine
El Volcán
El Teniente
Rancagua
Sewell
Maipú 17,464
Las Cabras
Peumo
San Fernando
Pichilemu
Santa Cruz
Butaendo
Aconcagua 22,831
San Felipe
Los Andes
Limache
ARGENTINA
PACIFIC OCEAN
72° 70° 34°
0 15 30 MILES

Buenos Aires inset

URUGUAY
Acevedo
San Pedro
Pergamino
Colón
Carabelas
Rojas
Junín
Chacabuco
Irala
G'ral. O'Brien
Los Toldos
Bragado
Alberti
Baradero
Sta. Lucía
Arrecifes
V. Lía
S. Antonio de Areco
Carmen de Areco
Capilla del Señor
Campana
Zárate
Tigre
San Fernando
San Isidro
DIST. FED.
BUENOS AIRES
Morón
Avellaneda
Quilmes
Lanús
Lomas de Zamora
Adrogué
La Plata
San Vicente
Magdalena
C'nl. Brandsen
Roque Pérez
Lobos
Cañuelas
Gral. Las Heras
Navarro
Chivilcoy
Mercedes
Luján
Rivas
Suipacha
Emilio Ayarza
Marcos Paz
Norberto de la Riestra
Salado
BUENOS AIRES
Joaquín Suárez
M. Garcia (Arg.)
Colonia
Nueva Palmira
Agraciada
Carmelo
Ibicuy
ENTRE RÍOS
60° 58° 34°
SCALE OF MILES
0 20 40 60

Rio de Janeiro inset

Baía de Guanabara
Ilha do Boqueirão
Pta. do Tubiacanga
I. de Paquetá
Ilha do Governador
Freguezia
Cocotá
Ilha dos Tavares
Ilha do Engenho
Baía de Guanabara
Neves
Niterói
Icaraí
S. Dumont
RIO DE JANEIRO
Duque de Caxias
São João de Meriti
S. João de Meriti
Anchieta
Pavuna
Vigário Geral
Saravatá
Pta. do Galeão
I. do Fundão
Ramos
I. do Bom Jesus
I. da Sapucaia
Ricardo de Albuquerque
Colégio
Irajá
Olaria
Penha
Vila Nova
Deodoro
Vila Militar
Madureira
Inhaúma
Piedade
Méier
Eng. Novo
Bangú
Realengo
Andaraí
Tijuca
Gloria
Botafogo
Copacabana
Sugar Loaf 1,296
Pta. das Palmas
Ilha das Palmas
Ilha Cagarra
Ilha Comprida
Sa. da Barata
Sa. do Engenho Velho
Pedra Branca 3,370
Rio Grande
Jacarepaguá
Pico da Tijuca 3,350
Morro da Taquara
Corcovado 2,310
Rio Comprido
L. Rodrigo de Freitas
Alto da Bôa Vista
Vargem Pequena
L. de Jacarepaguá
Lôa Tijuca
Gávea
Leblon
Ipanema
Pta. do Arpoador
Lagôa Marapendi
Pta. do Marisco
Ilha do Meio
Ilha Pontuda
I. da Alfavaca
RIO DE JANEIRO
ATLANTIC OCEAN
43°20′ 43°10′ 22°50′ 23°
SCALE OF MILES
0 2 4 6

ATLANTIC OCEAN
PACIFIC OCEAN

FALKLAND IS.
West Falkland
East Falkland
Stanley
Choiseul Sd.
Lively I.
Adventure Sd.
SOUTH SHETLAND IS.
Elephant I.
Clarence I.
SOUTH ORKNEY IS.
Coronation I.
Laurie I.

N

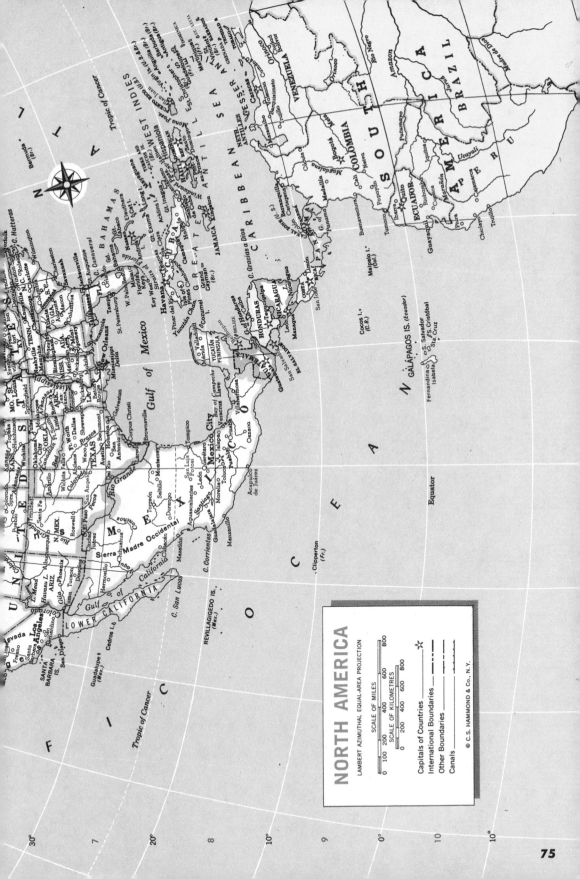

NORTH AMERICA

LAMBERT AZIMUTHAL EQUAL-AREA PROJECTION

SCALE OF MILES

0   100   200   400   600   800

SCALE OF KILOMETRES

0   200   400   600   800

Capitals of Countries .... ☆

International Boundaries ....

Other Boundaries ....

Canals ....

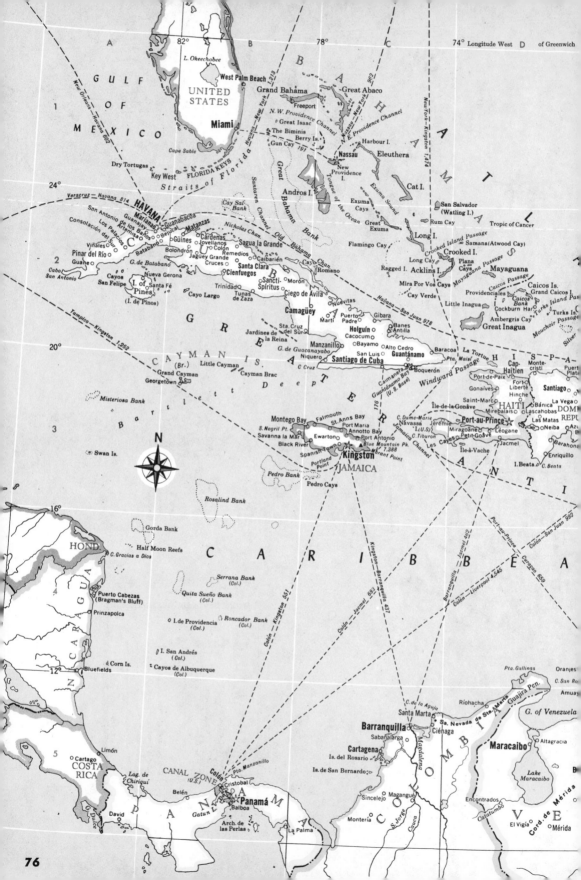

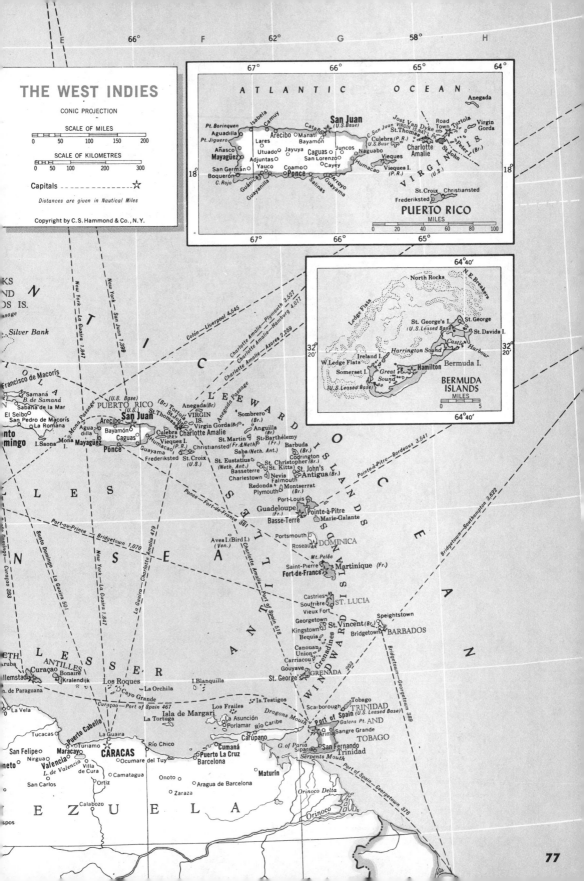

CENTRAL AMERICA

CONIC PROJECTION

SCALE OF MILES

0   25   50   100   150

SCALE OF KILOMETRES

0   25 50   100   150

Capitals of Countries .... ☆

International Boundaries ....

Canals ....

© Copyright HAMMOND INCORPORATED, Maplewood, N.J.

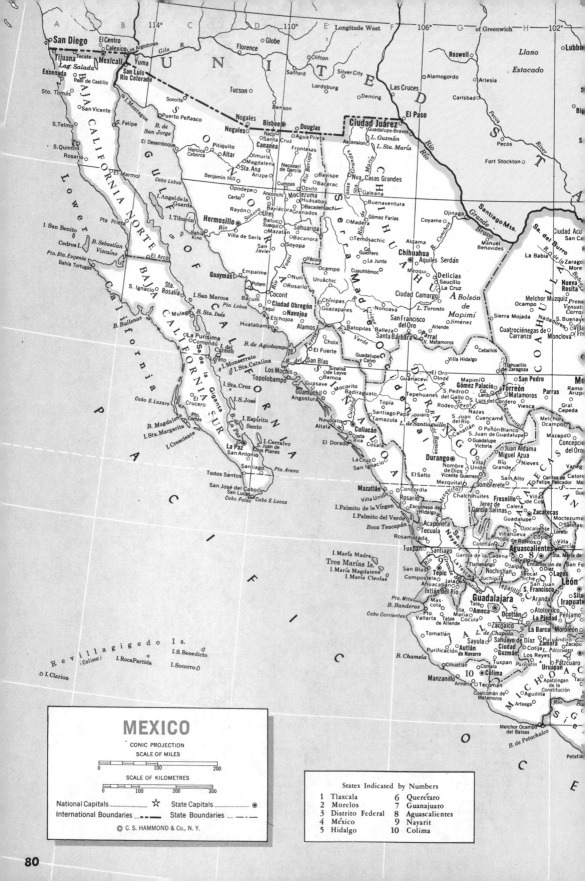

MEXICO

CONIC PROJECTION

SCALE OF MILES

0   100   200

SCALE OF KILOMETRES

0   100   200   300

National Capitals .... ☆   State Capitals ....◉
International Boundaries .. ▬ ▪ ▬   State Boundaries .... ▬ ·· ▬

© C. S. HAMMOND & Co., N.Y.

States Indicated by Numbers

1	Tlaxcala	6	Queretaro
2	Morelos	7	Guanajuato
3	Distrito Federal	8	Aguascalientes
4	México	9	Nayarit
5	Hidalgo	10	Colima

80

Map of
CANADA

SCALE OF MILES

| 0 | 100 | 200 | 300 | 400 | 500 |

✪ Capitals of Countries
◉ Capitals of Provinces
    and Territories
• Cities
▬▬ Boundaries of Countries
▬▬ Boundaries of Provinces
    and Territories
·········· Boundaries of Districts
▲ Mountain Peaks

ARCTIC OCEAN

BERING ASIA
U.S.S.R.

St. Lawrence
Island

Bering Strait

SEA

Nome

BEAUFORT SEA

Point Barrow

North Magnetic Pole
Queen Eliza

M'Clure Strait

Viscount Melvi
Sound

DISTRICT

Banks
Island

Amundsen
Gulf

Prince
of
Wales
Island

Victoria
Island

UNITED STATES

ALASKA

BROOKS RANGE

Yukon River

Mt. McKinley

ALASKA RANGE

Fairbanks

Anchorage

Alaska Peninsula

Kodiak
Island

Gulf of Alaska

YUKON TERRITORY

MACKENZIE MTS

Dawson

Mt.
Logan

Whitehorse

Inuvik

Coppermine

Great Bear
Lake

Port Radium

Mackenzie River

DISTRICT
OF MACKENZIE

NORTHWEST

Yellowknife

Fort
Providence

Great Slave
Lake

Fort Smith

Uranium City

Lake
Athabasca

Reindeer
Lake

PACIFIC OCEAN

Alexander

Juneau

Archipelago

COAST

BRITISH

ROCKY

Prince Rupert

Hazelton

Queen
Charlotte
Islands

Kitimat

COLUMBIA

MOUNTAINS

Prince
George

Fort
Nelson

Dawson
Creek

Peace River

Fort
McMurray

Peace
River

ALBERTA

SASKATCHEWAN

Prince
Albert

Flin Flon

MA

The Pas

Vancouver
Island

Kamloops

Fraser River

Edmonton

N.
Saskatchewan R.

Saskatoon

Saskatchewan R.

Victoria

Cape
Flattery

Vancouver

Calgary

Medicine
Hat

Regina

Winnipe

Seattle

Lethbridge

S.
Saskatchewan

Moose Jaw

Bran

CASCADE RANGE

Portland

Columbia

Spokane

Snake River

UNITED

MOUNTAINS

Helena

Missouri

Bismarck

STA

Boise

Snake River

Pierre

Ri

Longitude

110°

West of

100°

82

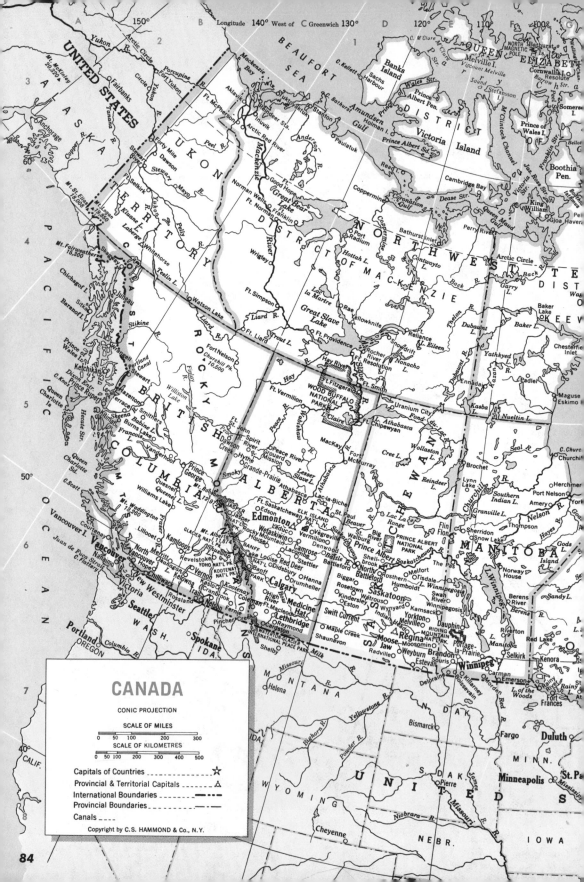

MARITIME PROVINCES

SCALE OF MILES

0 10 20 30 40 50

Provincial Capitals .... ⊛   Provincial Boundaries ----
County Seats .... ⊙   County Boundaries ---
International Boundaries -·-·-

Copyright by C. S. HAMMOND & CO., N. Y.

86

N

GULF OF

Brion I.   Bird Rock

Leslie
Grosse I.   East I.
Coffin I.
Grand Entry
MAGDALEN ISLANDS
(To Quebec)
Grindstone I.   Alright I.
Étang-du-Nord   House Har.
Grindstone I.   Pointe-Basse
Pleasant
Bay
Amherst I.   Entry I.
Southwest Cape   Havre-Aubert

CABOT STR.

C. Anguille
Codroy   South
Branch
NEWFOUNDLAND

C. Ray
Port-aux-Basques
Channel

ST.   LAWRENCE

North Point

. Kildare

cumpeque Bay

PRINCE EDWARD
ISLAND

St. Lawrence
C. St. Lawrence   St. Lawrence
Bay   Cape North
Bay St. Lawrence
Aspy Bay
Cape North   Dingwall
C. Egmont
Pleasant Bay   Neils Harbour
CAPE BRETON
HIGHLANDS
NAT'L
PARK
Chéticamp I.   Ingonish
Chéticamp   Bay Ingonish
Cape Smoky
Grand-Étang   Briton Cove

Cape Breton
Island

Molpeque B.
Stanley Bridge
Kensington   Glasgow
Eleanor   PRINCE EDW. I.
NAT'L PARK
Freetown   N. Rustico   Tracadie Bay
Emerald   Hunters River   Morell   St. Peters   East Point
Port   New Wiltshire   Mount   Bay   Elmira   South Lake
Borden   Crapaud   Parkdale   Stewart
Victoria   Cherry   Peake Station
Charlottetown   Valley
St. Peter   Pownal   Cardigan
Spear   Hillsborough   Vernon   Georgetown
Bridge   Sturgeon   Cardigan Bay
Monta   Murray Har.
Murray   Cape Bear
Prim   River   Murray Harbour
Point   Wood Is.

Margaree Harbour   Indian Brook
Sea Wolf
(Margaree I.)   Margaree Valley
North East Margaree   Englishtown   St. Ann's Bay   New Campbellton
Inverness   Scots-   St.   Sydney Mines   New Waterford
ville   Ann's   North   Dominion
Strathlorne   Middle   Sydney   Glace Bay
River   Nyanza   Reserve Mines
Mabou   L.   Baddeck   North   Port-   C. Morien
Ainslie   Sydney   Morien
McKinnon   Sydney   Mira Bay
Port Hood   Har.   Grand   CAPE BRETON   Scatari I.
Port Hood   Narrows   East Bay   Main-à-Dieu
Whycocomagh   Bras   Big   Cape Breton
Orangedale   d'Or   Pond
C. George   St.   River Denys   Lake   Shunacadie   Louisburg
Ballantynes   Judique   Sta.   West Bay   Irish Cove   Gabarouse
Cove   Georges   Havre-   Loch   Gabarus Bay
Long Point   Boucher   St.   Lomond   Cape Gabarus
Craigmore   Peters   Fourchu
Pictou I.   Bay   Hastings   Grand River
River John   Malignant   Frankville   Port   Ardoise
Caribou I.   Cove   Pomquet   Hawkesbury   L'Ardoise
Pictou Har.   Arisaig   Monastery   Grand River

Pugwash Har.
Pugwash
Port   Wallace
Howe   Malagash
Oxford Jct.   Tatamagouche
Westchester Sta.
Wallace
Denmark
River John
Pictou
Pictou Har.
Pictou Landing

Antigonish
ANTIGONISH
Trenton   St.
Westville   Andrews   Mulgrave   Bayfield
New Glasgow   Ohio   N. Lochaber   Lincolnville   Madame I.
Stellarton   Boylston
Wentworth Earltown   1,206   Bridgeville   Guysborough   Arichat
Sta.   Sunnybrae   Chedabucto Bay   Canso
Clondonderry   Belmont   West River   Queensport   Hazel Hill
North River   Station   Caledonia   Whitehead
Great   Kempt Town   Goshen   Larry's River
Village   Debert   Aspen   Sherbrooke   New Harbour
Brook-   Middle Stewiacke   Golden-   Isaac's Harbour
field   Upper   ville   Goldboro
Upper   Stewiacke   Port Hillford
Truro   Stewiacke   Liscomb   Goose I.
Debec   Liscomb Sec.   Liscomb I.
Musquodoboit R.   Moser   Barren I.
Stewiacke   River   Goose I.
Ecum Secum

Oldham   Mooseland
Goff's   Meaghers
Grant   Sheet
Milford   Elderbank   Harbour
Station   Ship
Shubenacadie   Har.
Bedford   Musquodoboit   Tangier
HALIFAX   Three Fathom Har.   Taylor Head
Hacketts Cove   Jeddore Har.
Peggy's Cove   Eastern Passage
Dartmouth   Halifax Har.
Ketch Harbour

ATLANTIC   OCEAN

54°
52°
Belle
Isle
C. Bauld
Cook's Har.   Griquet
St. Anthony
Cape   C. St. John   Roddickton
Onion   Englee   Bell I.

ATLANTIC

OCEAN

Flower's   Groais I.
Cove   Conche
Port   Roddickton
Saunders   Englee

Harbour
Deep
Daniel's   St. Barbe Is.
Harbour   Fleur-de-Lys

Cow Head   Partridge Pt.
White   C. St. John   Twillingate
Bay   La Scie   Fogo
Jackson's   Little Bay Is.   Joe Batts Arm
Arm   Baie-Verte   Fogo I.
King's   Spring-   Notre Dame Bay   Musgrave Harbour
Bonne Bay   Norris Pt.   Point   dale   C. Freels
Trout River   Hampden   Leamington   Newtown
Point Leamington   Lumsden
Bay of Islands   Robert's Arm   Campbellton   Greenspond
Lark Harbour   Botwood   Lewisporte   Wesley-
Deer   Howley   Bishop's   Norris Arm   ville   Bonavista
Lake   Windsor   Falls   Badger   Gander   Bay
Corner Brook   Buchans   Grand   L.
Red   Falls   Gambo   Glovertown   Bonavista
Indian   Millertown   Gander   Catalina
Stephenville   Victoria   TERRA NOVA   Port Union
Port-au-Port   L.   NAT'L PARK   Trinity   Trinity
St. George's   Meelpaeg   Head Bay   Port Blandford   Bay
Robinsons   L.   D'Espoir   Clarenville
Cape   Carbonear
St. George's   St. Alban's   Harbour Grace
Port-au-Port   Bay Roberts
St. Georges   South   Torbay
C. Anguille   Branch   Placentia
Codroy   Burgeo   Bay   St. JOHN'S
Port-aux-   Rose-Blanche   Ramea   Harbour Breton
Basques   Channel   Rames Is.   Fortune Bay   Placentia
Penguin   Brunette I.   St.
Is.   Grand Bank   Mary's Bay   Calvert
ST. PIERRE & MIQUELON   Fortune   Lawn   Ferryland
(Fr.)   Miquelon   Burin Bay   Lamaline   Renews
St-   Trepassey
Pierre   C. Race

58°   56°   54°

87

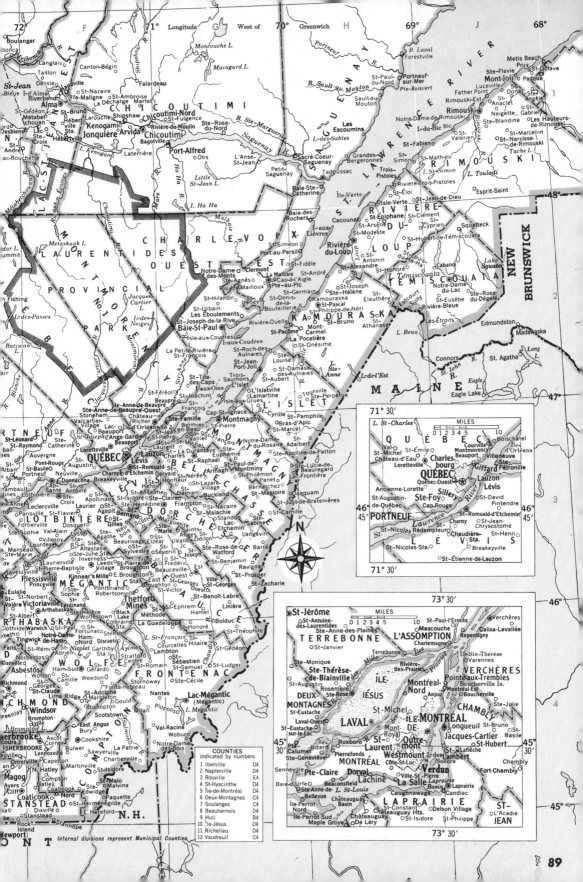

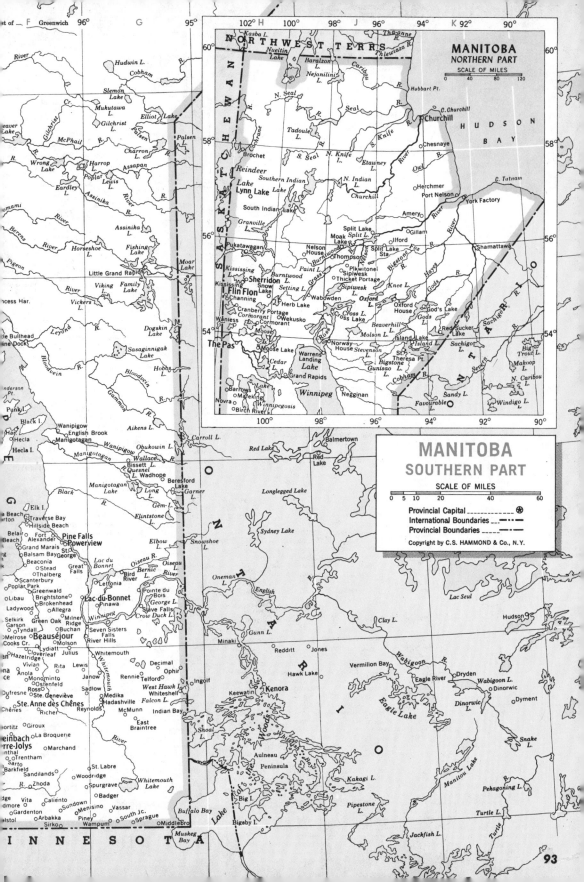

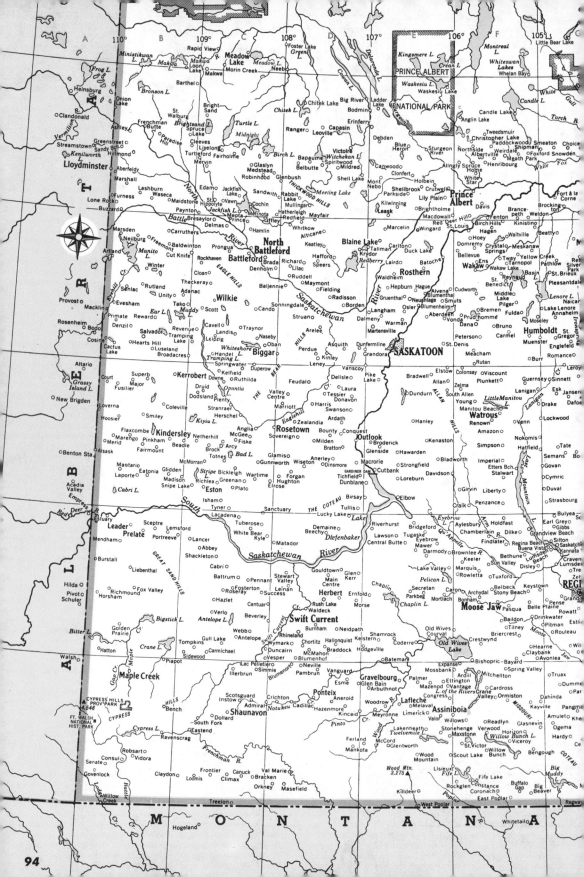

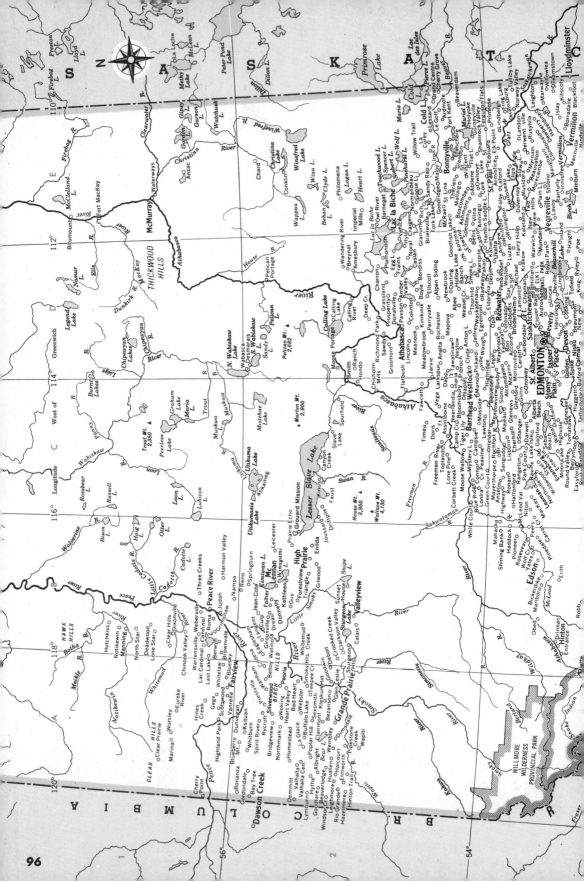

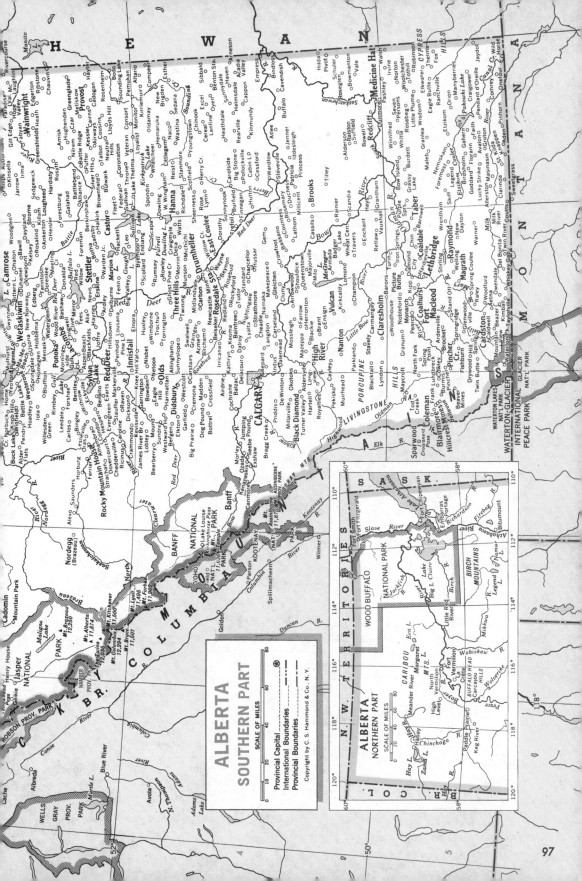

ALBERTA
SOUTHERN PART

SCALE OF MILES

Provincial Capital ⊛
International Boundaries
Provincial Boundaries

Copyright by C. S. Hammond & Co., N. Y.

BRITISH COLUMBIA
SOUTHERN PART

SCALE

0 15 30   60   90   120 MI.

0 15 30   60   90   120 KM.

Provincial Capital .... ⊛
State Capital .... ◉
International Boundaries .... ▬ ▪ ▬ ▪ ▬
Provincial Boundaries .... ▬ ▬ ▬

© C.S. HAMMOND & Co., N.Y.

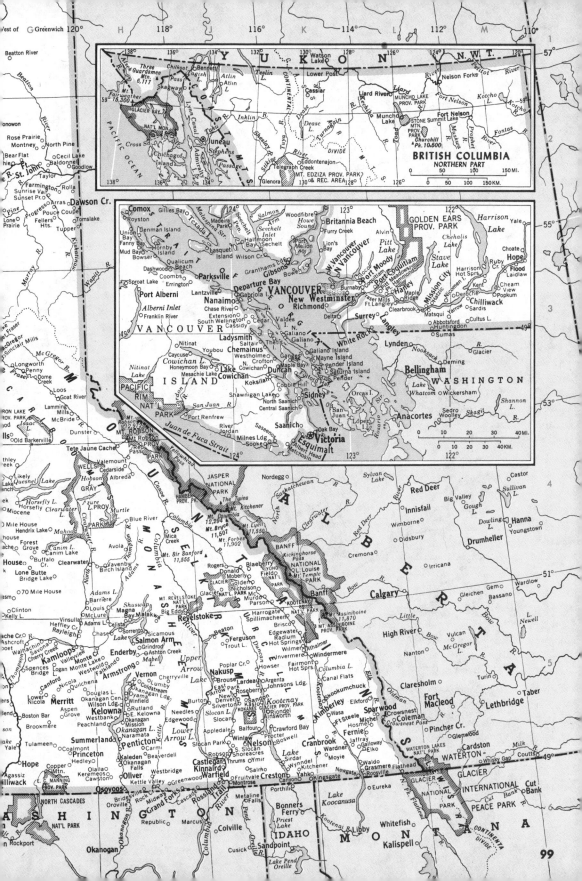

Map of
UNITED STATES
LAMBERT CONFORMAL CONIC PROJECTION
Copyright by C. S. HAMMOND & Co., N.Y.

SCALE OF MILES

| 0 | 50 | 100 | 200 | 300 |

Capitals of Countries
State and Provincial Capitals
International Boundaries
State Boundaries
Provincial Boundaries

Copyright by C. S. Hammond & Co., N.Y.

APPROXIMATE ELEVATIONS
10,000 ft.
5,000 ft.
2,000 ft.
1,000 ft.
500 ft.
Sea level
Depression

Longitude 90° West of Greenwich

101

UNITED STATES

POLYCONIC PROJECTION

SCALE OF MILES

0 50 100   200   300   400

SCALE OF KILOMETRES

0   100   200   300   400

Capitals of Countries ....☆
State Capitals ....△
International Boundaries ....

© Copyright HAMMOND INCORPORATED, Maplewood, N.J.

103

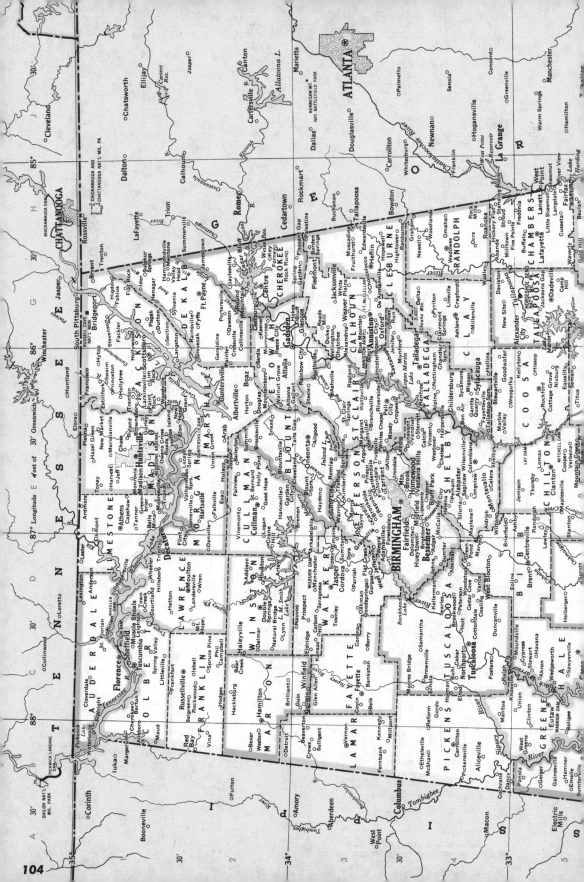

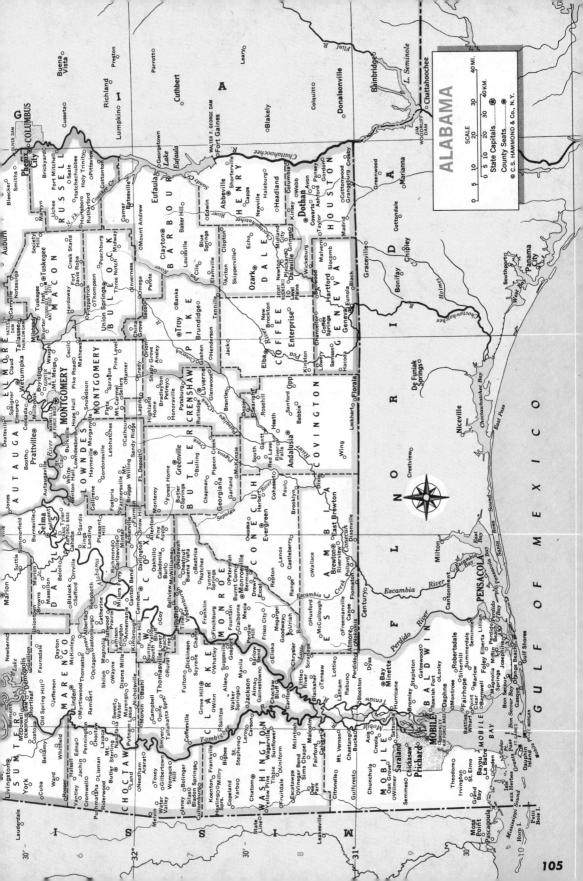

A map of Alaska.

Longitude 175° A 180° B 175° C 170° D 165° E 160° F 155° G

Inset map (upper left):

152° 150° 148° 146°

L. Louise
Talkeetna
Fish Lake
Montana
TALKEETNA
MTS.
Glennallen
Tazlina Glacier
Lodge
Nelchina
Tazlina L.
Caswell
Chickaloon
62°
Skwentna R.
Eureka Lodge
Willow
Jonesville
Eska
Sutton
CHUGACH
Mt. Gerdine
11,258
Skwentna
Houston
Wasilla
Palmer
Matanuska
Arm
Mt. Marcus
Baker
13,176
Susitna R.
Big Lake
Eklutna
Mt. Spurr
11,070
Beluga
ELMENDORF A.F.B.
Chugiak
Birchwood
Mt. Witherspoon
12,012
ANCHORAGE
FT. RICHARDSON
Spenard
Eagle River
Mt. Goode
10,610
Columbia Gl.
Valdez
Tyonek
Fire I.D.
Girdwood
Esther
Ellamar
Trading Bay
Turnagain Arm
Portage
Whittier
Tatitlek
Kustatan
Inlet
Hope
Perry
Prince
Cordova
Kalgin I.
Kenai
Port
Nellie Juan
Naked I.
William
Cohoe
Soldotna
Sterling
Cooper Moose
Landing Pass
Kenai
Sound
Hinchinbrook
Kasilof
Kenai
Knight I.
I.
60°
Clam Gulch
Tustumena L.
Seward
Bainbridge I.
Montague
Ninilchik
Anchor Pt.
Nikolaevsk
KENAI
Skilak B.
Blying Sound
Montague
I.
Kachemak Bay
Homer
Harding Icefield
Resurrection
Clear
Kachemak
Seldovia
KENAI FJORDS
MOUNTAINS
Pye I.
Port Graham
English Bay
Portlock
Nuka B.
NAT'L MON.
Chugach Is.
Barren Is.
Gore Pt.
GULF OF ALASKA
0 25 50 75 MI.
0 25 50 75 KM.
152° 150°

ARCTIC
Barrow
Pt. Barrow
Pt. Barrow Inlet
Pt. Franklin Peard
Tangent
Smith Bay
Wainwright
Icy Cape
ARCTIC
Point Lay
Kokolik R.
Utukok R.
C. Lisburne
Cape Lisburne
DE LONG MTS.
LOOKOUT RIDGE
Colville R.
BROOKS
Point Hope
Pt. Hope
Tingmerkpuk Mtn.
3,787
Noatak
Mtn.
4,500
NOATAK NAT'L MON.
GATES OF THE
ARCTIC
Kivalina
BAIRD MTS.
SCHWATKA MTS.
ENDICO
CAPE KRUSENSTERN
NAT'L MON.
KOBUK VALLEY
NAT'L MON.
Ambler
Kobuk
Kotzebue
Kiana
Shungnak
Kalla
Noorvik
WARING MTS.
Selawik
Arctic Circle
Hogatza
(Hog River)
C. Espenberg
Kotzebue Sound
Inland L.
Buckland
Huslia
CHUKCHI
SEA
Shishmaref
Inchoun
Uelen
C. Dezhnev
Little Diomede
Big Diomede I.
Diomede
Wales
BERING LAND BRIDGE
SEWARD PENINSULA
Haycock
Koyukuk
Melozitna R.
U.S.S.R.
Mechigmen
Port Clarence
Teller
Brevig Mission NAT'L MON.
Imuruk Basin
King I.
Tin City
Pt. Spencer
Council
White Mtn.
Moses Point
Koyuk
Nulato
Galena
Ruby
Long
Arakamchechen I.
Nome
Solomon
Bluff
Golovin
Elim
Norton
Ungalik
Kaltag
DAVIS
C. Darby
Denbigh
Shaktoolik
Providenyia
C. Chaplin
Koyuk
Unalakleet
KAIYUH MTS.
NORTON
SOUND
St. Lawrence I.
Gambell
Savoonga
Stuart I.
Stebbins
St. Michael
Innoko R.
Grayling
KUSKOKWIM MTS.
McGrath
Northeast Cape
Emmonak
(Emanguk)
Kotlik
Pastol Bay
Chaneliak
Anvik
Holikachuk
Shageluk
Farewell
Southeast Cape
Alakanuk
Sheldon Point
BERING
St. Marys
(Andreafski)
Holy Cross
Stony River
Mountain Village
Fortuna Ledge
(Marshall)
Crooked Creek
Sleetmute
SEA
Scammon Bay
C. Romanzof
Pitkas Point
Pilot Sta.
Russian Mission
Napamute
Kalskag
Hall I.
Glory of Russia Cape
C. Upright
Hooper Bay
Chevak
Kashunuk R.
Kalskag
Lower Kalskag
TAYLOR MTS.
St. Matthew
Hazen B.
Newtok
Akiak
Akiachak
Aniak Kuskokwim R.
Big River
LAKE CLARK NAT'L MON.
Nelson
(Akolmiut)
Akiak
Kwethluk
Kashegelok
Nogamut
C. Mohican
Mekoryuk
Tununak
Toksook Bay
Napaskiak
Chuathbaluk
Tikchik Lakes
Nunivak I.
Nash Harbor
Nightmute
Kipnuk
Chefornak
Tuntutuliak
Eek
Tikchik
Kwigillingok
Kongiganak
Kuskokwim Bay
Quinhagak
Nuyakuk L.S.
Koliganek
Iliamna
Nondalton
Mendenhall
Goodnews Bay
New Stuyahok
Ekwok
Iliamna L.
Kakhonak
Platinum
Togiak
Aleknagik
Levelock
Igiugig
Kukaklek L.
Dillingham
Nushagak
Clarks Pt.
C. Newenham
Manokotak
Naknek
King Salmon
Ekuk
VALLEY OF 10,000
SMOKES
Hagemeister I.
Togiak B.
Walrus I.
Kanakanak
Egegik
KATMAI
Mt. Katmai
Vol. 6,715
NAT'L MON.
C. Constantine
Pilot Point
Mt. Katmai
7,000
BRISTOL
BAY
Ugashik
Ugashik Lakes
BECHAROF NAT'L MON.
St. Paul I.
St. Paul
Walrus I.
Becharof L.
Otter I.
PRIBILOF IS.
Port Heiden
Mt. Chiginagak
7,000
Aniakchak Crater 4,275
ANIAKCHAK NAT'L MON.
St. George
St. George
Meshik
Chignik Lagoon
Chignik
Sutwik I.
Veniaminof Crater
8,225
Port Moller
Port Moller
Chignik B.
Chignik
Chiginik Lake
TRINITY
SHUMAGIN IS.
Nelson Lagoon
Herendeen Bay
Perryville
Mitrofania I.
Semidi Is.
Chirikof I.
Amak I.
Pavlof Vol. 8,905
Pavlof
Kupreanof Pt.
False Pass
Port Moller
Stepovak B.
Sand Point
Shishaldin Vol. 9,372
Unimak I.
Scotch Cap
Belkofski
Koniuji Is.
Akun
Unimak Pass
King Cove
Nagai Is.
Fauloff Harbor
Unalaska
ALEUTIAN
Akutan Pass
Deer I.
Cold B.
Sanak I.
Akutan
Tigalda I.
Akutan Vol. 6,680
Krenitzin Is.
Bogoslof I. Dutch Harbor
Fort Glenn
Mt. Vsevidof 7,050
Umnak I.
C. Izigan
Unalaska
Chuginadak I.
Is. of the Four
Mountains
Nikolski
FOX ISLANDS
Amukta Pass
Yunaska I.
Seguam Pass
Chagulak I.
Seguam I.
Amukta I.
ALEUTIAN
Amlia I.
Seguam Pass
Seguam

ALASKA
POLYCONIC PROJECTION
SCALE
0 50 100 150 200 MI.
0 50 100 150 200 KM.
State and Territorial Capitals..............⊛
Court Houses.......................................◉
International Boundaries................. — ∙ —
Senatorial District Boundaries........ — — —
© C.S. HAMMOND & Co., N.Y.

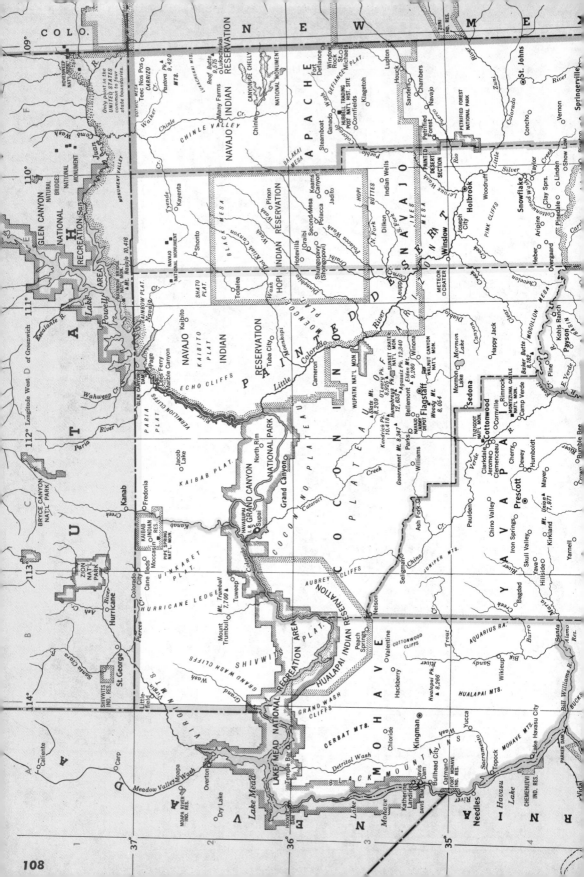

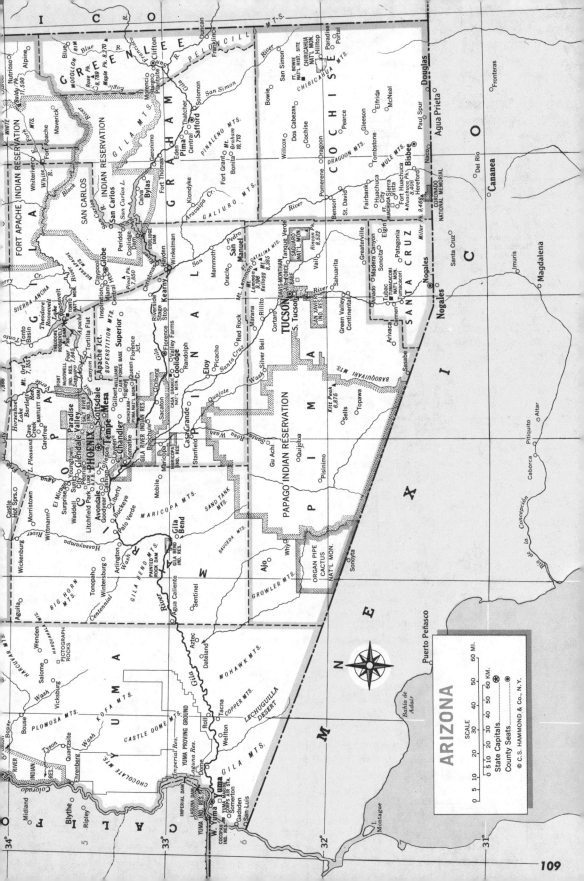

ARIZONA

SCALE
0 5 10 20 30 40 50 60 MI.
0 10 20 30 40 50 60 KM.
State Capitals........⊛
County Seats.........◉
© C.S. HAMMOND & CO., N.Y.

109

ARKANSAS

SCALE

0   5   10   20   30   40 MI.

0 5 10   20   30   40 KM.

State Capitals...............⊛

County Seats...............◉

© C.S. HAMMOND & Co., N.Y.

SACRAMENTO AND VICINITY

LOS ANGELES AND VICINITY

113

COLORADO

SCALE
0 5 10   20   30   40 MI.

0 5 10   20   30   40 KM.

State Capitals........⊛ County Seats........◉

© C.S. Hammond & Co., N.Y.

114

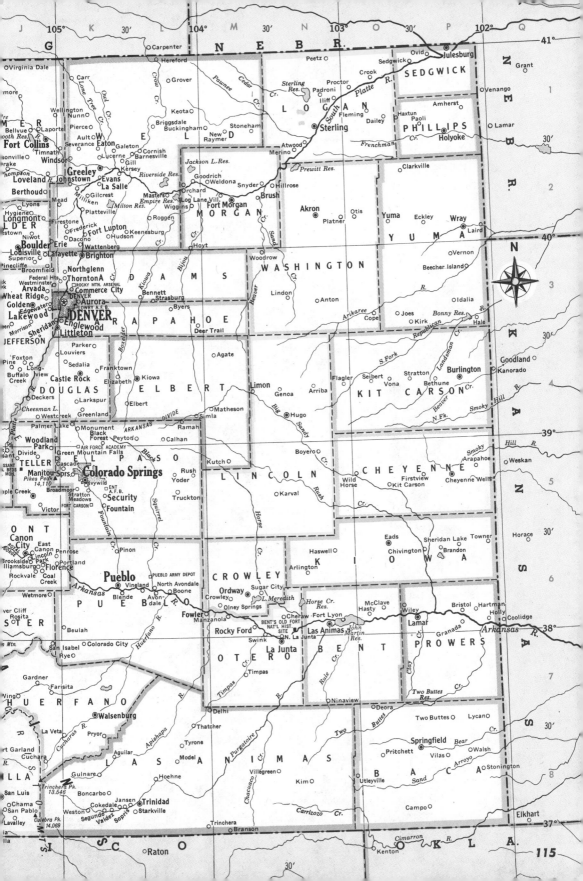

CONNECTICUT

SCALE

State Capitals..........................

© C.S. HAMMOND & Co., N.Y.

116

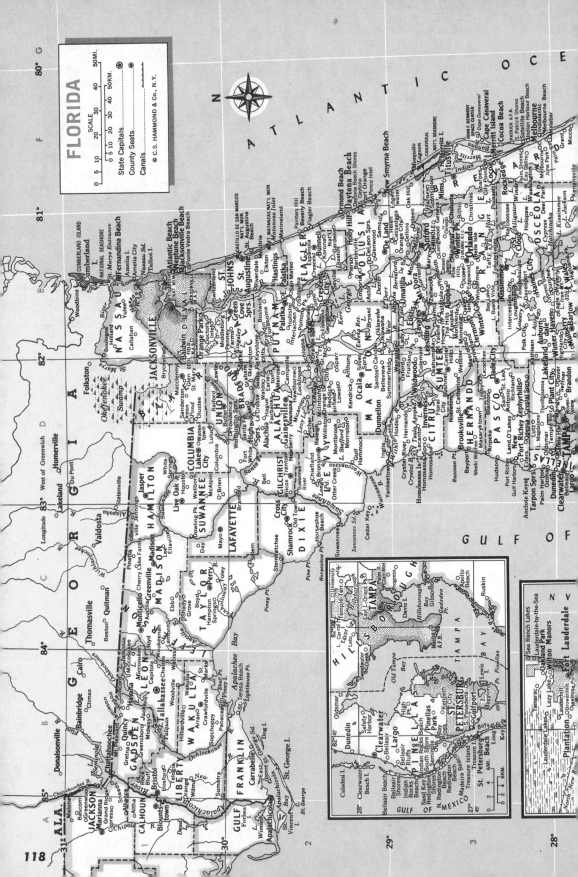

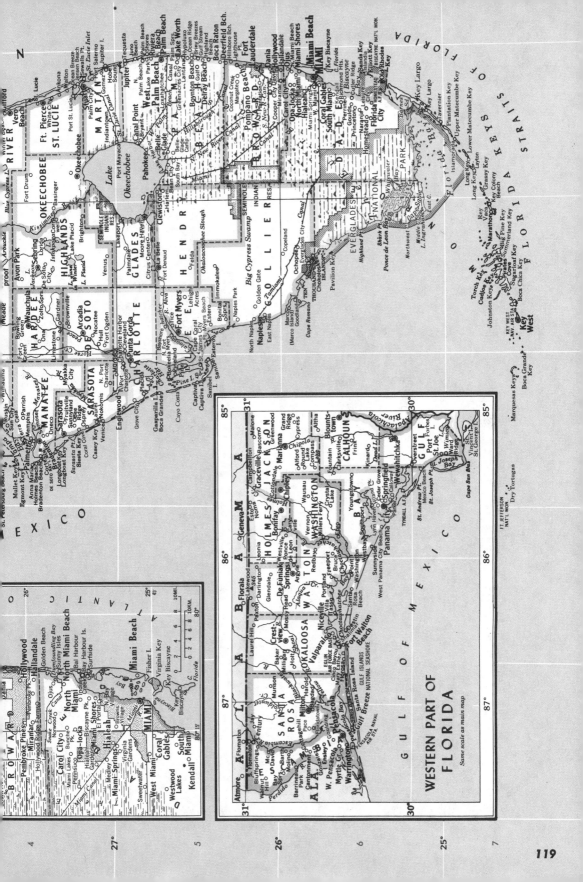

WESTERN PART OF FLORIDA

Same scale as main map

120

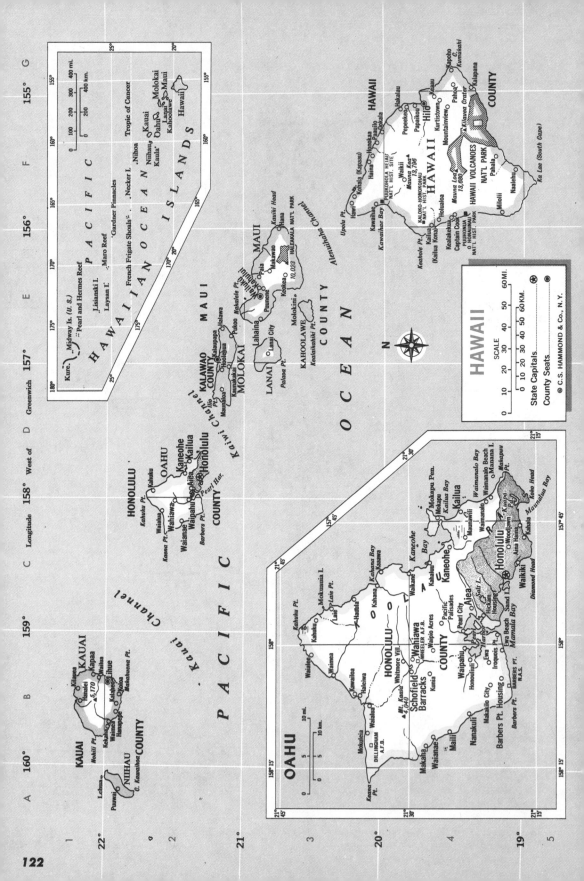

HAWAII

SCALE

10 20 30 40 50 60 MI.
0 10 20 30 40 50 60 KM.

⊛ State Capitals
⊙ County Seats

© C. S. HAMMOND & Co., N. Y.

HAWAIIAN ISLANDS

PACIFIC OCEAN

Midway Is. (U. S.)
Pearl and Hermes Reef
Kure
Lisianski I.
Laysan I.
Maro Reef
'Gardner Pinnacles'
French Frigate Shoals
Necker I.
Nihoa
Niihau
Kaula
Kauai
Oahu
Molokai
Lanai
Maui
Kahoolawe
Hawaii
Tropic of Cancer

400 mi.
400 km.
0 100 200 300
0 200 400

PACIFIC OCEAN

KAUAI

KAUAI COUNTY
Kilauea
Hanalei
Kapaa
Wailua
Lihue
Koloa
Waimea
Kekaha
Hanapepe
Kalaheo
Wailua
Makaweli Pt.
Nawiliwili Pt.
Kaena Pt.
Kawaihoa Pt.
5,170

NIIHAU
Lehua
Puuwai
C. Kawaihoa Pt.

Kauai Channel

OAHU
Kahuku
Kaneohe
Kailua
Aiea
Waipahu
Waianae
Wahiawa
Honolulu
Kaena Pt.
Kahuku Pt.
Barbers Pt.
Pearl Har.

HONOLULU COUNTY

Kaiwi Channel

MOLOKAI
Pukoo
Kaunakakai
Kaluaaha
Halawa
Kualapuu
Hoolehua
Ilio Pt.
Mo'omomi Pt.
Laau Pt.

KALAWAO COUNTY
Kalaupapa

MAUI COUNTY

MAUI
Wailuku
Kahului
Paia
Makawao
Keokea
Keanae
Hana
Lahaina
Puunene
Kaanapali
Kauiki Head
Nakalele Pt.
Kahakuloa Pt.
10,023
HALEAKALA NAT'L PARK

LANAI
Lanai City
Palaoa Pt.

KAHOOLAWE
Molokini
Kealaikahiki Pt.

Alenuihaha Channel

HAWAII

HAWAII COUNTY
Kohala (Kapaau)
Hawi
Honokaa
Paauilo
Ookala
Pepeekeo
Papaikou
Hilo
Kurtistown
Mountainview
Haina
Waikii
Pahoa
Opihikao
C. Kumukahi
Kalapana
Keaau
Kilauea Crater
Mauna Kea
13,796
Mauna Loa
13,680
PUUKOHOLA HEIAU NAT'L HIST. SITE
KALOKO-HONOKOHAU NAT'L HIST. PARK
Waimea
Kawaihae
Kawaihae Bay
Keahole Pt.
Kailua (Kailua Kona)
Keauhou
Kahaluu
Holualoa
Kealakekua
Captain Cook
PUUHONUA O HONAUNAU NAT'L HIST. PARK
Honaunau
HAWAII VOLCANOES NAT'L PARK
Pahala
Naalehu
Milolii
Upolu Pt.
Ka Lae (South Cape)

PACIFIC OCEAN

OAHU

HONOLULU COUNTY

Kahuku Pt.
Kahuku
Kaena Pt.
Mokuauia I.
Laie Pt.
Laie
Kahana
Hauula
Kaaawa
Kahaluu
Waiahole
Kaneohe Bay
Kailua Bay
Mokapu Pen.
Mokapu
Kailua
Waimanalo Bay
Waimanalo
Waimanalo Beach
Manana I.
Makapuu
Makapuu Pt.
Makaha
Waianae
Maili
Nanakuli
Barbers Pt. Housing
BARBERS PT. N.A.S.
Barbers Pt.
Makakilo City
Honouliuli
Ewa Beach
Ewa
Waipahu
Iroquois Pt.
Iroquois Pt.
Sand I.
Salt L.
Aiea
Pearl City
Pacific Palisades
Waipio Acres
WHEELER A.F.B.
Wahiawa
Whitmore Vill.
Schofield Barracks
Kunia
Waipahu
Mt. Kaala
4,040
Mokuleia
Waialua
Haleiwa
Kawailoa
Waimea
Waialee
Kaena Pt.
DILLINGHAM A.F.B.
Koolau
Waiawa
Waawa
Kaneohe
Honolulu
Woodlawn
Aina Haina
Kahala
Waikiki
Diamond Head
Koko Head
Maunalua Bay
Mamala Bay
HICKAM HOUSING
Makapuu

WAILUPE
Maumawili
Maunawili

10 mi.
10 km.
0 5
0 5

N

PACIFIC OCEAN

122

IDAHO

SCALE

0 — 20 — 40 — 60 — 80 MI.

0 — 20 — 40 — 60 — 80 KM.

State Capitals.............⊛

County Seats.............◉

© C.S. HAMMOND & Co., N.Y.

123

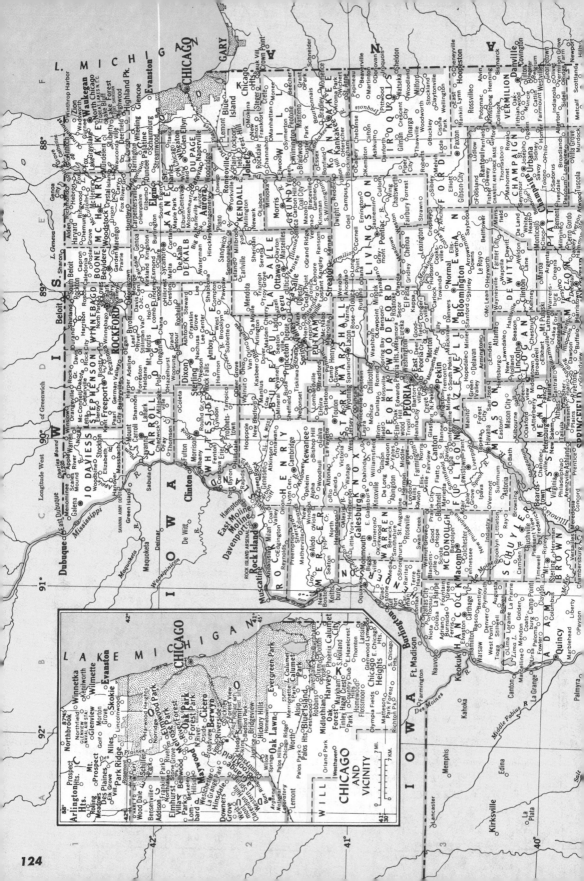

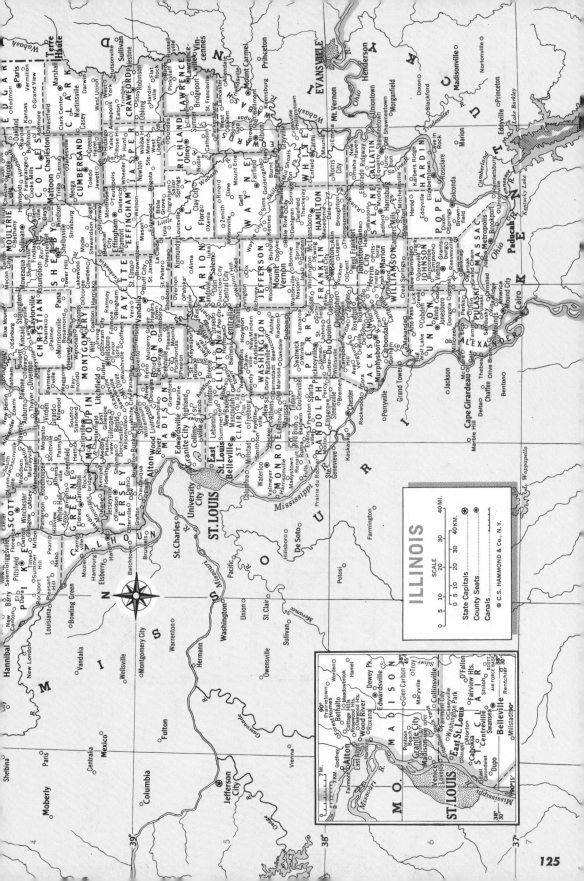

ILLINOIS

SCALE

0   10   20   30   40 MI.

0 5 10 20   30   40 KM.

State Capitals .... ✹

County Seats .... ◉

Canals ....

© C. S. HAMMOND & Co., N. Y.

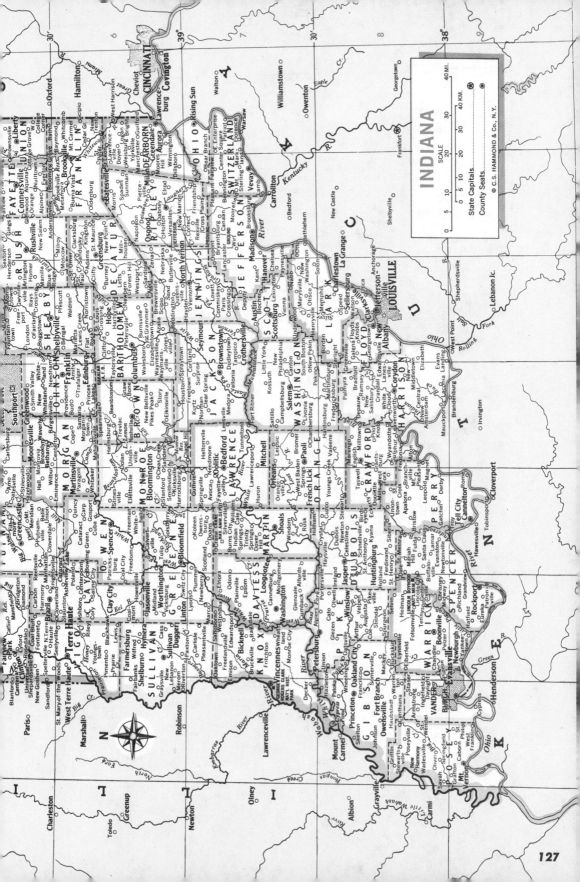

INDIANA

SCALE

State Capitals ⊛
County Seats ⊙

© C.S. HAMMOND & Co., N.Y.

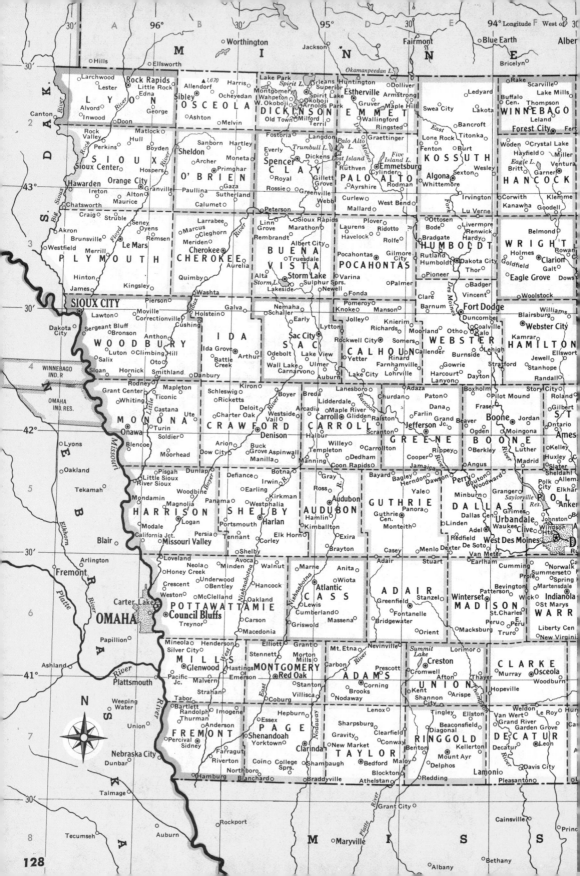

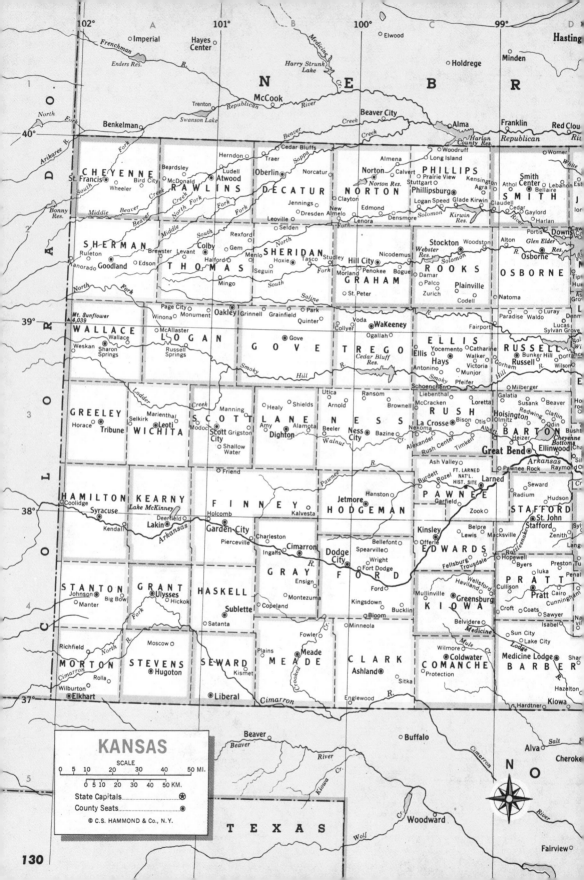

Kentucky map by C.S. Hammond & Co., N.Y.

LOUISIANA

SCALE

0 5 10   20   30   40 MI.

0 5 10   20   30   40 KM.

State Capitals.............⊛

Parish Seats..............◉

Canals....................

134

NEW ORLEANS, BATON ROUGE AND VICINITY

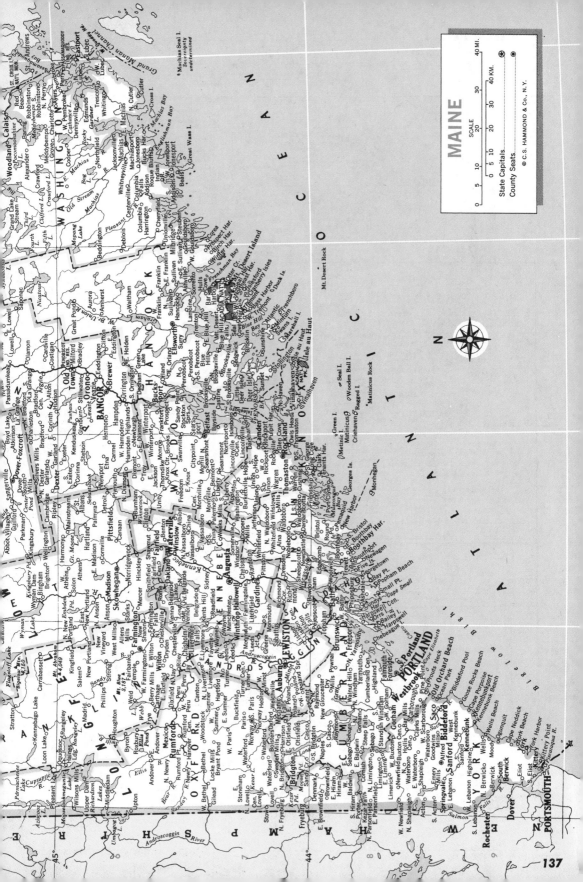

MARYLAND
and DELAWARE

SCALE

0   5   10   20   30MI.

0 5 10   20   30 KM.

National Capital .... ⊛
State Capitals .... ⊛
County Seats .... ⊙
Canals ....

WESTERN PART
OF
MARYLAND
Same scale as main map

© C.S. HAMMOND & Co., N.Y.

139

MASSACHUSETTS
and
RHODE ISLAND

SCALE

0   5   10   15   20 MI.

0   5   10   15   20 KM.

State Capitals..................................⊛
County Seats & Courthouses.......◉
Canals...

© C.S. HAMMOND & Co., N.Y.

143

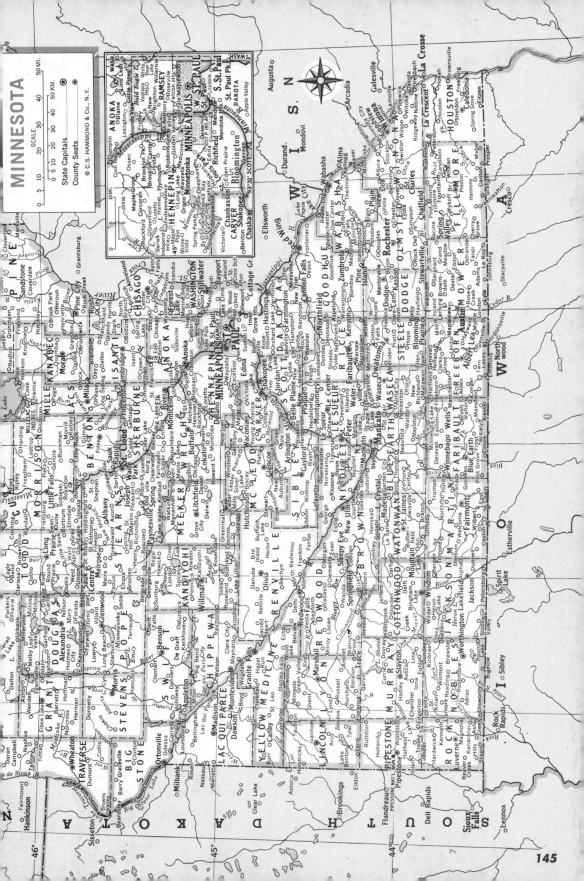

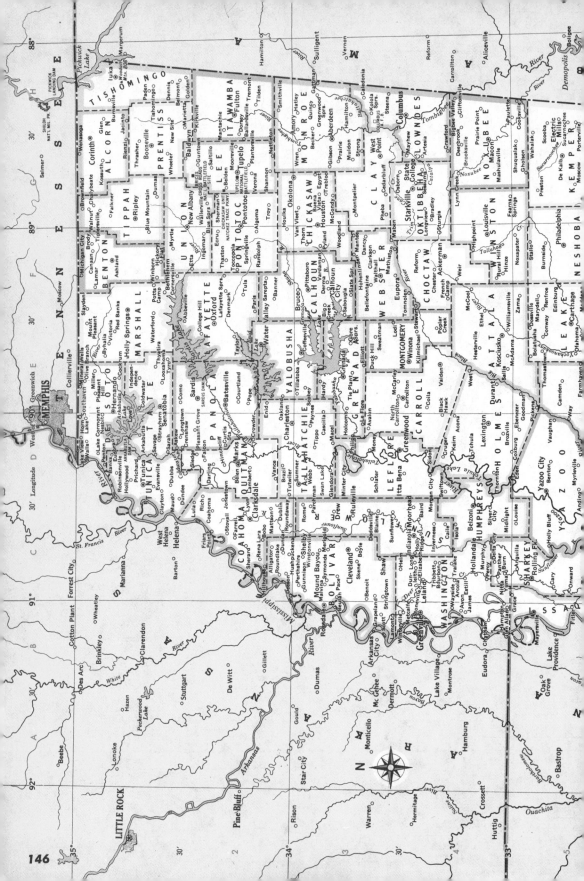

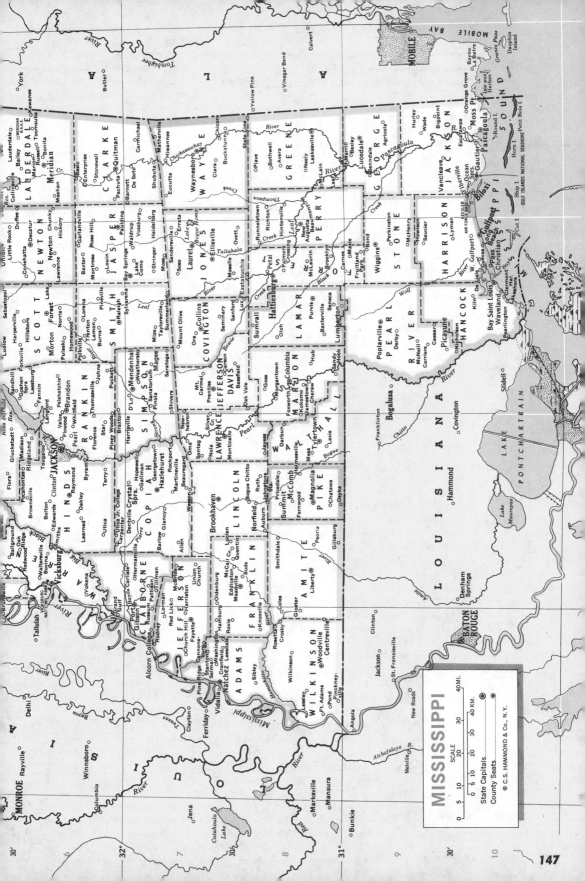

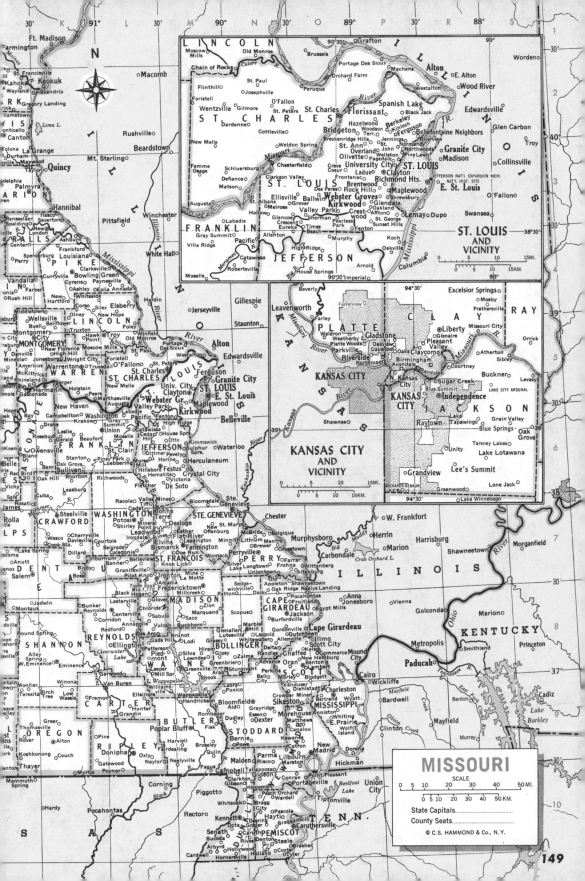

ST. LOUIS AND VICINITY

LINCOLN

Moscow Mills   Old Monroe   Brussels   Grafton
Chain of Rocks   Cuivre R.   Portage Des Sioux   Machens   Alton   E. Alton   Worden
Flinthill   St. Paul   Orchard Farm   Westaton   Wood River
Foristell   Josephville   Peruque   Spanish Lake   Edwardsville
Wentzville   Gilmore   O'Fallon   St. Charles   Florissant   Black Jack   Glen Carbon
ST. CHARLES   St. Peters   Hazelwood   Berkeley   Kinloch   Ferguson   Granite City   Troy
Dardenne   Bridgeton   Woodson   Terr.   Jennings   Northwoods   Madison
New Melle   Cottleville   Breckenridge Hills   St. Ann   Normandy   Pine Lawn   Collinsville
Weldon Spring   Overland   St. John   Northwoods
Schluersburg   Creve   Olivette   Pagedale   Riverview
Femme   Chesterfield   Coeur   Ladue   University City   ST. LOUIS
Osage   Clarkson Valley   Des Peres   Frontenac   Clayton   JEFFERSON NAT'L EXPANSION MEM.   O'Fallon
Defiance   Matson   St. Albans   Ellisville   Ballwin   Rock Hill   Richmond Hts.   NAT'L HIST. SITE   E. ST. LOUIS
Augusta   Melrose   Webster Groves   Maplewood   Shrewsbury
Hollow   Glencoe   Valley Park   Kirkwood   Glendale   Lemay   Dupo
FRANKLIN   Labadie   Crescent   Sherman   Oakland   Affton   St. George   Swansea
Gray Summit   Eureka   Times   Peerless   Sunset Hills
Allenton   Beach   Park   Fenton
Villa Ridge   Murphy   Koch   ST. LOUIS
Pacific   High Ridge   Oakville   AND
Moselle   Catawissa   Big   House Springs   Columbia   VICINITY
Robertsville   Arnold   38°30'
JEFFERSON   Imperial   90°

SCALE   0   5   10   15 MI.
0   5   10   15 KM.

KANSAS CITY AND VICINITY

Excelsior Springs
Leavenworth   Beverly   Farley   Mosby   Prathersville
Ferryview   Waldron   PLATTE   Weatherby   Gladstone   CLAY   Orrick
Platte Woods   Glenaire   Liberty   Missouri City   RAY
Parkville   Oakwood   Pleasant   Valley
Riverside   Northmoor   Oaks   Claycomo   Atherton   Sibley
KANSAS CITY   Avondale   Birmingham   Randolph   Courtney   Buckner   Levasy
Kansas   Sugar Creek   Lake City Arsenal
Shawnee   City   Blue Summit   Independence   JACKSON
Raytown   Lake   Tapawingo   Grain Valley
KANSAS CITY   Unity   Blue Springs   Oak Grove
AND   Tarsney Lakes   Lake Lotawana
VICINITY   Grandview   Lee's Summit   Greenwood   Lone Jack   38°
RICHARDS-GEBAUR   Lake Winnebago   94°30'

SCALE   0   5   10   15 MI.
0   5   10   15 KM.

MISSOURI

SCALE
0   5   10   20   30   40   50 MI.
0   5   10   20   30   40   50 KM.

State Capitals ....
County Seats ....

© C.S. HAMMOND & Co., N.Y.

149

151

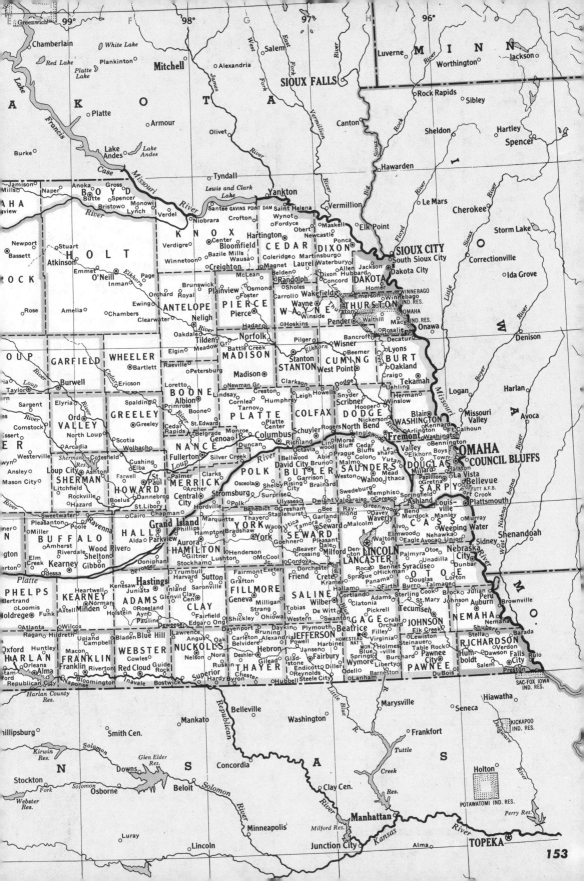

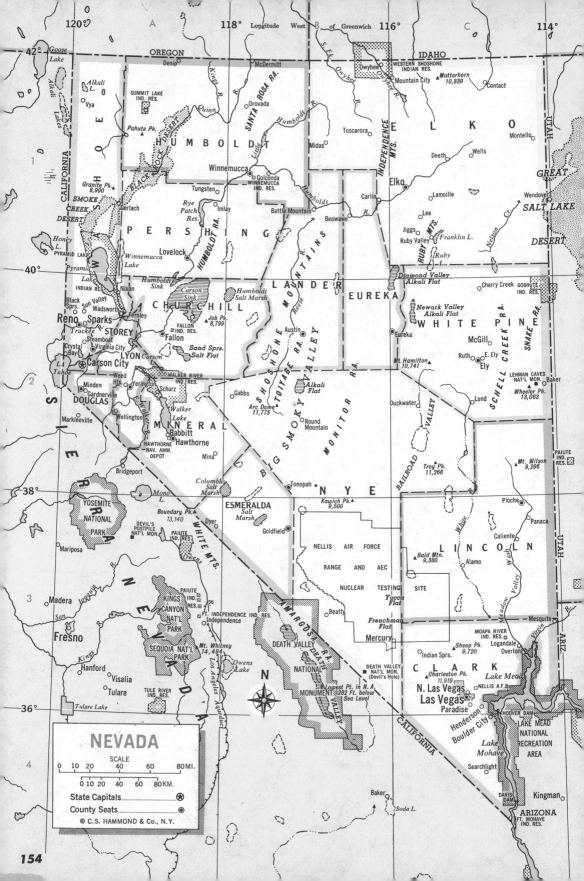

NEVADA

SCALE

0 10 20 40 60 80 MI.

0 10 20 40 60 80 KM.

State Capitals..............⊗

County Seats..............◉

© C.S. HAMMOND & CO., N.Y.

154

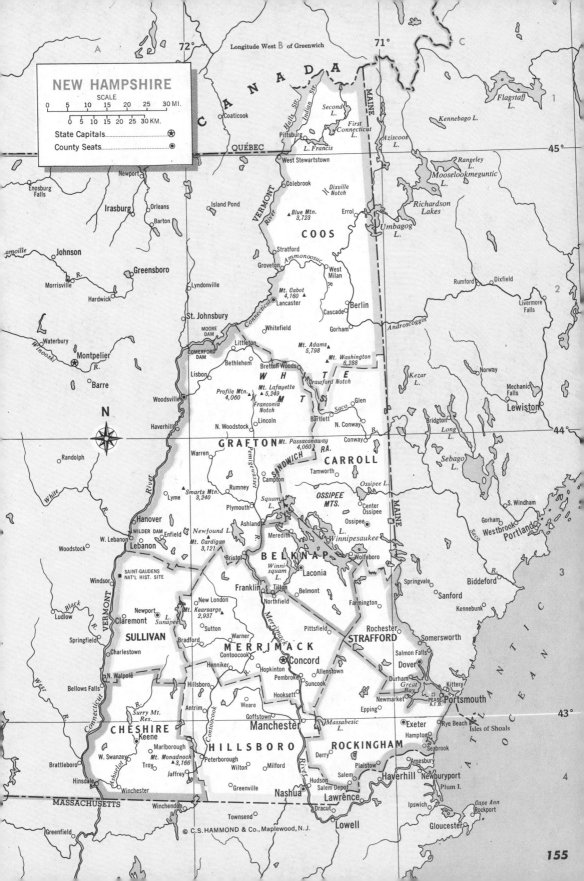

NEW HAMPSHIRE

SCALE

0 5 10 15 20 25 30 MI.

0 5 10 15 20 25 30 KM.

State Capitals..................⊛

County Seats....................◉

C A N A D A

Longitude West B of Greenwich

QUÉBEC

VERMONT

MAINE

Flagstaff L.

Coaticook

Halls Str.

Indian Str.

Second L.

First Connecticut L.

Kennebago L.

Pittsburg

L. Francis

West Stewartstown

Aziscoos L.

Rangeley L.

Mooselookmeguntic L.

Newport

Colebrook

Dixville Notch

Richardson Lakes

Enosburg Falls

Island Pond

Blue Mtn. 3,723

Errol

Umbagog L.

Irasburg

Orleans

COOS

Barton

Johnson

Greensboro

Stratford

Groveton

Ammonoosuc

West Milan

Berlin

Rumford

Dixfield

Morrisville

Hardwick

Lyndonville

Mt. Cabot 4,160

Lancaster

Cascade

Gorham

Androscoggin

Livermore Falls

St. Johnsbury

Whitefield

MOORE DAM

Littleton

Bretton Woods

Mt. Adams 5,798

Mt. Washington 6,288

Kezar L.

Norway

Waterbury

Winooski R.

COMERFORD DAM

Bethlehem

W H I T E

Crawford Notch

Mechanic Falls

Montpelier

Lisbon

Profile Mtn. 4,060

Mt. Lafayette 5,249

M T S.

Saco

Glen

Lewiston

Barre

Woodsville

Franconia Notch

Lincoln

Bartlett

N. Conway

Bridgton

Long L.

Haverhill

N. Woodstock

Mt. Passaconaway 4,060

Conway

Sebago L.

Randolph

GRAFTON

SANDWICH RA.

CARROLL

White R.

Warren

Tamworth

Ossipee L.

S. Windham

Rumney

Campton

OSSIPEE MTS.

Gorham

Lyme

Smarts Mtn. 3,240

Squam L.

Center Ossipee

Westbrook

Pemigewasset

Plymouth

Ashland

Ossipee

Portland

Hanover

Newfound L.

Meredith

L. Winnipesaukee

WILDER DAM

Enfield

Mt. Cardigan 3,121

Saco

Woodstock

W. Lebanon

Bristol

BELKNAP

Wolfeboro

Lebanon

Winni- squam L.

Springvale

Biddeford

Windsor

SAINT-GAUDENS NAT'L HIST. SITE

Franklin

Laconia

Sanford

Ludlow

Black R.

Newport

L. Sunapee

Mt. Kearsarge 2,937

Tilton

Belmont

Kennebunk

Claremont

New London

Northfield

Farmington

Springfield

Sutton

Warner

Rochester

Somersworth

Charlestown

SULLIVAN

Bradford

MERRIMACK

Pittsfield

STRAFFORD

Salmon Falls

Contoocook

Concord

Dover

Bellows Falls

N. Walpole

Henniker

Hopkinton

Allenstown

Durham

Great Bay

Kittery

West R.

Hillsboro

Pembroke

Suncook

Newmarket

PEASE A.F.B.

Portsmouth

Antrim

Weare

Hooksett

Epping

Goffstown

VERMONT

Surry Mt. Res.

Massabesic L.

Exeter

Rye Beach

Isles of Shoals

CHESHIRE

Marlborough

Peterborough

Manchester

Derry

ROCKINGHAM

Hampton

Keene

Mt. Monadnock 3,166

Wilton

Milford

Seabrook

W. Swanzey

Troy

HILLSBORO

Greenville

Plaistow

Amesbury

Haverhill

Newburyport

Brattleboro

Jaffrey

Hudson

Salem

Ashuelot R.

Salem Depot

Lawrence

Plum I.

Hinsdale

Winchester

Nashua

Dracut

Ipswich

Gloucester

Cape Ann Rockport

MASSACHUSETTS

Winchendon

Townsend

Lowell

Greenfield

© C.S. HAMMOND & Co., Maplewood, N.J.

A T L A N T I C   O C E A N

N

155

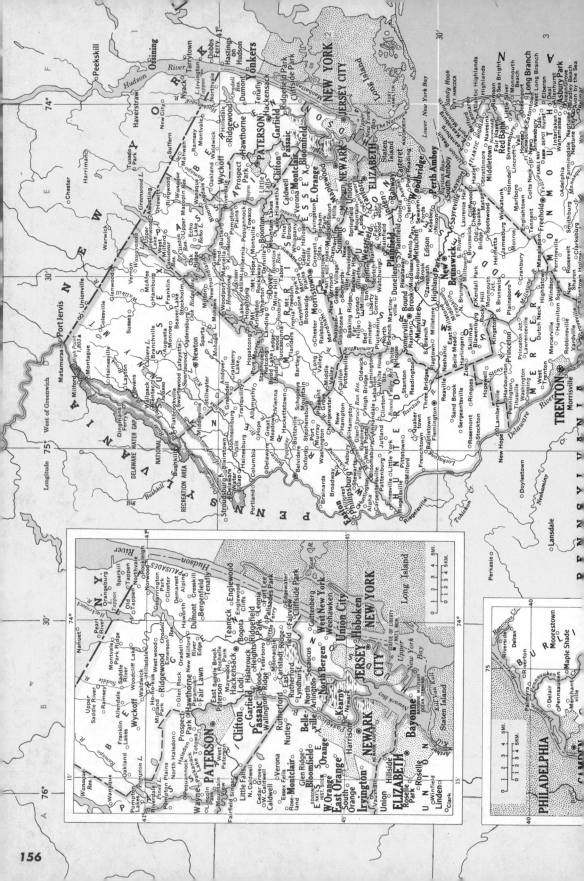

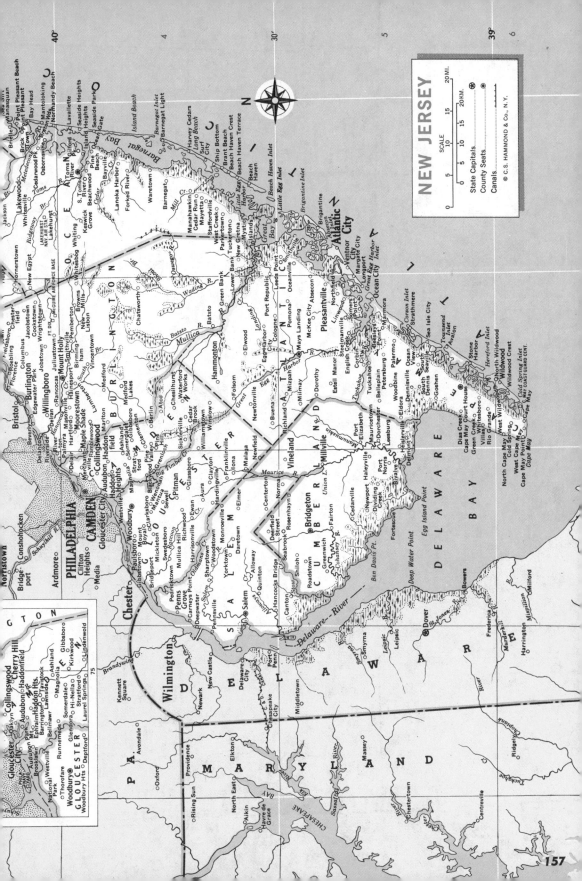

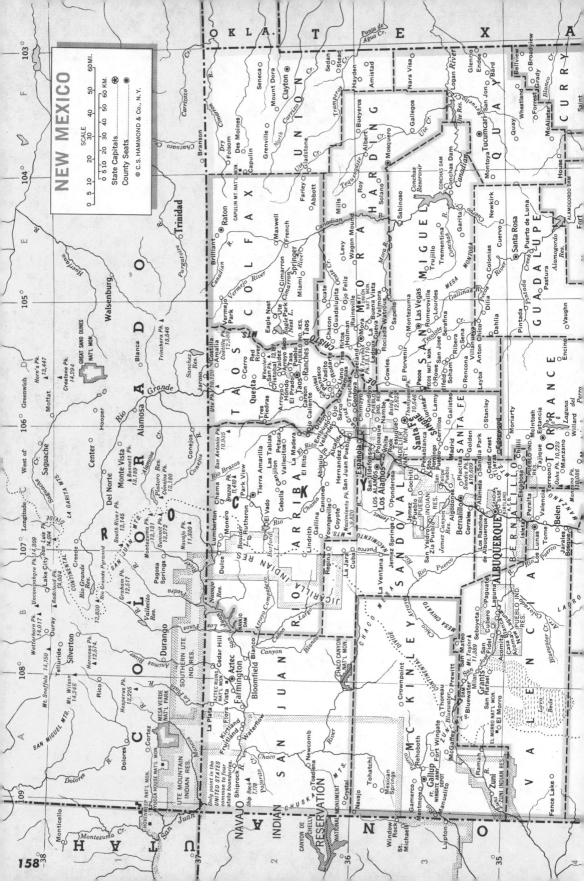

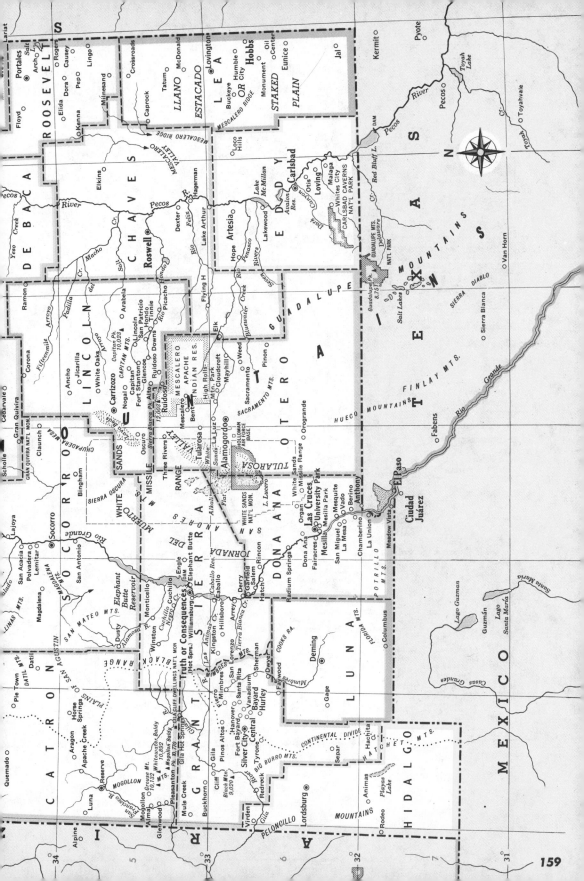

SOUTHEASTERN PART OF NEW YORK
Same scale as main map

NEW YORK

SCALE
0 5 10   20   30   40 MI.
0 5 10 20   30   40 KM.

State Capitals .... ✪
County Seats .... ◉
Canals .... ——

© C.S. HAMMOND & Co., N.Y.

160

161

WESTERN PART OF
NORTH CAROLINA
Same scale as main map.

162

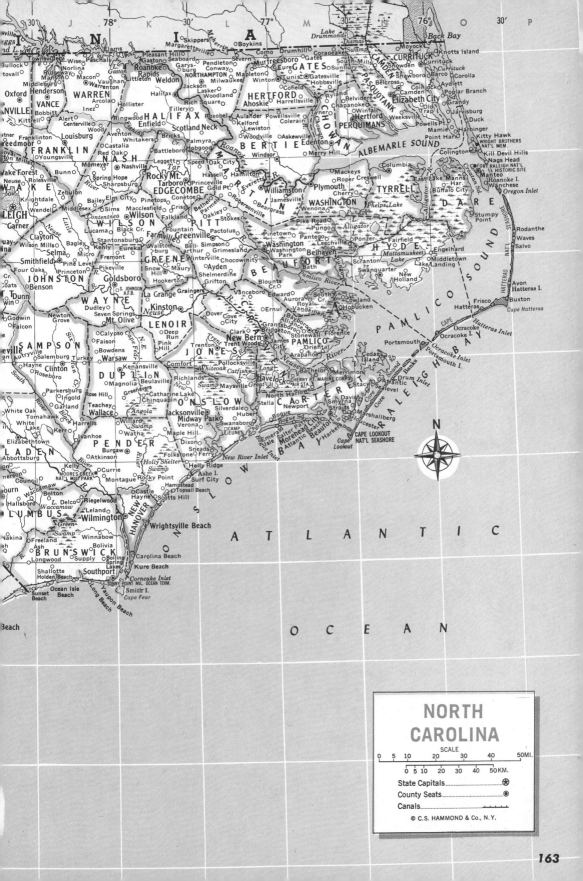

NORTH CAROLINA

SCALE
0 5 10 20 30 40 50 MI.
0 5 10 20 30 40 50 KM.

State Capitals..........⊛
County Seats..........◉
Canals..........

© C.S. HAMMOND & Co., N.Y.

163

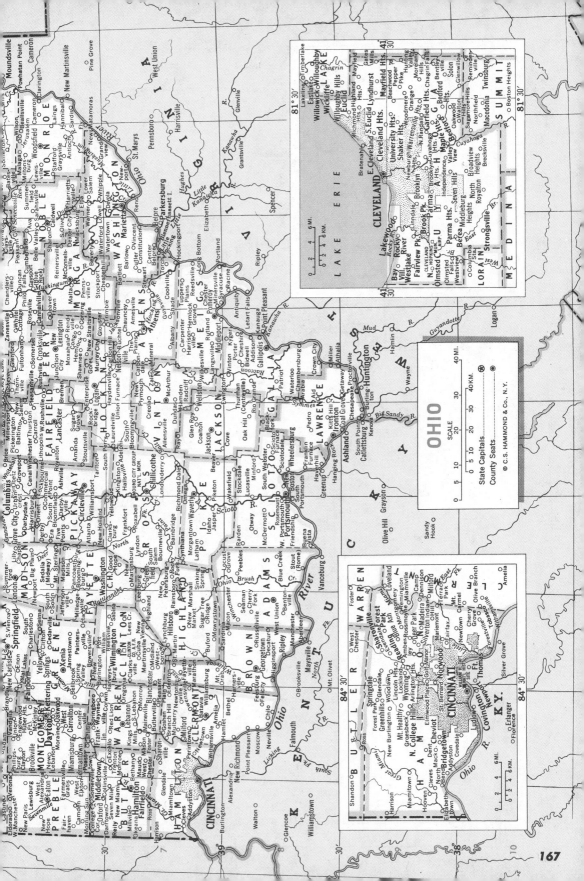

OHIO

SCALE

State Capitals ⊛
County Seats ○

© C. S. HAMMOND & Co., N.Y.

167

OKLAHOMA

SCALE
0 5 10   20   30   40 MI.
0 5 10   20   30   40 KM.

State Capitals.................................✪
County Seats.................................⊛

© C.S. HAMMOND & Co., N.Y.

169

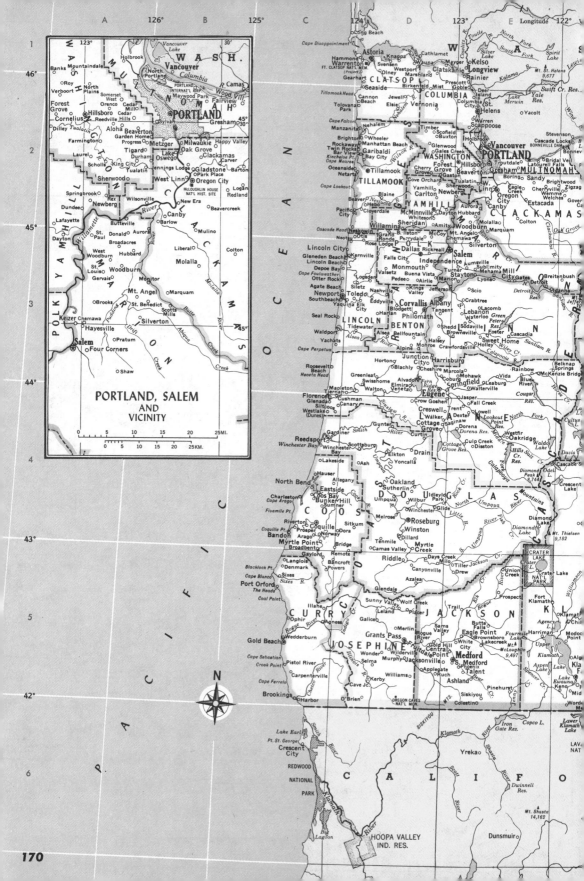

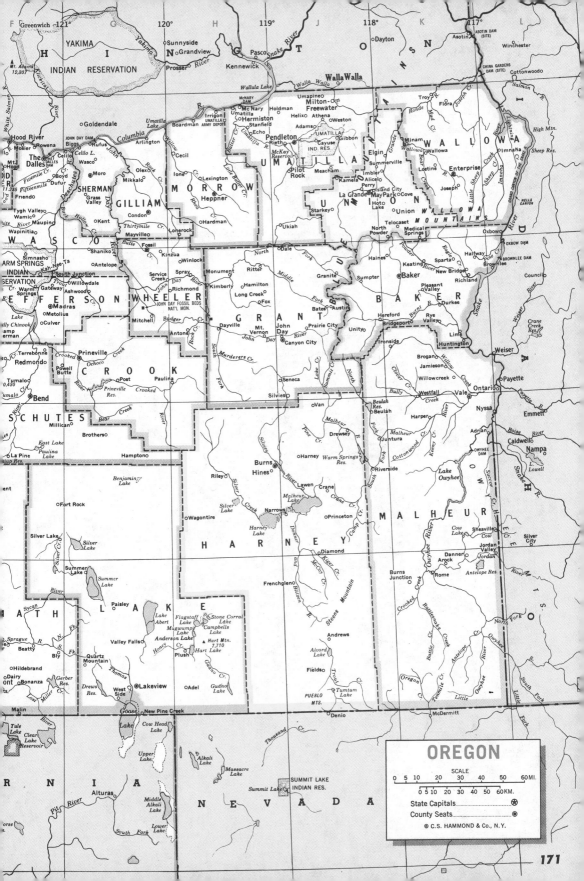

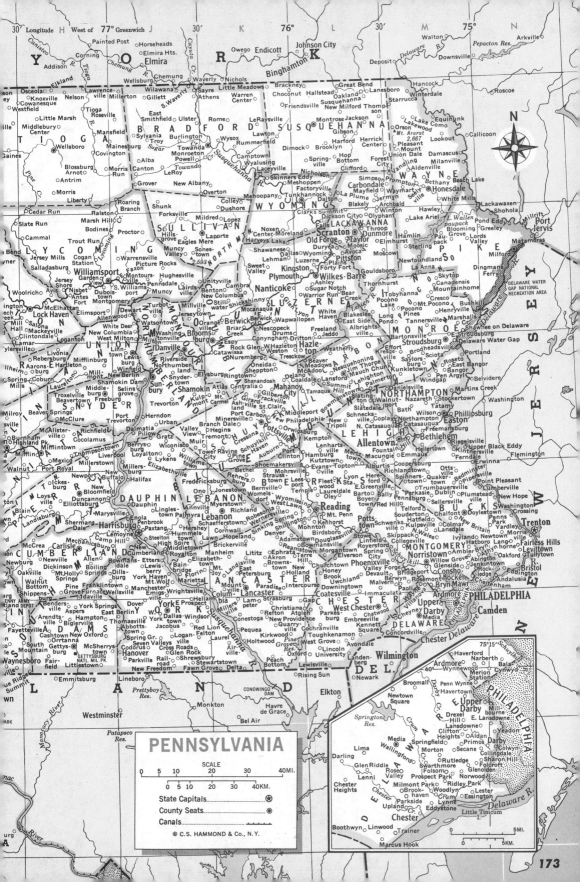

PENNSYLVANIA

SCALE
0   5 10   20   30   40MI.
0 5 10   20   30   40KM.

State Capitals............⊛
County Seats.............◉
Canals....................

© C.S. HAMMOND & Co., N.Y.

173

SOUTH CAROLINA

SCALE

0 5 10 20 30 40MI.

0 5 10 20 30 40 KM.

State Capitals..................⊛

County Seats..................⊚

Canals

© C.S. HAMMOND & Co., N.Y.

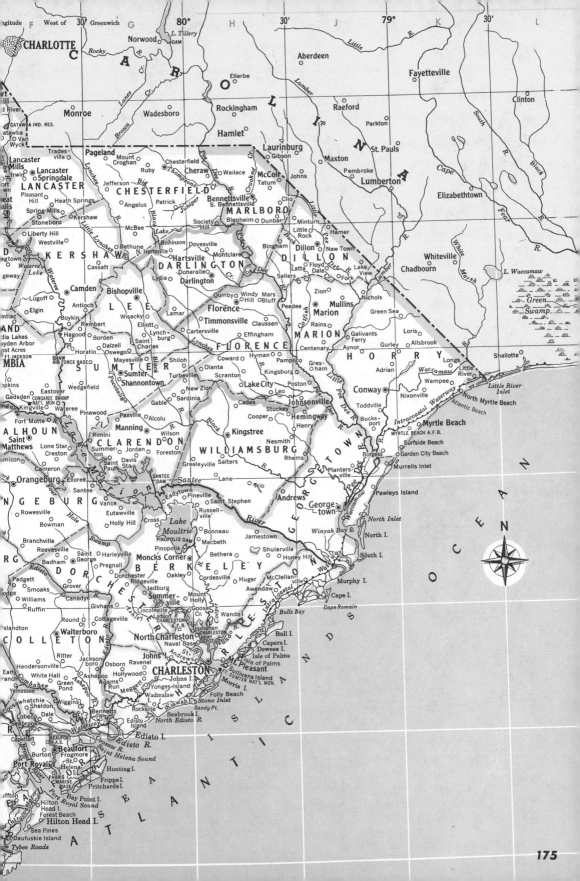

SOUTH DAKOTA

SCALE

0 5 10   20   40   60 MI.

0 5 10 20   40   60 KM.

State Capitals................. ✪

County Seats.................. ◉

© C.S. HAMMOND & Co., N.Y.

Napoleon

A K O T A

Lisbon

Bois de Sioux

Fergus Falls

Edgeley
La Moure

Wahpeton
Breckenridge

Ashley
Ellendale

Monango
Oakes
Ludden
Forman
Wild
Rice
Hankinson
Fairmount

M
I
N

Artas
Greenway
Longlake
Long L.
Hecla
Mud Lake Res.
Newark
Kidder
Hillhead
White Rock
Rosholt
New Effington

Herreid
Mound City

M PBELL
MC PHERSON
Eureka
Leola
Frederick
Houghton
Columbia Road Res.
Claremont

MARSHALL
Britton
Amherst

Claire City
Hammer
Victor
Peever
Wheaton

Hillsview
Hosmer
Wetonka
Barnard
Westport
Olumbia
Putney
Tacoma Park
Langford

Buffalo L.
Eden
Pisga
Dry Wood
Wist

ROBERTS
Sisseton

L. Traverse
Browns Valley

LWORTH
Bowdle
Roscoe
Ipswich
Mina
Aberdeen
Bath
Groton
Pierpont
Grenville
Roslyn
Webster
L. Parker

Wilmot
Graceville
Big Stone City
Ortonville

Java
EDMUNDS
Loyalton
Warner
Stratford
Verdon
Holmquist
Waubay
Summit
Marvin
Corona

Minnesota
Milbank
Appleton

OTTER
Hoven
Tolstoy
Onaka
Norbeck
Chelsea
Northville
Mellette
Crandall
Swan L.
South Shore

GRANT
Big Stone L.

Gettysburg
Lebanon
Seneca
FAULK
Faulkton
Athol
Ashton
Turton
Crocker
Bradley
Wallace
Florence
Rauville
Troy
Strandburg
Revillo

LLY
Onida
Miranda
Rockham
Zell
Redfield
Frankfort
Garden City
Raymond
Clark
CODINGTON
Watertown
Kranzburg
Goodwin
Altamont
Gary

HYDE
Holabird
Highmore
Miller
St. Lawrence
Hitchcock
Bonilla
Naples
Vienna
Thomas
Hazel
HAMLIN
Hayti
Clear Lake
Castlewood
DEUEL
Astoria

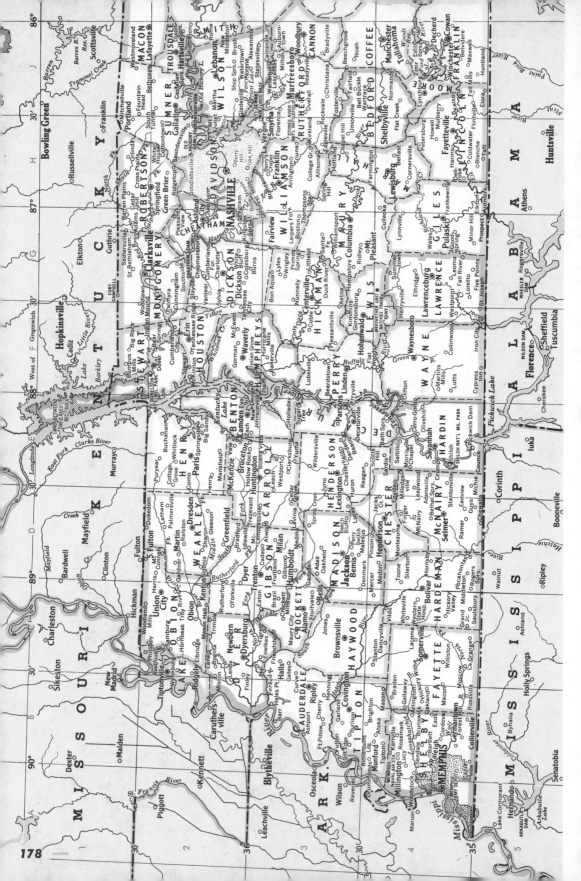

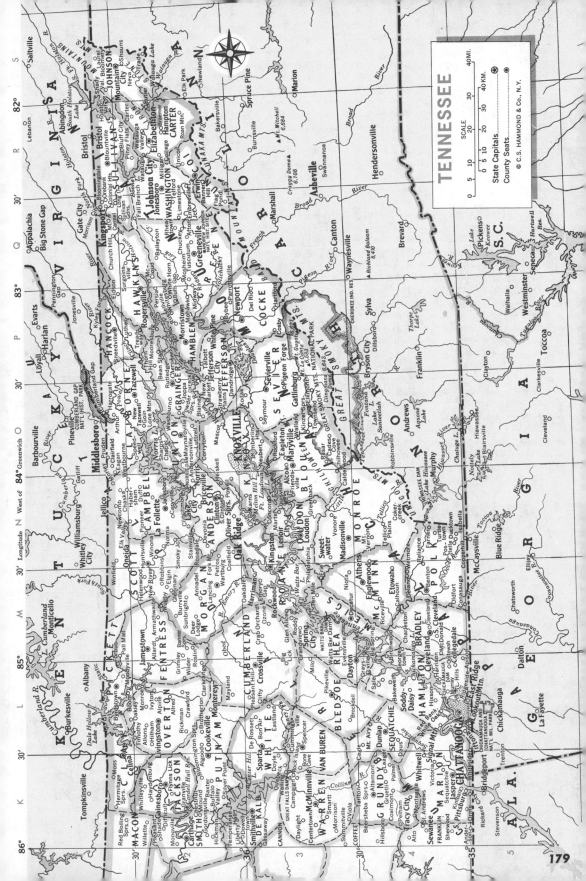

TENNESSEE

SCALE

State Capitals.............. ✶
County Seats............... ◉

© C. S. HAMMOND & Co., N.Y.

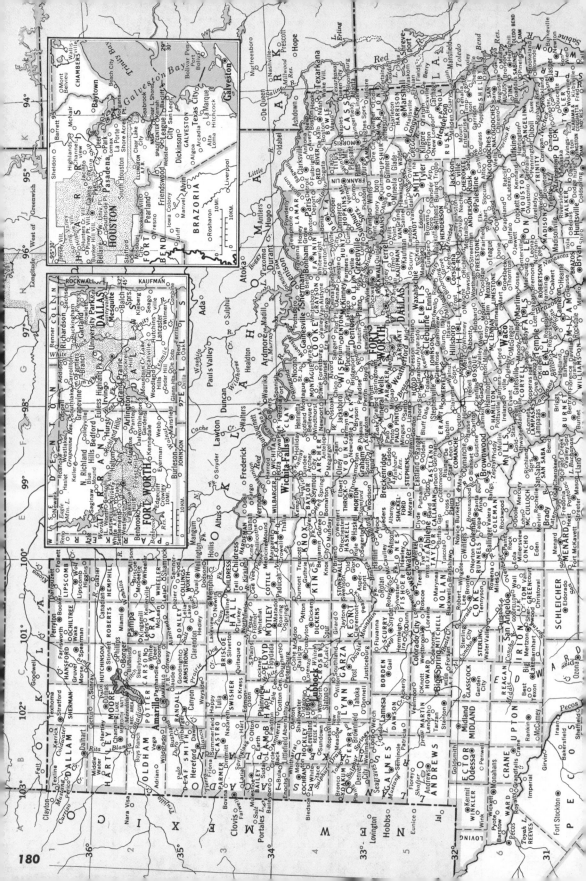

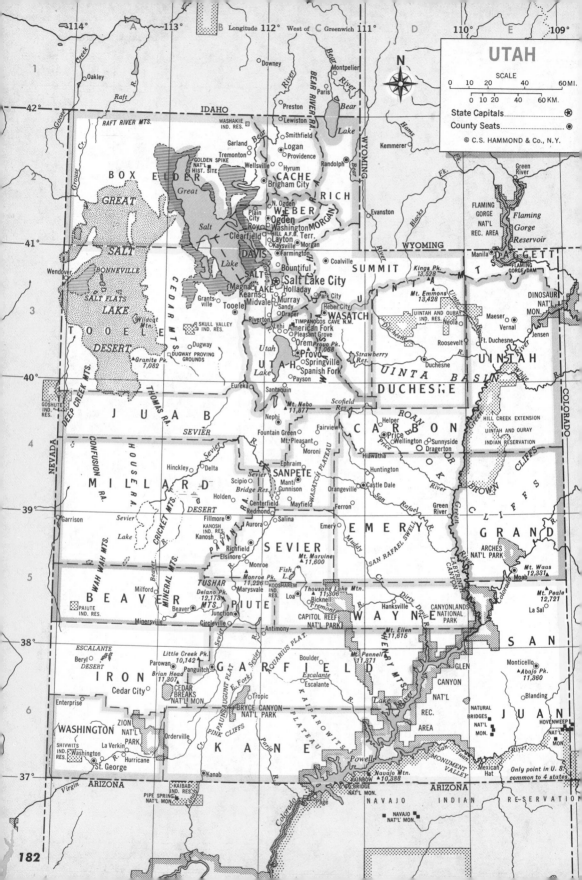

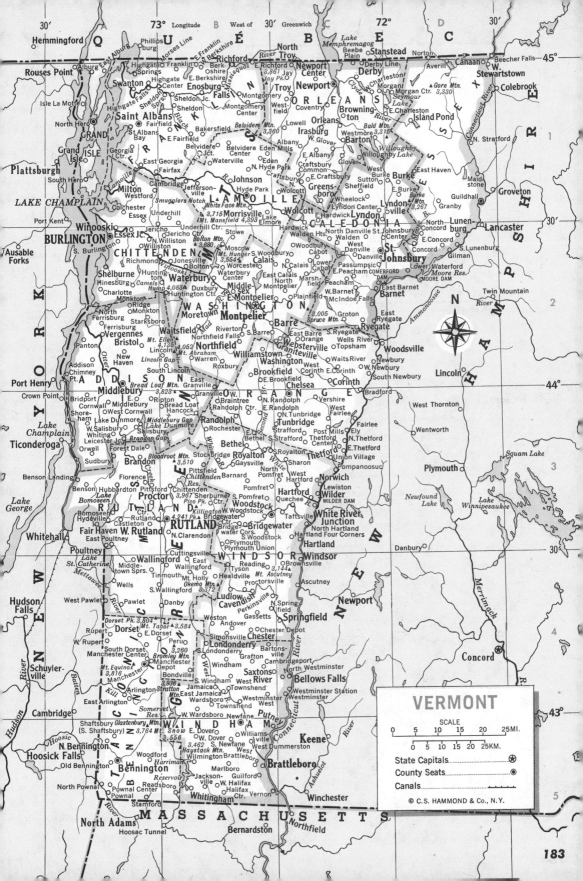

VERMONT

SCALE

0 5 10 15 20 25 MI.

0 5 10 15 20 25 KM.

State Capitals............⊛

County Seats.............⊙

Canals....................

© C.S. HAMMOND & Co., N.Y.

183

WESTERN PART OF VIRGINIA
Same scale as main map.

KENTUCKY

Martin
McVeigh
Pikeville
Wayland
Fishtrap Res.
Hurley
Big Rock
Jaeger
Welch
Meyersdale
WEST VIRGINIA
Marrowbone
Weeksbury
Russell
Breaks
Stacy
War
Cumberland
Ridgeley
Hazard
Jenkins
Harman
Maxie
Grundy
Vansant
Oakwood
Whitewood
BUCHANAN
Patterson
CHESAPEAKE & OHIO CANAL NAT'L HIST. PARK
Hyden
Whitesburg
Georges Fork
Clinchco
Birchleaf
Rowe
Jewell Ridge
Amonate
Bandy
Bishop
Piedmont
Keyser
Pound
McClure
Nora
Clintwood
Drill
Swords
Red Ash
TAZEWELL
Tazewell
Pounding Mill
Romney
WISE
Stonega
Andover
Coeburn
St. Paul
Dante
Honaker
Rosedale
Cedar Bluff
Richlands
Moorefield
Wardensville
Star Tanne
Lebanon
Zeppo
Twilao
Harlan
Appalachia
Norton
Tacoma
Banner
Castlewood
Cleveland
Elk Garden
Clinchburg
Broadford
Glade Spr.
SMYTH
Marion
CUMBERLAND MOUNTAIN
Big Stone Gap
East Stone Gap
Dungannon
Hansonville
Meadowview
Emory
Seven Mile Ford
Chilhowie
Petersburg
PINE MT.
Keokee
Pennington Gap
Blackmore
Holston
RUSSELL
WASHINGTON
Saltville
Mt. Rogers 5,729
Fork
Gibson Sta.
St. Charles
Dryden
Duffield
Fort Blackmore
Nickelsville
Holston
Abingdon
Komarock
Damascus
LEE
Rose Hill
Jonesville
Clinchport
Mendota
Greendale
SCOTT
Benhams
Whitetop
CUMBERLAND GAP NAT'L HIST. PK.
Ewing
Powell
Blackwater
Duffield
Hiltons
Weber City
Bristol
South Holston Lake
N.C.
TENNESSEE

KENTUCKY

Spencer
Clendenin
Gassaway
Mill Creek
Franklin
Durbin
Shenandoah

Clay
Sutton Lake
Blue Grass
SHENANDOAH
Mt. Jackson
Quicksburg
New Market

Charleston
Webster Springs
Hightown
Doe Hill
Monterey
Head Waters
Harrisonburg
Timberville
Broadway
Singers Glen
Lacey Spr.
Linville

Summersville
Richwood
Vanderpool
Mc Dowell
Mustoe
HIGHLAND
Dayton
Keezletown
Pleasant Val.
Elkton
ROCKINGHAM
Bridgewater
McGaheysville

Montgomery
Summersville Lake
Marlinton
Hillsboro
Bolar
Burnsville
Williamsville
Mt. Solon
West Augusta
Weyers Cave
Mt. Sidney
Port Republic
Grottoes
Stanardsville
GRE

Fayetteville
Dorothy
Marfrance
Deerfield
Churchville
Verona
Ft. Defiance
New Hope
Free Union
Boones

Mt. Hope
East Rainelle
Warm Springs
BATH
Hot Sprs.
Millboro Sprs.
Craigsville
AUGUSTA
Augusta Sprs.
Staunton
Crimora
Greenville
Crozet
White Hall
Charlotte
ALBEMAR

Beckley
Lewisburg
Healing Sprs.
Millboro
Goshen
Waynesboro
Middlebrook
Stuarts Draft
Afton
Batesville
North Garden

Pineville
Mullens
White Sulphur Springs
ALLEGHANY
Clifton Forge
Selma
Raphine
Vesuvius
Steeles Tavern
Spottswood
Fairfield
Covesville
Nellysford
Scottsville

Guyandotte
Ronceverte
Covington
Iron Gate
Colliers-town
ROCKBRIDGE
NELSON
Tyro
Faber
Esmon

Welch
Keystone
Hinton
Alleghany
Sweet Chalybeate
Glen Wilton
Lowmoor
Lexington
Buena Vista
Massies Mill
Lowesville
Roseland
Piney R.
Shipman
Arrington
Norwood
Howardsville

Union
Bluestone Lake
Greenbrier
Paint Bank
New Castle
Buchanan
Eagle Rock
Natural Br.
Glasgow
Natural Bridge Sta.
Forks of Buffalo
Clifford
Tye R.
BUCKING

Pocahontas
Boissevain
Princeton
Narrows
Goldbond
Kimballton
Ripplemead
Craig Springs
Springwood
Big Island
Pedlar Mills
Amherst
Gladstone
Riverville
Buckingham
Andersonville

Bishop
Bluefield
Rich Creek
Glen Lyn
Troutville
Fincastle
BOTETOURT
AMHERST
Monroe
Madison Hts.
Bent Cr.

TAZEWELL
Bastian
Crandon
Pearisburg
Eggleston
CRAIG
Catawba
Daleville
Cloverdale
Lithia
Coleman Falls
Lynchburg
APPOMATTOX
Appomattox

Burkes Garden
Ceres
Mechanicsburg
Newport
GILES
Blacksburg
Lafayette
Elliston
Hollins
Troutville
Montvale
Thaxton
Big Goode
Concord
APPOMATTOX C.H. NAT'L HIST. PARK
Evergreen
Pamplin
Hampden
Sydney
PRINCE

Ceres
BLAND
Bland
N. Pulaski
Dublin
Fairlawn
Shawsville
ROANOKE
Salem
Vinton
Blue Ridge
Bedford
Lowry
Forest
Rustburg
Evington
Gladys
Cullen
Charlotte C.H.
Darling-ton

SMYTH
WYTHE
Max Meadows
Draper
Pilot
Bent Mtn.
Roanoke
Hardy
Moneta
Huddleston
Lynch Sta.
Leesville
Red House
CAMPBELL

Marion
Atkins
Crockett
Wytheville
Barren Sprs.
Foster Falls
Austinville
PULASKI
Radford
Christiansburg
Copper Hill
Wirtz
Boones Mill
Smith Mountain Lake
Altavista
Naruna
Brookneal
Phenix
CHARLOTTE

Marion
Speedwell
Ivanhoe
Hillsville
Willis
Indian Valley
FLOYD
Floyd
Callaway
Gladehill
Penhook
Pittsville
Leesville
Long Island
Hurt
ME

Seven Mile Ford
Sugar Grove
Elk Creek
Woodlawn
Laurel Fork
Meadows of Dan
Stanleytown
Union Hall
Waidsboro
Naruna
Cedar Spr.
CARROLL
PATRICK
FRANKLIN
PITTSYLVANIA
Callands
Chatham
Java
Vernon Hill
Halifax
Clover
Wylliesburg

Mt. Rogers 5,729
GRAYSON
Trout Dale
Fries
Galax
Woolwine
Fancy Gap
HENRY
Collinsville
Fieldale
Axton
Republican Grove
Nathalie
Randolph
Crystal Hill
Red Oak
Skipwith

Volney
Mouth of Wilson
Independence
Cana
Claudville
Stuart
Patrick Spr.
Martinsville
Bassett
Henry
Ringgold
South Boston
Scottsburg
Clarksville
Buffalo Jct.

Whitetop
Sparta
Lambsburg
Ararat
Spencer
Ridgeway
Keeling
Blairs
Sutherlin
Alton
Virgilina

NORTH CAROLINA
W. Jefferson
Dobson
Mt. Airy
Danbury
Mayodan
Eden
Hyco Res.
Yanceyville
Roxboro
Buggs Isl

184

VIRGINIA

SCALE

0 5 10 20 30 40 MI.

0 5 10 20 30 40 KM.

National Capital .... ⊛
State Capitals .... ⊛
County Seats .... ⊙
Canals ....

185

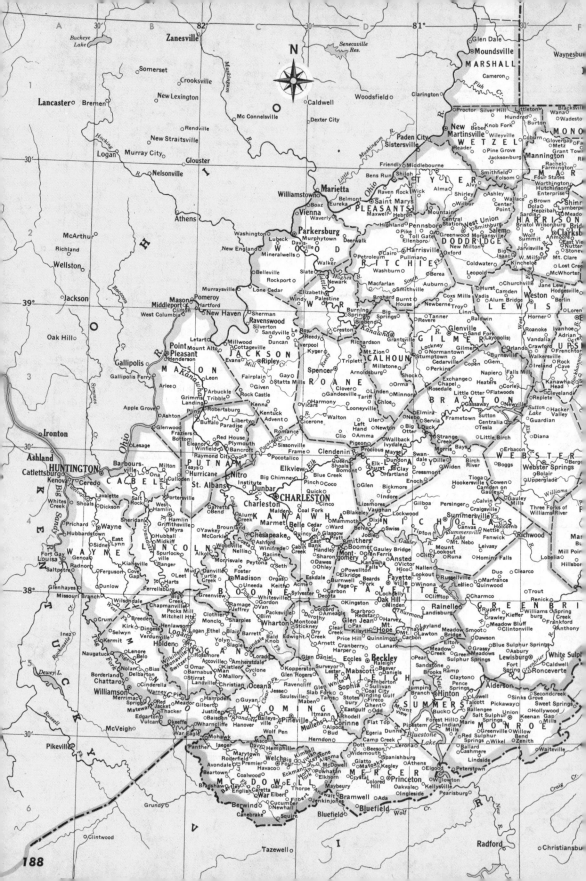

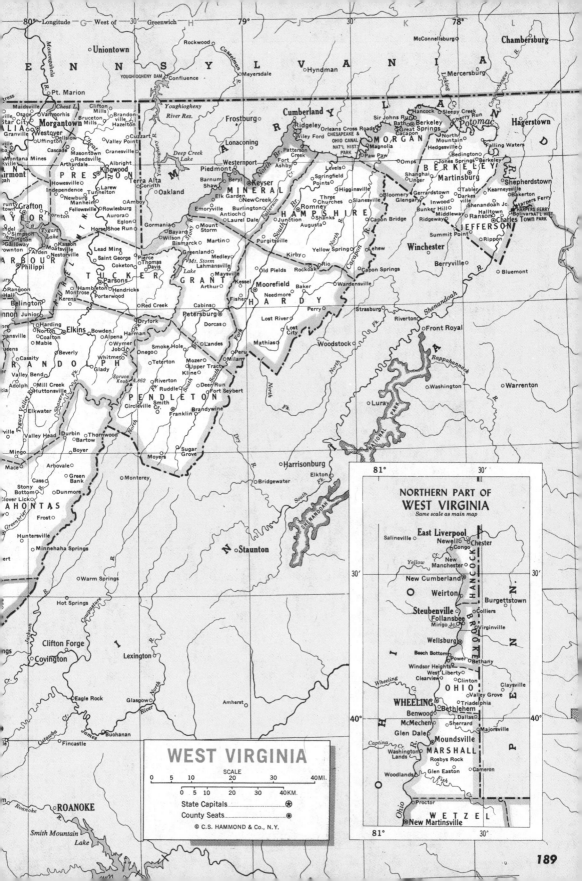

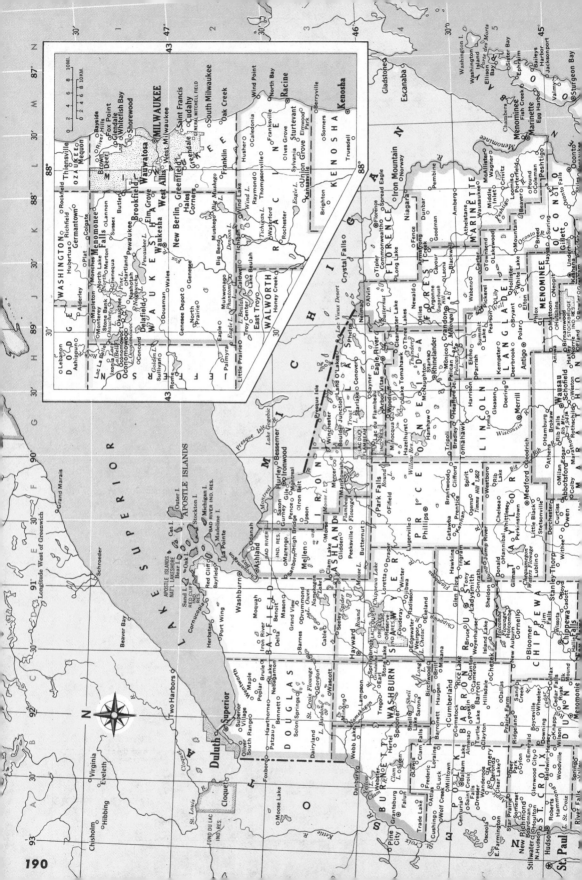

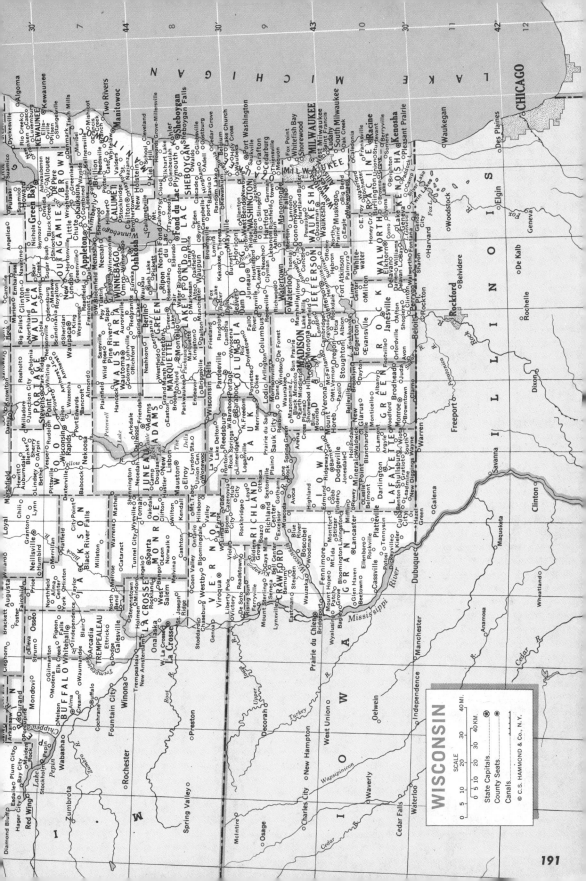

WISCONSIN

© C.S. HAMMOND & CO., N.Y.

SCALE

State Capitals ⊛
County Seats ⊙
Canals

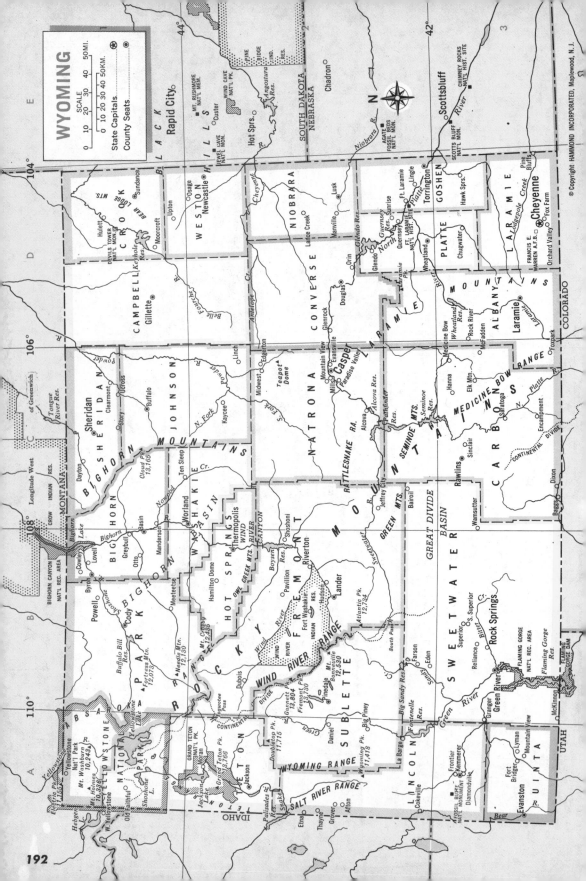

GLOSSARY OF GEOGRAPHICAL TERMS

A. = Arabic Camb. = Cambodian Ch. = Chinese Dan. = Danish Du. = Dutch
Finn. = Finnish Fr. = French Ger. = German Ice. = Icelandic It. = Italian
Jap. = Japanese Mong. = Mongol Nor. = Norwegian Per. = Persian
Port.=Portuguese Russ.=Russian Sp.=Spanish Sw.=Swedish Turk. =Turkish

Å	Nor., Sw.	Stream
Abajo	Sp.	Lower
Ada, Adasi	Turk.	Island
Altiplano	Sp.	Plateau
Älv, Alf, Elf	Sw.	River
Arrecife	Sp.	Reef
Baai	Du.	Bay
Bahía	Sp.	Bay
Bahr	Arabic	Marsh, Lake, Sea, River
Baia	Port.	Bay
Baie	Fr.	Bay, Gulf
Bañados	Sp.	Marshes
Barra	Sp.	Reef
Belt	Ger.	Strait
Ben	Gaelic	Mountain
Berg	Ger., Du.	Mountain
Bir	Arabic	Well
Boca	Sp.	Gulf, Inlet
Bolshoi, Bolshaya	Russ.	Big
Bolsón	Sp.	Depression
Bong	Korean	Mountain
Bucht	Ger.	Bay
Bugt	Dan.	Bay
Bukhta	Russ.	Bay
Burnu, Burun	Turk.	Cape, Point
By	Dan., Nor., Sw.	Town
Cabo	Port., Sp.	Cape
Campos	Port.	Plains
Canal	Port., Sp.	Channel
Cap, Capo	Fr., It.	Cape
Catarátas	Sp.	Falls
Central, Centrale	Fr., It.	Middle
Cerrito, Cerro	Sp.	Hill
Ciénaga	Sp.	Swamp
Ciudad	Sp.	City
Col	Fr.	Pass
Cordillera	Sp.	Mt. Range
Côte	Fr.	Coast
Cuchilla	Sp.	Mt. Range
Dağ, Dagh	Turk.	Mountain
Dağlari	Turk.	Mt. Range
Dal	Nor., Sw.	Valley
Darya	Per.	Salt Lake
Dasht	Per.	Desert, Plain
Deniz, Denizi	Turk.	Sea, Lake
Desierto	Sp.	Desert
Eiland	Du.	Island
Elv	Dan., Nor.	River
Emi	Berber	Mountain
Erg	Arabic	Dune, Desert
Est, Este	Fr., Port., Sp.	East
Estrecho, Estreito	Sp., Port.	Strait

Étang	Fr.	Pond, Lagoon, Lake
Fjørd	Dan., Nor.	Fiord
Fleuve	Fr.	River
Gebel	Arabic	Mountain
Gebirge	Ger.	Mt. Range
Gobi	Mongol	Desert
Gol	Mongol, Turk.	Lake, Stream
Golf	Ger., Du.	Gulf
Golfe	Fr.	Gulf
Golfo	Sp., It., Port.	Gulf
Gölü	Turk.	Lake
Gora	Russ.	Mountain
Grand, Grande	Fr., Sp.	Big
Groot	Du.	Big
Gross	Ger.	Big
Grosso	It., Port.	Big
Guba	Russ.	Bay, Gulf
Gunto	Jap.	Archipelago
Gunung	Malay	Mountain
Higashi, Higasi	Jap.	East
Ho	Ch.	River
Hoek	Du.	Cape
Holm	Dan., Nor., Sw.	Island
Hu	Ch.	Lake
Hwang	Ch.	Yellow
Île	Fr.	Island
Insel	Ger.	Island
Irmak	Turk.	River
Isla	Sp.	Island
Isola	Sp.	Island
Jabal, Jebel	Arabic	Mountains
Järvi	Finn.	Lake
Jaure	Sw.	Lake
Jezira	Arabic	Island
Jima	Jap.	Island
Joki	Finn.	River
Kaap	Du.	Cape
Kabir, Kebir	Arabic	Big
Kanal	Russ., Ger.	Canal, Channel
Kap, Kapp	Nor., Sw., Ice.	Cape
Kawa	Jap.	River
Khrebet	Russ.	Mt. Range
Kiang	Ch.	River
Kita	Jap.	North
Klein	Du., Ger.	Small
Kô	Jap.	Lake
Ko	Thai.	Island
Koh	Camb., Khmer	Island
Köping	Sw.	Borough
Körfez, Körfezi	Turk.	Gulf
Kuh	Per.	Mountain

Kul..................... Sinkiang Turki...Lake
Kum...................Turk. ....Desert
Lac....................Fr. ....Lake
Lago...................Port., Sp., It. ..Lake
Lagôa.................Port. ....Lagoon
Laguna...............Sp. ....Lagoon
Lagune...............Fr. ....Lagoon
Llanos.................Sp. ....Plains
Mar...................Sp., Port. ....Sea
Mare..................It. ....Sea
Meer..................Du. ....Lake
Meer..................Ger. ....Sea
Mer...................Fr. ....Sea
Meseta...............Sp. ....Plateau
Minami...............Jap. ....Southern
Misaki.................Jap. ....Cape
Mittel.................Ger. ....Middle
Mont..................Fr. ....Mountain
Montagne...........Fr. ....Mountain
Montaña............Sp. ...Mountains
Monte.................Sp., It., Port.
Mountain
More..................Russ. ....Sea
Muong................Siamese ....Town
Mys...................Russ. ....Cape
Nam...................Burm., Lao......River
Nevado..............Sp. ......Snow covered
peak
Nieder................Ger. ....Lower
Nishi, Nisi...........Jap. ....West
Nizhni,
Nizhnyaya.......Russ. ....Lower
Nor....................Mong. ....Lake
Nord..................Fr., Ger. ....North
Norte.................Sp., It., Port. North
Nos...................Russ. ....Cape
Novi, Novaya.......Russ. ....New
Nusa...................Malay ....Island
O.......................Jap. ....Big
Ö.......................Nor., Sw ....Island
Ober...................Ger. ....Upper
Occidental,
Occidentale......Sp., It. ....Western
Oeste.................Port. ....West
Oriental..............Sp., Fr. ....Eastern
Orientale.............It. ....Eastern
Ost.....................Ger. ....East
Ostrov................Russ. ....Island
Ouest..................Fr. ....West
öy......................Nor. ....Island
Ozero.................Russ. ....Lake
Pampa................Sp. ....Plain
Paso....................Sp. ....Pass
Passo.................It., Port. ....Pass
Pequeño.............Sp. ....Small
Peski..................Russ. ....Desert
Petit...................Fr. ....Small
Pic......................Fr. ....Mountain
Pico....................Port., Sp. ..Mountain,
Peak
Pik......................Russ. ....Peak
Pointe.................Fr. ....Point
Poluostrov...........Russ. ....Peninsula

Ponta..................Port. ....Point
Presa..................Sp. ....Reservoir
Proliv..................Russ. ....Strait
Pulou, Pulo.........Malay ....Island
Punta..................Sp., It., Port.
Point
Ras.....................Arabic ....Cape
Ría.....................Sp. ....Estuary
Río.....................Sp. ....River
Rivier, Rivière.....Du., Fr. ....River
Rud.....................Per. ....River
Saki....................Jap. ....Cape
Salto...................Sp., Port. ....Falls
San.....................Ch., Jap., Korean
Hill
See.....................Ger. ....Sea, Lake
Selvas.................Sp., Port. ......Forest
Serra...................Port. ....Mts.
Serranía..............Sp. ....Mts.
Severni,
Servernaya......Russ. ....North
Shan...................Ch., Jap. ....Hill, Mts.
Shima.................Jap. ....Island
Shoto..................Jap. ....Islands
Sierra..................Sp. ....Mountains
Sjö.....................Nor., Sw. Lake, Sea
Spitze.................Ger. ....Mt. Peak
Sredni,
Srednyaya........Russ. ....Middle
Stad....................Dan., Nor., Sw.
City
Stari, Staraya.....Russ. ....Old
Su.......................Turk. ....River
Sud, Süd.............Sp., Fr., Ger. ..South
Sul.......................Port. ....South
Sungei................Malay ....River
Sur......................Sp. ....South
Tagh...................Turk. ......Mt. Range
Tal......................Ger. ....Valley
Tandjong,
Tanjung...........Malay.....Cape, Point
Tso......................Tibetan ....Lake
Val......................Fr. ....Valley
Velho..................Port. ....Old
Verkhni...............Russ. ....Upper
Vesi....................Finn. ....Lake
Vishni,
Vishnyaya........Russ. ....High
Vostochni,
Vostochnaya... Russ. ..East, Eastern
Wadi..................Arabic.......Dry River
Wald..................Ger. ....Forest
Wan...................Jap. ....Bay
Yama..................Jap. ....Mountain
Yug, Yuzhni,
Yuzhnaya........ Russ.
South, Southern
Zaliv...................Russ. ....Bay, Gulf
Zapadni,
Zapadnaya.......Russ. ....Western
Zee....................Du. ....Sea
Zemlya...............Russ. ....Land
Zuid....................Du. ....South

WORLD
STATISTICAL TABLES
and
DISTRIBUTION MAPS

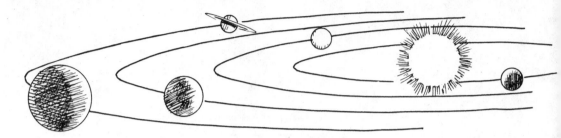

Elements of the Solar System

	Mean Distance From Sun in Miles	Period of Revolution Around Sun	Period of Rotation on Axis	Equatorial Diameter in Miles	Surface Gravity (Earth=1)	Mean Density (Water=1)	Number of Satellites
SUN	....	....	25.4 days	864,000	27.95	1.4	....
MERCURY	36,001,000	87.97 days	59 days	3,100	0.38	5.3	0
VENUS	67,272,000	224.70 days	247 days	7,700	0.88	4.9	0
EARTH	93,003,000	365.26 days	23h 56m	7,927	1.00	5.5	1
MARS	141,708,000	687 days	24h 37m	4,200	0.39	4.0	2
JUPITER	483,880,000	11.86 years	9h 50m	88,698	2.65	1.3	12
SATURN	887,141,000	29.46 years	10h 14m	75,060	1.17	0.7	10
URANUS	1,782,000,000	84.02 years	10h 45m	29,200	1.05	1.3	5
NEPTUNE	2,792,000,000	164.79 years	15h 48m	27,700	1.23	1.6	2
PLUTO	3,664,000,000	248.5 years	6.4 days	8,700?	0.7	?	0

Dimensions of the Earth

Superficial area	192,251,000	sq. miles
Land surface	52,970,000	" "
North America	9,363,000	" "
South America	6,885,700	" "
Europe	4,057,000	" "
Asia	17,128,500	" "
Africa	11,707,000	" "
Australia	2,941,500	" "
Water surface	139,781,000	" "
Atlantic Ocean	31,862,000	" "
Pacific Ocean	64,186,000	" "
Indian Ocean	28,350,000	" "
Arctic Ocean	5,427,000	" "
Equatorial circumference	24,894	miles
Meridional circumference	24,811	"
Equatorial diameter	7,926.677	"
Polar diameter	7,899.988	"
Equatorial radius	3,963.34	"
Polar radius	3,949.99	"
Volume of the Earth	260,000,000,000	cubic miles
Mass, or weight	5,890,000,000,000,000,000,000	tons
Mean distance from the Sun	93,003,000	miles

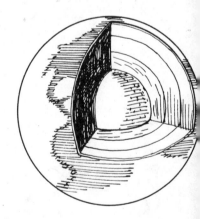

The Moon is the Earth's natural satellite. The mean distance which separates the Earth from the Moon is 237,087 miles. The Moon's true period of revolution (sidereal month) is 27⅓ days. The Moon rotates on its own axis once during this time. The phase period or time between new moons (synodic month) is 29½ days. The Moon's diameter is 2,160 miles, its density is 3.3 and its surface gravity is 0.2.

Principal Lakes and Inland Seas

	AREA IN SQ. MILES		AREA IN SQ. MILES
Caspian Sea	143,243	Lake Peipus	1,400
Lake Superior	31,700	Lake Tana	1,219
Lake Victoria	26,724	Great Salt Lake	1,100
Aral Sea	25,676	Lake Iliamna	1,000
Lake Huron	23,010	Vättern	733
Lake Michigan	22,300	Dead Sea	400
Lake Tanganyika	12,650	Lake Balaton	228
Lake Baykal	12,162	Lake Geneva	224
Great Bear Lake	12,096	Lake of Constance	208
Lake Nyasa	11,555	Lake Tahoe	193
Great Slave Lake	11,269	Lake Garda	143
Lake Erie	9,910	Lake Como	56
Lake Winnipeg	9,417	Lake of Lucerne	44
Lake Ontario	7,340	Lake of Zürich	34
Lake Ladoga	7,104		
Lake Balkhash	7,027		
Lake Chad	5,300		
Lake Onega	3,710		
Lake Titicaca	3,200		
Lake Nicaragua	3,100		
Lake Athabasca	3,064		
Reindeer Lake	2,568		
Lake Turkana (Rudolf)	2,463		
Issyk-Kul'	2,425		
Vanern	2,156		
Lake Winnipegosis	2,075		
Lake Albert	2,075		
Kariba Lake	2,050		
Lake Urmia	1,815		
Lake of the Woods	1,679		

Oceans and Seas of the World

	AREA IN SQ. MILES	GREATEST DEPTH IN FEET	VOLUME IN CUBIC MILES
Pacific Ocean	64,186,000	36,198	167,025,000
Atlantic Ocean	31,862,000	28,374	77,580,000
Indian Ocean	28,350,000	25,344	68,213,000
Arctic Ocean	5,427,000	17,880	3,026,000
Caribbean Sea	970,000	24,720	2,298,400
Mediterranean Sea	969,000	16,896	1,019,400
South China Sea	895,000	15,000	....
Bering Sea	875,000	15,800	788,500
Gulf of Mexico	600,000	12,300	....
Sea of Okhotsk	590,000	11,070	454,700
East China Sea	482,000	9,500	52,700
Japan Sea	389,000	12,280	383,200
Hudson Bay	317,500	846	37,590
North Sea	222,000	2,200	12,890
Black Sea	185,000	7,365	....
Red Sea	169,000	7,200	53,700
Baltic Sea	163,000	1,506	5,360

Longest Rivers of the World

	LENGTH IN MILES		LENGTH IN MILES		LENGTH IN MILES
Nile, Africa	4,145	Purus, S.A.	1,995	Kolyma, U.S.S.R.	1,562
Amazon, S.A.	3,915	Yukon, Alaska-Canada	1,979	Ganges, Asia	1,550
Mississippi-Missouri, U.S.A.	3,710	St. Lawrence, Canada-U.S.A.	1,900	Ural, U.S.S.R.	1,509
Yangtze, China	3,434	Rio Grande, U.S.A.-Mexico	1,885	Japurá, S.A.	1,500
Ob-Irtysh, U.S.S.R.	3,362	Syr-Dar'ya, U.S.S.R.	1,859	Arkansas, U.S.A.	1,450
Yenisey-Angara, U.S.S.R.	3,100	São Francisco, Brazil	1,811	Colorado, U.S.A.-Mexico	1,450
Hwang (Yellow), China	2,903	Indus, Asia	1,800	Negro, S.A.	1,400
Amur, Asia	2,744	Danube, Europe	1,775	Dnieper, U.S.S.R.	1,368
Lena, U.S.S.R.	2,734	Salween, Asia	1,770	Irrawaddy, Burma	1,325
Congo, Africa	2,718	Brahmaputra, Asia	1,700	Orange, Africa	1,350
Mackenzie-Peace, Canada	2,635	Euphrates, Asia	1,700	Ohio-Allegheny, U.S.A.	1,306
Mekong, Asia	2,600	Tocantins, Brazil	1,677	Kama, U.S.S.R.	1,262
Niger, Africa	2,585	Si, China	1,650	Columbia, U.S.A.-Canada	1,243
Paraná, S.A.	2,450	Amu-Dar'ya, Asia	1,616	Red, U.S.A.	1,222
Murray-Darling, Australia	2,310	Zambezi, Africa	1,600	Don, U.S.S.R.	1,222
Volga, U.S.S.R.	2,194	Nelson, Canada	1,600	Brazos, U.S.A.	1,210
Madeira, S.A.	2,013	Orinoco, S.A.	1,600	Saskatchewan, Canada	1,205
		Paraguay, S.A.	1,584	Peace-Finlay, Canada	1,195
				Tigris, Asia	1,181
				Darling, Australia	1,160
				Angara, U.S.S.R.	1,135
				Sungari, Asia	1,130
				Pechora, U.S.S.R.	1,124
				Snake, U.S.A.	1,038
				Churchill, Canada	1,000
				Pilcomayo, S.A.	1,000
				Uruguay, S.A.	1,000
				Magdalena, Colombia	1,000
				Platte-N. Platte, U.S.A.	990
				Oka, U.S.S.R.	918
				Canadian, U.S.A.	906
				Tennessee, U.S.A.	900
				Colorado, Texas, U.S.A.	894
				Dniester, U.S.S.R.	876

Great Ship Canals

	LENGTH IN MILES	MIN. DEPTH IN FEET
Volga-Baltic, U.S.S.R.	225	....
Baltic-White Sea, U.S.S.R.	140	16
Suez, Egypt	100.76	42
Albert, Belgium	80	16.5
Moscow-Volga, U.S.S.R.	80	18
Volga-Don, U.S.S.R.	62	....
Göta, Sweden	54	10
Kiel, West Germany	53.2	38
Panama, Canal Zone	50.72	41.6
Houston Ship, U.S.A.	50	36
Amsterdam-Rhine, Netherlands	45	41
Beaumont-Port Arthur, U.S.A.	40	32
Manchester Ship, England	35.5	28
Chicago Sanitary and Ship, U.S.A.	33.8	20
Welland, Canada	27.6	27
Juliana, Netherlands	21	11.8
Chesapeake and Delaware, U.S.A.	19	35
Cape Cod, U.S.A.	17.4	32
Lake Washington, U.S.A.	8	30
Corinth, Greece	3.5	26.25
Sault Ste. Marie, U.S.A.	1.8	27
Sault Ste. Marie, Canada	1.4	27

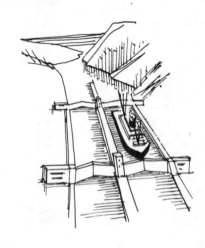

Principal Mountains of the World

	FEET			FEET
Everest, Nepal-China . . .	29,028		Kazbek, U.S.S.R.	16,512
K2 (Godwin Austen), India .	28,250		Djaja, Indonesia	16,503
Kanchenjunga, Nepal-India .	28,208		Blanc, France	15,771
Lhotse, Nepal-China	27,923		Klyuchevskaya Sopka, U.S.S.R.	15,584
Makalu, Nepal-China . . .	27,824		Rosa (Dufourspitze), Italy-	
Dhaulagiri, Nepal	26,810		Switzerland	15,203
Nanga Parbat, India . . .	26,660		Ras Dashan, Ethiopia . . .	15,157
Annapurna, Nepal	26,504		Matterhorn, Switzerland . .	14,688
Nanda Devi, India	25,645		Whitney, California	14,494
Kamet, India	25,447		Elbert, Colorado	14,433
Tirich Mir, Pakistan	25,230		Rainier, Washington	14,410
Minya Konka, China . . .	24,902		Blanca Peak, Colorado . . .	14,345
Muztagh Ata, China	24,757		Markham, Antarctica . . .	14,272
Communism Peak, U.S.S.R. .	24,599		Shasta, California	14,162
Pobeda Peak, U.S.S.R. . . .	24,406		Pikes Peak, Colorado . . .	14,110
Chomo Lhari, Bhutan-China .	23,997		Finsteraarhorn, Switzerland .	14,022
Muztagh, China	23,891		Tajumulco, Guatemala . . .	13,845
Aconcagua, Argentina . . .	22,831		Mauna Kea, Hawaii . . .	13,796
Ojos del Salado, Chile-Arg. .	22,572		Mauna Loa, Hawaii	13,680
Tupungato, Chile-Argentina .	22,310		Toubkal, Morocco	13,665
Mercedario, Argentina . . .	22,211		Jungfrau, Switzerland . . .	13,642
Huascarán, Peru	22,205		Cameroon, Cameroon . . .	13,350
Llullaillaco, Chile-Arg. . . .	22,057		Gran Paradiso, Italy . . .	13,323
Ancohuma, Bolivia	21,489		Robson, British Columbia .	12,972
Illampu, Bolivia	21,276		Grossglockner, Austria . . .	12,461
Chimborazo, Ecuador . . .	20,561		Fuji, Japan	12,389
McKinley, Alaska	20,320		Cook, New Zealand	12,349
Logan, Yukon	19,850		Pico de Teide, Canary Is. . .	12,172
Cotopaxi, Ecuador	19,347		Semeru, Java, Indonesia . .	12,060
Kilimanjaro, Tanzania . . .	19,340		Mulhacen, Spain	11,411
El Misti, Peru	19,101		Etna, Italy	11,053
Huila, Colombia	18,865		Lassen Peak, California . .	10,457
Citlaltépetl (Orizaba), Mexico	18,855		Kosciusko, Australia	7,316
El'brus, U.S.S.R.	18,510		Mitchell, North Carolina . .	6,684
Demavend, Iran	18,376			
St. Elias, Alaska-Yukon . . .	18,008			
Popocatépetl, Mexico . . .	17,887			
Dykh-Tau, U.S.S.R.	17,070			
Kenya, Kenya	17,058			
Ararat, Turkey	16,946			
Vinson Massif, Antarctica . .	16,864			
Maraherita (Ruwenzori), Africa	16,795			

Principal Islands of the World

	AREA IN SQ. MILES
Greenland	840,000
New Guinea	305,000
Borneo	290,000
Madagascar	226,400
Baffin	195,928
Sumatra	164,000
Philippines	115,707
New Zealand	103,736
Great Britain	88,764
Honshu	88,000
Victoria	83,896
Ellesmere	75,767
Celebes	72,986
Java	48,842
Newfoundland	42,031
Cuba	40,533
Luzon	40,420
Iceland	39,768
Mindanao	36,537
Molucca Islands	32,307
Novaya Zemlya	31,900
Ireland	31,743
Sakhalin	29,500
Hispaniola	29,399
Hokkaido	28,983
Banks	27,038
Tasmania	26,383
Ceylon	25,332
Svalbard	23,957
Devon	21,331
Bismarck Arch.	18,976
Tierra del Fuego	17,900
Melville	16,274
Southampton	15,913
Solomon Islands	15,600
New Britain	14,100
Taiwan (Formosa)	13,836
Kyushu	13,770
Hainan	13,127
Prince of Wales	12,872
Vancouver	12,079
Timor	11,527

	AREA IN SQ. MILES
Sicily	9,926
Somerset	9,570
Sardinia	9,301
Fiji Islands	7,055
Shikoku	6,860
New Caledonia	6,530
Kuril Islands	6,025
New Hebrides	5,700
Bahama Islands	5,382
Falkland Islands	4,618
Jamaica	4,232
Hawaii	4,038
Cape Breton	3,981
Cyprus	3,572
Puerto Rico	3,435
Corsica	3,352
New Ireland	3,340
Crete	3,218
Galápagos Islands	3,075
Wrangel	2,819
Hebrides	2,812
Canary Islands	2,808
Kerguélen	2,700
Prince Edward	2,170
Trinidad and Tobago	1,980
Balearic Islands	1,936
Ryukyu Islands	1,767
Madura	1,752
Cape Verde Islands	1,557
South Georgia	1,450
Long I., New York	1,401
Socotra	1,400
Samoa	1,209
Gotland	1,153
Réunion	969
Azores	902
Isle of Pines	849
Macías Nguema Biyogo	779
Tenerife	745
Maui	729
Mauritius	720
Zanzibar	641

	AREA IN SQ. MILES
Oahu	608
Guadeloupe	584
Åland Is.	581
Kauai	553
Shetland Islands	552
Rhodes	542
Caroline Islands	463
Martinique	425
Tahiti	402
Pemba	380
Orkney Islands	372
Madeira Islands	307
Dominica	290
Tonga	270
Molokai	261
St. Lucia	238
Corfu	229
Bornholm	227
Isle of Man	227
Singapore	226
Guam	212
Isle Royale	196
Virgin Islands	192
Curaçao	182
Barbados	166
Isle of Wight	145
Lanai	140
St. Vincent	131
Maltese Islands	122
Grenada	120
Tobago	116
Martha's Vineyard	93
Seychelles	85
Channel Islands	74
St. Helena	47
Nantucket	46
Ascension	34
Hong Kong	30
Manhattan, New York	22
Bermuda Islands	21

Eckert Projection (equal-area)

Copyright by C. S. HAMMOND & CO., N. Y.

DENSITY OF POPULATION. One of the most outstanding facts of human geography is the extremely uneven distribution of people over the Earth. One-half of the Earth's surface has less than 3 people per square mile, while in the lowlands of India, China, Java and Japan rural density reaches the incredible congestion of 2000-3000 per square mile. Three-fourths of the Earth's population live in four relatively small areas; Northeastern United States, North-Central Europe, India and the Far East.

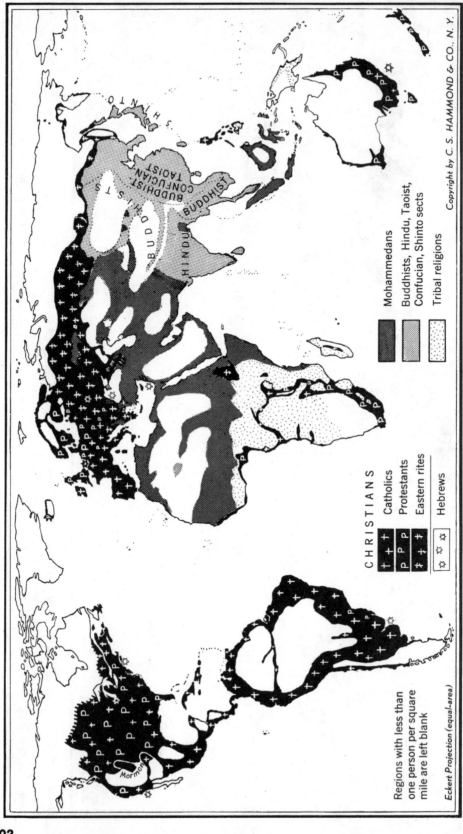

RELIGIONS. *Most people of the Earth belong to four major religions: Christians, Mohammedans, Brahmans, Buddhists and derivatives. The Eastern rites of the Christians include the Greek Orthodox, Greek Catholic, Armenian, Syrian, Coptic and more minor churches. The lamaism of Tibet and Mongolia differs a great deal from Buddhism in Burma and Thailand. In the religion of China the teachings of Buddha, Confucius and Tao are mixed, while in Shinto a great deal of ancestor and emperor worship is added. About 11 million Hebrews live scattered over the globe, chiefly in cities and in the state of*

CHRISTIANS

Catholics +++

Protestants P P P

Eastern rites ✢✢✢

Hebrews ✡ ✡ ✡

Regions with less than one person per square mile are left blank

Eckert Projection (equal-area)

Mohammedans

Buddhists, Hindu, Taoist, Confucian, Shinto sects

Tribal religions

Copyright by C. S. HAMMOND & CO., N. Y.

LANGUAGES. Several hundred different languages are spoken in the World, and in many places two or more languages are spoken, sometimes by the same people. The map above shows the dominant languages in each locality. English, French, Spanish, Russian, Arabic and Swahili are spoken by many people as a second language for commerce or travel.

Copyright by C. S. HAMMOND & CO., N. Y.

Eckert Projection (equal-area)

Legend:

E English

Spanish, Portuguese

Russian

other Indo-European languages

Semitic & Hamitic Languages

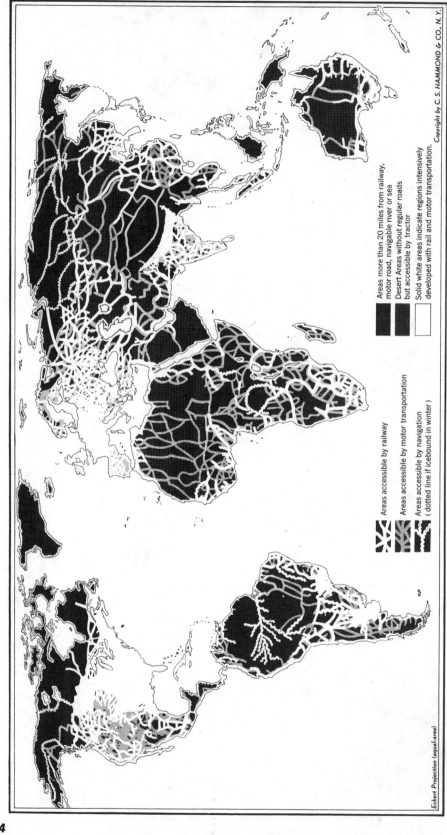

Eckert Projection (equal-area)

Copyright by C. S. HAMMOND & CO., N. Y.

Areas accessible by railway

Areas accessible by motor transportation

**Areas accessible by navigation
(dotted line if icebound in winter)**

Areas more than 20 miles from railway,
motor road, navigable river or sea

Desert Areas without regular roads
but accessible by tractor

Solid white areas indicate regions intensively
developed with rail and motor transportation.

ACCESSIBILITY. Many regions in the world are far from railways, roads, navigable rivers or the seas. Their economic development is retarded because their products can be brought to the world's markets only at great expense. Such areas are in the tundra (alpine), the boreal forest and in the equatorial rain forest regions. Desert areas, if not too mountainous, can be crossed by tractors. The largest inaccessible area is in Tibet, on account of high mountains, the alpine climate and isolationist attitude of the people. Airplane transportation is helping to bring these inaccessible areas into the orbit of civilization.

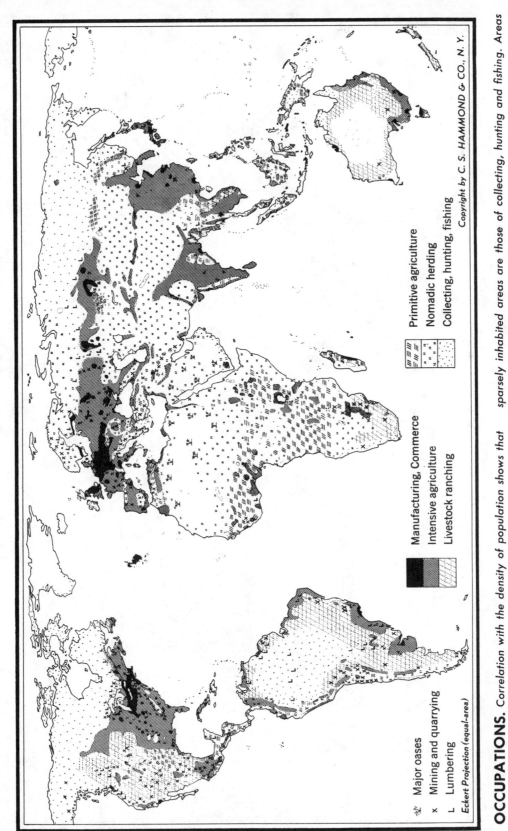

OCCUPATIONS. Correlation with the density of population shows that the most densely populated areas fall into the regions of manufacturing and intensive farming. All other economies require considerable space. The most sparsely inhabited areas are those of collecting, hunting and fishing. Areas with practically no habitation are left blank.

Manufacturing, Commerce

Intensive agriculture

Livestock ranching

Primitive agriculture

Nomadic herding

Collecting, hunting, fishing

⚒ Major oases

× Mining and quarrying

L Lumbering

Eckert Projection (equal-area)

Copyright by C. S. HAMMOND & CO., N. Y.

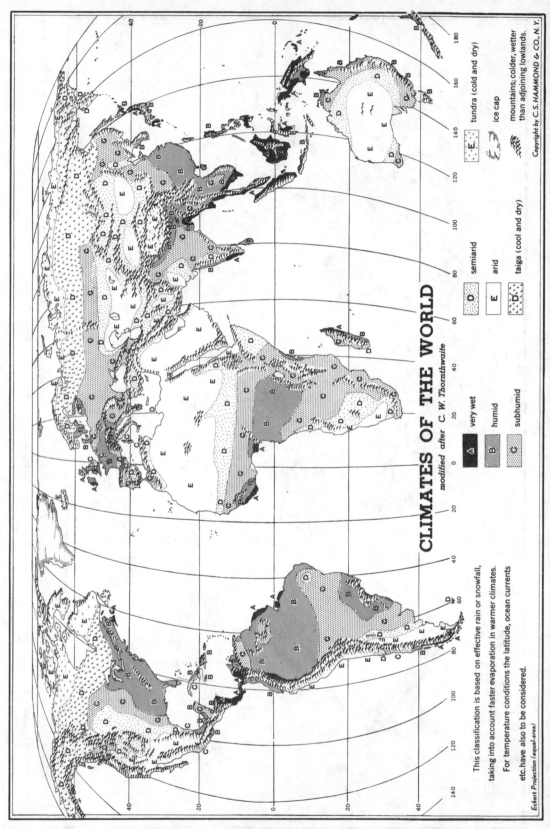

CLIMATES OF THE WORLD

modified after C. W. Thornthwaite

This classification is based on effective rain or snowfall,
taking into account faster evaporation in warmer climates.

For temperature conditions the latitude, ocean currents
etc. have also to be considered.

Eckert Projection (equal-area)

	very wet
A	very wet
B	humid
C	subhumid

D	semiarid
E	arid
D	taiga (cool and dry)

E. tundra (cold and dry)

ice cap

mountains; colder, wetter
than adjoining lowlands.

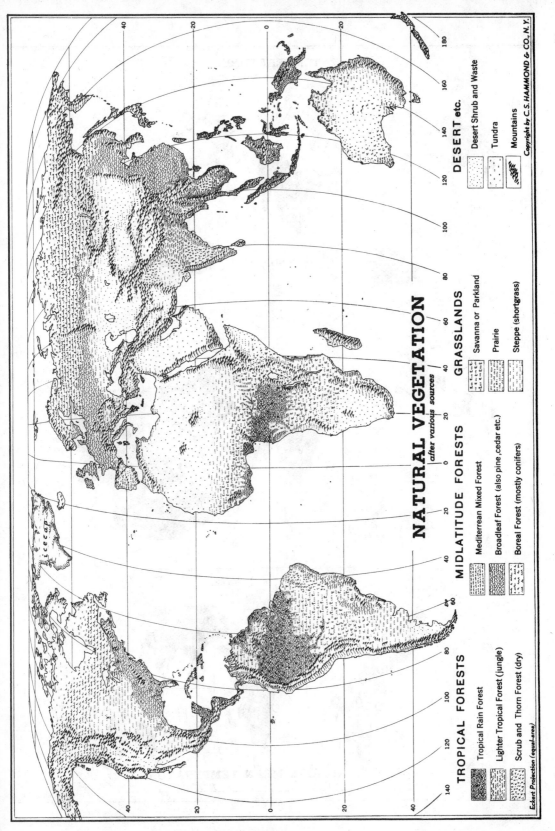

NATURAL VEGETATION
(after various sources)

TROPICAL FORESTS

- Tropical Rain Forest
- Lighter Tropical Forest (jungle)
- Scrub and Thorn Forest (dry)

MIDLATITUDE FORESTS

- Mediterrean Mixed Forest
- Broadleaf Forest (also pine, cedar etc.)
- Boreal Forest (mostly conifers)

GRASSLANDS

- Savanna or Parkland
- Prairie
- Steppe (shortgrass)

DESERT etc.

- Desert Shrub and Waste
- Tundra
- Mountains

Eckert Projection (equal-area)

Copyright by C. S. HAMMOND & CO., N.Y.

207

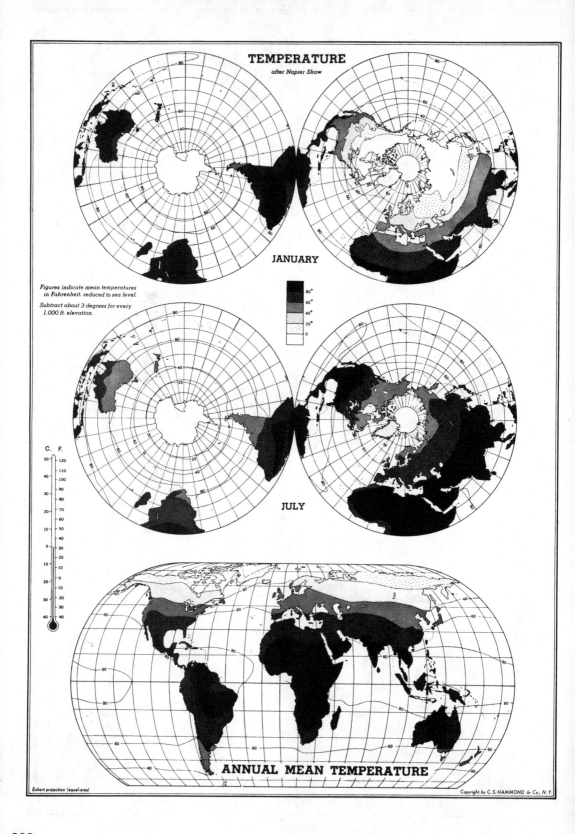

TEMPERATURE

after Napier Shaw

JANUARY

*Figures indicate mean temperatures
in Fahrenheit, reduced to sea level.*

*Subtract about 3 degrees for every
1,000 ft. elevation.*

JULY

ANNUAL MEAN TEMPERATURE

Eckert projection (equal-area)

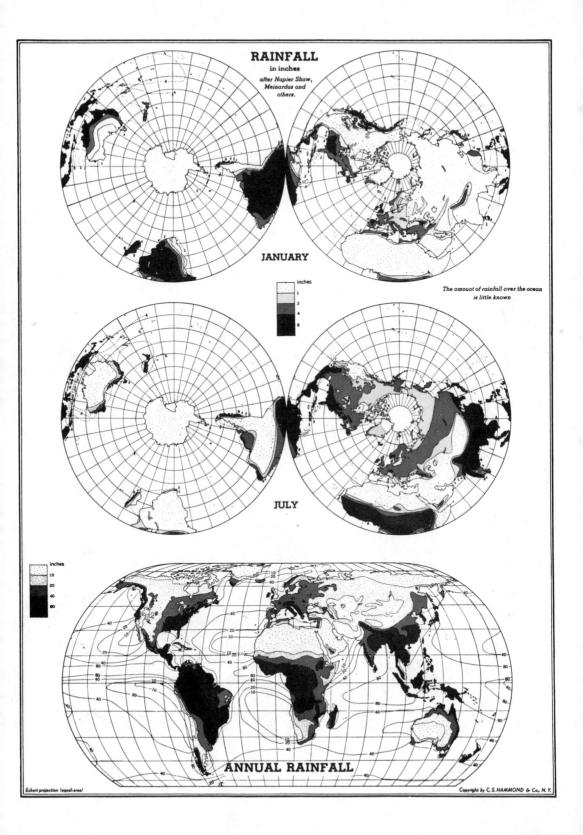

RAINFALL
in inches
*after Napier Shaw,
Meinardus and
others.*

JANUARY

inches
1
2
4
8

*The amount of rainfall over the ocean
is little known*

JULY

inches
10
20
40
80

ANNUAL RAINFALL

Eckert projection (equal-area)

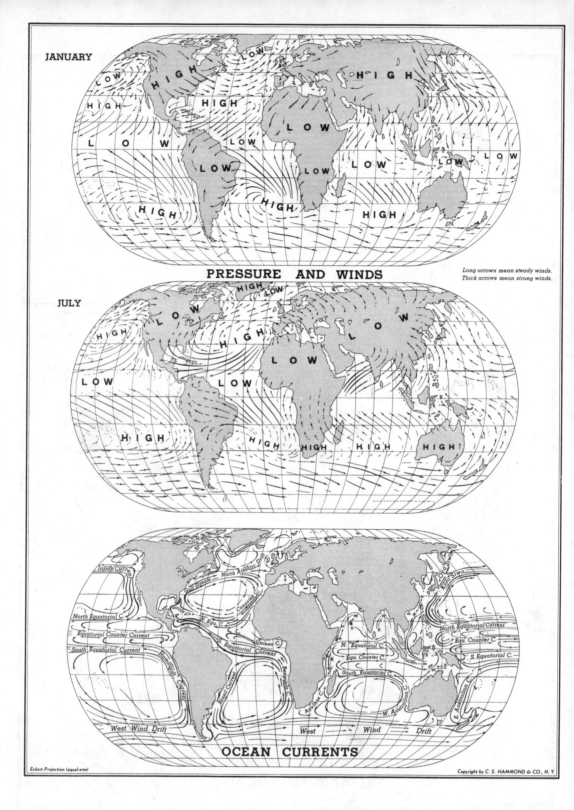

JANUARY

PRESSURE AND WINDS

Long arrows mean steady winds.
Thick arrows mean strong winds.

JULY

OCEAN CURRENTS

Eckert Projection (equal-area)

Copyright by C. S. HAMMOND & CO., N. Y.

Illustrated

Social and Economic Tables

of the World

N.Y. State Dep't of Commerce

The headline events of the last half-century have made the average person acutely curious of the vast world beyond his country's borders. This new national concern for the external world and its problems is one of the hopeful signs pointing to a better future for mankind. However, no matter how well-intentioned our concern for international relations may be, it is of no value unless it is grounded on an intelligent appreciation of the great diversity of social, economic and political forms extant throughout the globe.

On the following pages the editors have presented information on the world's nations, products, peoples and governments arranged in easily-found tabular form. This arrangement by tables makes comparison between political units a simpler task. These data, used with the maps in this atlas, complete the story of the nations of the world.

Social and Economic Tables

POLITICAL DIVISION	GOVERNMENT	MONETARY UNIT	LANGUAGE	RELIGION
AFGHANISTAN	Independent republic with a president, prime minister and cabinet; under martial law.	afghani	Pushtu (Afghan) Dari (Persian) Turkic languages	Islam
ALBANIA	Soviet-type republic with a head of state, premier, cabinet and unicameral legislature; controlled by the Communist party.	lek	Albanian	Islam Eastern Orthodoxy Roman Catholicism
ALGERIA	Centralized republic under a president, premier, council of ministers, and an elected unicameral legislature.	Algerian dinar	Arabic French Berber	Islam
AMERICAN SAMOA	U.S. territory with an elected governor and bicameral legislature.	U.S. dollar	English Samoan	Protestantism
ANDORRA	Co-principality of the president of France and the Spanish bishop of Seo de Urgel, with an elected Syndic General and a general council.	French franc and Spanish peseta	Catalan Spanish French	Roman Catholicism
ANGOLA	Centralized republic under a president, assisted by a premier, cabinet and revolutionary council.	kwanza	Portuguese Bantu languages	Tribal religions Roman Catholicism
ANTIGUA	Associated British state, with governor, prime minister, cabinet and bicameral legislature.	East Caribbean dollar	English	Protestantism
ARGENTINA	A republic with a president, at present under a military government.	Argentine peso	Spanish	Roman Catholicism
AUSTRALIA	Independent British Commonwealth member with a governor-general, prime minister, cabinet, and a bicameral parliament, composed of a senate and a house of representatives.	Australian dollar	English	Protestantism Roman Catholicism
AUSTRIA	A federal republic with a president, chancellor, cabinet, and a partly elected bicameral parliament.	schilling	German	Roman Catholicism
BAHAMAS	Independent British Commonwealth member, with a governor-general, prime minister, cabinet and bicameral general assembly.	Bahamian dollar	English	Protestantism Roman Catholicism
BAHRAIN	Independent state with an emir, prime minister and cabinet.	Bahraini dinar	Arabic	Islam
BANGLADESH	Independent republic in the British Commonwealth, with a president, prime minister, cabinet and unicameral parliament.	taka	Bengali English Urdu	Islam Hinduism Christianity Buddhism

MAJOR PRODUCTS

Wheat, barley, corn, rice, sugar beets, nuts & seeds, fruits, cotton, tobacco; livestock; timber; natural gas, salt, copper, lead, talc, coal, lapis lazuli; hides & skins (karakul), wool, textiles, leather, carpets, cement.

Corn, tobacco, wheat, potatoes, cotton, sugar beets, fruits; livestock; fish; timber; petroleum, bitumen, lignite, nickel, copper, iron ore, chromite; textiles, wool, tobacco products, chemicals.

Wheat, barley, oats, corn, grapes, olives, dates, figs, citrus fruits, vegetables, tobacco; fish; livestock; timber; iron ore, petroleum, phosphates, zinc, natural gas, mercury, lead; hides, wine, olive oil, cork, food & tobacco products, leather, textiles, chemicals, machinery, iron & steel, refined petroleum.

Taro, breadfruit, yams, bananas, arrowroot, pineapples, coconuts, oranges; fish; livestock; canned fish, copra, mats.

Tobacco, potatoes, oats, barley; livestock; timber; iron ore, lead; dairy, tobacco, wood & wool products.

ALGERIA: A native letter writer in the streets of Constantine, the country's third largest city.
TWA—Trans World Airlines

Coffee, corn, sugarcane, peanuts, tobacco, rice, palm products, cotton, sisal; iron ore, petroleum, diamonds; fish; livestock; timber; refined petroleum, cement, paper, tires, refined sugar, food products, chemicals.

Sugar, cotton, rice, molasses, fruits, vegetables; fish; processed sugar and cotton, rum.

Wheat, corn, millet, cotton, sugarcane, tobacco, fruits; livestock; timber; petroleum, natural gas, zinc, silver, lead, coal, iron ore, tungsten; wine, vegetable oils, dairy products, meat & meat products, wool, hides, textiles, wood and metal products, iron & steel, machinery, autos, chemicals, leather, petroleum products, cement.

Wheat, oats, barley, fruits, vegetables; livestock; gold, coal, petroleum, copper, iron, lead, silver, bauxite, uranium, zinc; timber, iron & steel, wool, electrical equipment, appliances, chemicals, petroleum products, optical & agricultural implements, machinery, textiles, leather, airplanes, engines, ships, processed meat, sugar, dairy products, building materials, autos, tires.

Rye, wheat, corn, oats, barley, potatoes, sugar beets, hops, flax, tobacco, grapes; livestock; timber; iron ore, copper, lead, graphite, coal, petroleum, salt, magnesite; wine, processed foods, dairy products, iron & steel, aluminum, machinery, tools, chemicals, paper, textiles, cement.

Tomatoes, pineapples, sugarcane, vegetables, sponges, citrus fruits, bananas; fish, crawfish, shells; timber; salt; handcraft products, cement, pulpwood, processed fish, rum, refined petroleum, drugs.

Vegetables, fruits, dates; fish, shellfish; petroleum; refined petroleum, processed aluminum, electrical goods, cement, flour.

Rice, sugarcane, jute, cotton, oilseeds, tobacco, tea, chilies, fruit; timber; cattle, fish; natural gas, coal; textiles, hides & skins, flour, refined petroleum, steel, chemicals, refined sugar, handicrafts, paper, leather goods, jute products.

AUSTRALIA: The country's first oil field at Moonie, Queensland, is in a sheep herding region.
Australian Government

Social and Economic Tables

POLITICAL DIVISION	GOVERNMENT	MONETARY UNIT	LANGUAGE	RELIGION
BARBADOS	Independent British Commonwealth member, with a governor-general, prime minister, cabinet and a bicameral parliament.	Barbadian dollar	English	Protestantism
BELGIUM	Constitutional, hereditary monarchy, with a king, premier, cabinet, and a bicameral parliament.	Belgian franc	French (Walloon) Flemish (Dutch)	Roman Catholicism
BELIZE	Internally self-governing British colony with governor, prime minister, cabinet and bicameral legislature.	Belize dollar	English; Spanish Mayan; Creole	Roman Catholicism Protestantism
BENIN	Republic, at present under a head of state and a committee of the ruling party.	CFA franc	French Sudanese languages	Tribal religions Islam Christianity
BERMUDA	Partly self-governing British colony with a governor, prime minister, cabinet and a bicameral legislature.	Bermuda dollar	English	Protestantism
BHUTAN	Monarchy with a king, councils, and a unicameral assembly.	Indian rupee; ngultrum	Dzongka Nepali	Buddhism Hinduism
BOLIVIA	Centralized constitutional republic, with a president and cabinet, presently ruled by decree.	Bolivian peso	Spanish Quechua Aymará	Roman Catholicism
BOTSWANA	Constitutional republic within the British Commonwealth, with a president, cabinet, a unicameral parliament and an advisory house of chiefs.	pula	English Setswana Sindebele Bushman Afrikaans	Tribal religions Protestantism
BRAZIL	Federal republic with a president, vice-president, appointive cabinet and a bicameral legislature, at present ruled by decree.	cruzeiro	Portuguese Italian German Japanese	Roman Catholicism
BRUNEI	Internally self-governing British protected sultanate, with a chief minister, cabinet, and councils.	Brunei dollar	Malay English	Islam
BULGARIA	Soviet-type republic with a cabinet, state council and unicameral parliament, which elects a presidium whose chairman is chief of state. Actual control is by the Communist party.	lev	Bulgarian Turkish Greek	Eastern Orthodoxy Islam
BURMA	One-party socialist republic with a unicameral assembly, prime minister and cabinet, and a state council with its chairman the president.	kyat	Burmese Karen; Kachin Shan; Chin English Hindi; Tamil Chinese	Buddhism Tribal religions
BURUNDI	One-party republic with a president, premier, and revolutionary council.	Burundi franc	French; Kirundi Kiswahili	Tribal religions Roman Catholicism
CAMBODIA (KAMPUCHEA)	Communist state with a president, vice-president and a revolutionary council.	—	Khmer French	Buddhism

MAJOR PRODUCTS

Sugarcane, vegetables, cotton; fish; manjak (asphalt); sugar, molasses, rum, edible oils, margarine.

Wheat, rye, oats, barley, potatoes, sugar beets, tobacco, vegetables, fruit, hops; livestock, poultry; fish; coal, iron, zinc, lead, dolomite; coke, iron & steel, machinery, metal products, textiles, lace, glass, chemicals, petroleum & uranium refining, sugar, beer, paper, wine, wool, cut diamonds, dairy products, aircraft, cement, autos.

Rice, corn, bananas, vegetables, citrus fruits, cocoa, sugarcane; cattle; hard and softwoods; fish, shellfish; rum, meat, fruit & fish products.

Palm products, tobacco, peanuts, cotton, corn, copra, coffee, castor oil, kapok, millet; livestock; fish; gold, diamonds, bauxite, iron ore; oil seed milling, textiles.

Lily bulbs, onions, bananas, citrus fruits, vegetables, potatoes; coral; poultry, fish; limestone; perfume, pharmaceuticals, concrete.

Rice, wheat, barley, millet, corn, fruits; timber; cattle, yaks; handicrafts, dairy products.

Potatoes, corn, wheat, barley, rice, cassava, sugarcane, cotton, coffee, fruits; timber; livestock; tin, zinc, lead, silver, antimony, copper, natural gas, petroleum, tungsten, gold, sulphur; hides & skins, textiles, chemicals, cement, beer, tobacco products.

Kaffir cotton, sorghum, millet, corn, wheat, beans, fruits & nuts; livestock; diamonds, nickel, copper, coal, salt, talc, manganese ore; hides & skins, meat & dairy products, leather goods, brewing.

Coffee, corn, rice, wheat, cotton, cocoa, sugarcane, soybeans, cassava, rubber, fibers, carnauba wax, medicinal plants, fruits & nuts, tobacco; livestock; timber; iron & manganese ore, diamonds, lead & zinc, bauxite, gold & silver, mica, asbestos, chromite, tungsten, petroleum, quartz, beryllium, copper, coal; meat products, hides, textiles, chemicals, petrochemicals, drugs, paper, lumber, machinery, autos, metal products, iron & steel, sugar, aluminum, tires, cement.

Rice, sago, rubber, jelutong, cutch, tapioca, bananas; timber; livestock; petroleum, natural gas; boat building, cloth, brass and silverware, refined petroleum.

Wheat, corn, barley, cotton, tobacco, sugar beets, potatoes, seeds, fruits, vegetables; timber; livestock; fish; iron ore, copper, lead, coal, manganese, petroleum, zinc; food, leather & tobacco products, sugar, refined minerals & petroleum, textiles, wine, iron & steel, machinery, cement.

Rice, corn, cotton, pulses, sugarcane, tobacco, fruits & nuts, jute, rubber, sesame; livestock; timber (teak); petroleum, lead, zinc, tungsten, nickel, silver, copper, precious stones; sugar, food, tobacco & wood products, drugs, chemicals, textiles, cement, refined petroleum, steel.

Coffee, tea, cotton, corn, beans, fruits & nuts, sweet potatoes, sorghum; cattle; fish; timber; nickel; hides & skins, textiles, cement, beer, soap, shoes, food products.

Rice, tobacco, corn, beans, sugarcane, rubber, cotton; cattle; fish; timber; phosphates, gold, precious stones; food products, textiles, sugar, glass, drugs.

BELGIUM: The Grand' Place in Brussels, with its flower market surrounded by Gothic and Renaissance architecture.

Belgian Gov't Info. Ctr.

BRAZIL: Baling cotton for export by rail and sea in the state of São Paulo.

Pan American Union

Social and Economic Tables

POLITICAL DIVISION	GOVERNMENT	MONETARY UNIT	LANGUAGE	RELIGION
CAMEROON	One-party republic, with a president, prime minister, cabinet, and unicameral elected assembly.	CFA franc	French; English Sudanese and Bantu languages	Tribal religions Christianity Islam
CANADA	Independent confederation of the British Commonwealth, with a governor-general, prime minister, cabinet and a bicameral parliament, composed of an appointed senate and an elected house of commons.	Canadian dollar	English French	Protestantism Roman Catholicism
CAPE VERDE	Republic, ruled by the president as chairman of the only political party; prime minister and cabinet.	Cape Verdean escudo	Portuguese	Roman Catholicism
CENTRAL AFRICAN EMPIRE	Constitutional monarchy, with an emperor, premier and cabinet.	CFA franc	French; Sangho Sudanese and Bantu languages	Tribal religions Christianity Islam
CHAD	Republic with a head of state and a cabinet.	CFA franc	French, Arabic Bantu and Sudanese languages	Tribal religions Islam Roman Catholicism
CHILE	Republic ruled by a president and an advisory council of state.	Chilean peso	Spanish	Roman Catholicism
CHINA (PEOPLE'S REPUBLIC)	Nominal republic, ruled by a prime minister & cabinet (state council); controlled by Communist party's politburo, headed by the standing committee and its chairman.	yuan	Chinese Mongol Turkic languages Tibetan	Confucianism Buddhism Taoism Islam
CHINA (REPUBLIC OF): TAIWAN	Republic with a president, prime minister, cabinet, a legislative yuan and a national assembly, the latter electing the president.	new Taiwan dollar (yuan)	Chinese	Confucianism Buddhism Taoism Christianity Tribal religions
COLOMBIA	A centralized federal republic with a president, vice-president, appointive cabinet, and elective bicameral congress.	Colombian peso	Spanish	Roman Catholicism
COMOROS	Republic with a president, premier, cabinet and unicameral legislature.	CFA franc	Arabic French Kiswahili	Islam
CONGO	Republic of the French Community, with a president, premier and a presidium.	CFA franc	French Sudanese and Bantu languages	Tribal religions Roman Catholicism
COOK ISLANDS	Internally self-governing state associated with New Zealand with a commissioner, prime minister, cabinet and legislative assembly.	New Zealand dollar	Polynesian dialects English	Protestantism
COSTA RICA	Constitutional republic with president, cabinet and elected unicameral assembly.	colón	Spanish	Roman Catholicism

of the World

MAJOR PRODUCTS

Cocoa, coffee, rubber, nuts, tea, rice, tobacco, palm products, cotton; livestock; fish; timber; bauxite, gold, petroleum; hides & skins, wood, rubber & tobacco products, textiles, beer, food products, palm oil.

Wheat, oats, barley, corn, potatoes, vegetables, sugar beets, tobacco, fruits, oilseeds; livestock, poultry; fish, shellfish; timber; furs; gold, copper, nickel, zinc, lead, silver, potash, molybdenum, platinum, iron ore, titanium, cobalt, radium, uranium, petroleum, natural gas, coal, asbestos, salt, gypsum, sulphur; hydroelectric power; foods, apparel, meat & dairy products, transportation equipment, iron & steel, aluminum, metal products, lumber, pulp, paper & wood products, textiles, electric goods, chemicals, autos, cement, processed minerals, refined petroleum, machinery.

Coffee, bananas, nuts, oilseeds, corn; livestock; salt, lime; hides & skins, preserved fish, sugar, cement.

Coffee, cotton, peanuts, tobacco, corn, rice, sorghum; timber; livestock; gold, diamonds, uranium; wood & palm products, textiles, flour, soap, beer.

Millet, sorghum, rice, cotton, vegetables, dates, cassava, peanuts, gum arabic, ivory, ostrich feathers; livestock; fish; natron (salt); hides, cloth, meat products.

Cereal grains, seeds, sugar beets, potatoes, vegetables, fruits, tobacco; livestock; fish; timber; copper, nitrates, iron ore, manganese, silver, gold, molybdenum, zinc, coal, petroleum; chemicals, petrochemicals, wood & metal products, textiles, paper, pulp, drugs, wine, iron & steel, food & leather products, cement.

Rice & cereal grains, soybeans, fruits, vegetables, nuts, oilseeds, tea, silk, cotton, sugarcane, tobacco; livestock, poultry; fish; timber; iron ore, petroleum, coal, tungsten, tin, antimony, magnetite, manganese, molybdenum, natural gas, mercury, bauxite, lead, zinc; meat & food products, textiles, apparel, ceramics, cement, iron & steel, machinery, metal products, aluminum, chemicals, vehicles, armaments.

Rice, sugarcane, tea, sweet potatoes, bananas, pineapples, mushrooms, soybeans, tobacco; livestock; fish; timber; coal, natural gas; food & wood products, cement, glass, chemicals, petrochemicals, steel, bicycles, sugar, electric & electronic goods, machinery, metal products, textiles, apparel.

Coffee, rice, cotton, sugarcane, bananas, cacao, wheat, corn, tobacco, rubber, fibers; livestock; fish; timber; petroleum, gold, platinum, emeralds, silver, salt; sugar, food & tobacco products, beer, textiles, cement, iron & steel, machinery, metal & leather products, chemicals, meat.

Sugarcane, vanilla, rice, root vegetables, copra, sisal, coffee, essential oils (ylang, citronella), cloves, cacao, perfume plants; timber; rum distilling.

Palm products, coffee, cocoa, bananas, tobacco, sugarcane, rice, corn, peanuts, fruits; livestock; timber; petroleum, potash, lead, zinc, gold; hardwoods & wood products, textiles, beer, cement, sugar, food products.

Citrus fruits, coconuts, copra, oilseeds, tomatoes, arrowroot, pineapples, breadfruit, taro, kumaras, plantains, yams; mother-of-pearl, textiles, processed fruits.

Coffee, bananas, cocoa, corn, sugarcane, rice, potatoes, tobacco; cattle; tuna; timber; gold, salt, bauxite; dairy, tobacco & food products; electrical goods, beef, sugar, textiles, furniture, cement, apparel.

CHILE: Bathers and cabanas on the Pacific sands of Las Salinas, a popular beach at Viña del Mar.

Hamilton Wright

COLOMBIA: One of the country's principal products, coffee, drying under the tropical sun.

Pan American Union

Social and Economic Tables

POLITICAL DIVISION	GOVERNMENT	MONETARY UNIT	LANGUAGE	RELIGION
CUBA	Communist republic with a president, cabinet and an elected legislature, but with dictatorial powers held by the president and council of state.	Cuban peso	Spanish	Roman Catholicism
CYPRUS	British Commonwealth republic, at present divided into Greek and Turkish states, each with a president and unicameral legislature.	Cyprus pound	Greek Turkish English	Greek Orthodoxy Islam
CZECHOSLOVAKIA	Soviet-type republic with a president, premier, cabinet, bicameral legislature, and Czech and Slovak National Councils, with actual power residing in the Communist party presidium.	koruna	Czech and Slovak	Roman Catholicism Protestantism
DENMARK	Constitutional, hereditary monarchy with a queen, a unicameral elective legislature and an appointed cabinet and premier.	krone	Danish	Protestantism
DJIBOUTI	Independent republic with a president, premier and a unicameral assembly.	Djibouti franc	Hamitic languages French Arabic	Islam
DOMINICA	Independent British Commonwealth republic, with a president, prime minister, cabinet and a unicameral parliament.	East Caribbean dollar	English French patois	Roman Catholicism Protestantism
DOMINICAN REPUBLIC	Republic with a president, vice-president, appointed cabinet, and bicameral legislature.	Dominican peso	Spanish	Roman Catholicism
ECUADOR	Constitutional republic with a president, cabinet and unicameral legislature.	sucre	Spanish Indian languages (Quechua, etc.)	Roman Catholicism
EGYPT	Arab republic with a president, appointed prime minister, cabinet, and a partly elected unicameral assembly.	Egyptian pound	Arabic	Islam Christianity
EL SALVADOR	Republic with a president, cabinet, and unicameral legislature.	colón	Spanish	Roman Catholicism
ENGLAND AND WALES	Integral part of the United Kingdom, with executive power nominally residing in the Crown, but actually exercised by the prime minister, cabinet and bicameral parliament, composed of a house of lords and a house of commons.	pound sterling	English Welsh	Protestantism Roman Catholicism
EQUATORIAL GUINEA	One-party centralized republic with a president and a unicameral national assembly.	ekuele	Spanish Fang; Bubi	Tribal religions Roman Catholicism
ETHIOPIA	Military state, with the chairman of the military council as head of state, and a cabinet.	birr	Amharic Hamitic languages	Coptic Christianity Islam Tribal religions
FALKLAND ISLANDS	British colony with a governor, executive & legislative councils.	pound sterling	English	Protestantism Roman Catholicism
FIJI	Independent British Commonwealth member with a governor-general, prime minister, cabinet, and a bicameral parliament.	Fiji dollar	English; Fijian Hindi; Chinese Polynesian dialects	Protestantism Roman Catholicism Hinduism Islam

218

of the World

MAJOR PRODUCTS

Sugarcane, tobacco, coffee, rice, fruits; cattle; timber; fish; nickel, iron ore, chromite, manganese, copper; sugar, tobacco, meat & food products, textiles, cement, chemicals, steel, refined petroleum & metals, electrical goods, rum.

Wheat, barley, grapes, raisins, olives, potatoes, carobs, nuts, citrus fruits, tobacco, vegetables; fish; livestock; copper & concentrates, iron pyrites, asbestos, chromite, gypsum, marble; tobacco, leather & food products, cement, wine, textiles, refined petroleum.

Wheat, rye, oats, barley, corn, sugar beets, potatoes; livestock; timber; coal, iron ore, magnesite, uranium, lead, salt; munitions, machinery, metal, rubber, leather & wood products, cement, iron & steel, textiles, shoes, porcelain, paper, chemicals, aircraft, autos, glass & glassware, beer, apparel, sugar, food products.

Barley, oats, rye, wheat, potatoes, sugar beets, vegetables; poultry, livestock; stone, clay, iron ore; meat & meat products, dairy products, canned foods, beverages, machinery, transportation equipment, metal & rubber products, chemicals, apparel, shoes, furniture, glassware, earthenware, electrical goods, ships, cement, paper, tobacco products.

Salt; hides & skins; livestock; boats.

Bananas, citrus fruits, timber, pumice, edible and essential oils, copra.

Sugarcane, cacao, coffee, tobacco, bananas, rice, fruits, corn; cattle; lumber; nickel, bauxite; nickel & petroleum refining, chocolate, sugar, meat, cigars, textiles, cement, beer, flour, peanut oil, leather goods, rum.

Rice, cocoa, coffee, sugarcane, corn, bananas, cotton, cinchona; livestock; fish & shellfish; timber; petroleum, gold, silver; food, rubber, leather & wood products, textiles, toquilla (panama) hats, sugar, beer, cement, chemicals & petrochemicals, drugs, glass.

Cotton, cereal grains, sugarcane, fruits, vegetables; livestock; fish; petroleum, phosphates, salt, iron ore, manganese, limestone; cotton ginning, iron & steel, refined petroleum, food processing, textiles, chemicals, cement, petrochemicals, sugar.

Coffee, cotton, cereal grains, cacao, tobacco, henequén, sugarcane; fish, shellfish; livestock; timber; silver; sugar, textiles, food products, drugs, chemicals, electric goods.

Potatoes, vegetables, cereal grains, hay, hops, fruits; livestock, poultry; fish; coal, petroleum, natural gas, iron ore, copper, lead, nickel, tin; dairy products, wool, cotton & linen textiles, electrical goods, vehicles, steel, scientific instruments, cutlery, foods & beverages, leather & tobacco products, apparel, chemicals, petrochemicals, pottery, china, machinery, locomotives, knitwear, drugs.

Cocoa, coffee, bananas, sugarcane, palm oil & kernels; timber, cabinet woods; fish; copra, beverages, soap.

Coffee, wheat, corn, barley, durra, teff, pulses, oilseeds, chat, civet, fruits, vegetables, sugarcane, spices; poultry, livestock; gold, platinum; hides & skins, meat & food products, textiles, cement, sugar, refined petroleum, drugs.

Oats, vegetables, hay; sheep; wool, hides & skins, tallow, animal & vegetable oil.

Sugarcane, coconuts, rice, fruits, cotton, rubber, ginger, oilseeds, vegetables, bananas, cocoa, corn, tobacco; livestock; timber; fish; gold, silver, manganese; sugar, copra, coconut oil, molasses, candlenut oil, cement, beer, meat products, flour, shipbuilding.

DENMARK: Amalienborg Palace in Copenhagen, the queen's residence, and the statue of King Frederik V.

Danish Nat'l Travel Office

FRANCE: Fresh fruits and vegetables occupy a market in Paris, near the right bank of the Seine.

TWA—Trans World Airlines

Social and Economic Tables

POLITICAL DIVISION	GOVERNMENT	MONETARY UNIT	LANGUAGE	RELIGION
FINLAND	Constitutional republic with a president, premier, cabinet, and a unicameral parliament.	markka	Finnish Swedish	Protestantism
FRANCE	A constitutional republic with a president, premier, bicameral elective legislature and appointive council of ministers.	franc	French	Roman Catholicism
FRENCH GUIANA	Overseas department of France governed by a prefect with an elective general council.	French franc	French	Roman Catholicism
FRENCH POLYNESIA	Overseas territory of France, with a governor, government council, and an elected territorial assembly.	CFP franc	Polynesian dialects French	Protestantism Roman Catholicism
GABON	One-party republic of the French Community with a president, appointed prime minister, and unicameral national assembly.	CFA franc	French Bantu languages	Roman Catholicism Tribal religions Islam
GAMBIA	Republic of the British Commonwealth, with a president, vice-president, cabinet and unicameral legislature.	dalasi	English Sudanese languages	Islam Tribal religions Protestantism
GERMANY	Divided country with two governments. The western democratic Federal Republic has a president, chancellor, cabinet & bicameral parliament. The eastern Democratic Republic is ruled by the chairman of the state council, a prime minister & cabinet, & a unicameral legislature; actual power resides in the head of the Communist party.	West German Deutsche mark East German Ostmark (GDR mark)	German	Protestantism Roman Catholicism
GHANA	Republic of the British Commonwealth, with a military council and appointed cabinet.	cedi	English Sudanese languages	Tribal religions Protestantism Islam
GIBRALTAR	Partly self-governing British colony, with governor, cabinet, house of assembly and local council.	pound sterling	English Spanish	Roman Catholicism
GILBERT ISLANDS (KIRIBATI)	Self-governing British colony, with a governor and local councils.	Australian dollar	English Gilbertese	Protestantism Roman Catholicism
GREAT BRITAIN	See: England and Wales, Northern Ireland, Scotland.			
GREECE	Constitutional republic, with a president, premier, and unicameral parliament.	drachma	Greek	Greek Orthodoxy
GREENLAND (KALÂTDLIT-NUNÂT)	Self-governing community of Denmark with a premier and elected legislature.	Danish krone	Danish Greenlandic Eskimo	Protestantism
GRENADA	Independent British Commonwealth member with a governor-general, premier and revolutionary council.	East Caribbean dollar	English French patois	Roman Catholicism Protestantism
GUADELOUPE	Overseas department of France with a prefect and elected general council.	French franc	French French patois (Creole)	Roman Catholicism
GUAM	Unincorporated U.S. territory, with an elected governor, advisory staff, and a unicameral legislature.	American dollar	English Chamorro Spanish	Roman Catholicism

of the World

MAJOR PRODUCTS

Hay, potatoes, cereal grains; livestock, poultry, reindeer; timber; fish; copper, iron ore, titanium, zinc, nickel; lumber, plywood, furniture, pulp, paper, wood products, textiles, food & dairy products, meat, chemicals, china, glass, machinery, ships, transportation equipment, electrical & metal products, vehicles, apparel, iron & steel.

Sugar beets, potatoes, cereal grains, turnips, fruits, nuts, grapes, buckwheat; livestock; fish; coal, iron ore, bauxite, pyrites, potash, salt, sulphur, natural gas; iron & steel, chemicals, machinery, metal & leather goods, autos, aircraft, ships, aluminum, porcelain, food & dairy products, apparel, cosmetics, perfumes, sugar, wines & spirits, electric & electronic goods, lace, silk, cotton, rayon, wool & linen textiles.

Rice, bananas, sugarcane, corn, manioc; timber; livestock; shrimp; bauxite, gold; hides, shoes, rum, fish glue.

Coconuts, bananas, pineapples, oranges, vanilla, sugarcane, coffee, bamboo; fish; mother-of-pearl, sugar, rum, copra.

Coffee, cocoa, rubber, corn, rice, bananas, cassava; timber; fish; manganese, uranium, petroleum, iron ore, gold, natural gas, lead, zinc, copper, diamonds, phosphates; refined petroleum, processed metals, textiles, plywood.

Peanuts, rice, millet, sorghum, fruits, palm kernels; livestock; fish; textiles, peanut oil refining, fish processing, palm products, beverages.

Cereal grains, potatoes, sugar beets, fruits, hops; livestock; fish; timber; coal, lignite, iron ore, potash, salt, uranium, lead, zinc, natural gas, fluorspar; iron & steel, autos, bicycles, machinery, aluminum, cement, electrical & transportation equipment, ships, metal & electronic products, cotton & woolen textiles & yarn, rayon fiber, precision & optical instruments, shoes, apparel, food products, sugar, beer, wine, chemicals, sulphuric acid, soda, ammonia, synthetic rubber, drugs, petrochemicals.

Cocoa, coconuts, kola nuts, fruits, tobacco, coffee, peanuts, rubber; livestock; fish; timber; gold, diamonds, manganese, bauxite; aluminum, refined petroleum, textiles.

Fish; ship repairing, beer, local food processing.

Coconuts, breadfruit; phosphate of lime; pearl shell, fish; pigs, poultry; copra, palm products.

Cereal grains, tobacco, sugar beets, cotton, fruits, olives; livestock; sponges, fish; iron ore, emery, manganese, magnesite, marble, silver, nickel, bauxite, salt, chromite; textiles, olive oil, processed meat, fruit & vegetables, dairy, wood & leather products, steel, machinery, refined aluminum & petroleum, chemicals, wine, olive oil, cement, drugs.

Grass for fodder; cod and other fish; sheep, furs; cryolite, lead, zinc; processed fish, skins.

Cocoa, nutmeg, coffee, mace, limes, bananas, sugarcane, coconuts, vegetables, cotton; fish; livestock; timber; sugar, cotton ginning, copra, lime oil, rum, beer, cigarettes.

Sugarcane, bananas, pineapples, mangoes, avocados, coffee, cotton, sisal, cocoa, vanilla, cassava; fish; rum, sugar.

Coconuts, corn, bananas, citrus fruits, mangoes, papayas, breadfruit, sweet potatoes, cassava, vegetables, sugarcane, pineapples; livestock, poultry; fish; dairy & coconut products.

GREECE: An "evzone," one of the uniquely uniformed guards at the palace in Athens.

J. Walter Thompson

GUATEMALA: Removing the nuts from the pods at a cacao "finca," or plantation, is the first stage of processing chocolate.

I.I.A.A.

221

Social and Economic Tables

POLITICAL DIVISION	GOVERNMENT	MONETARY UNIT	LANGUAGE	RELIGION
GUATEMALA	Republic with a president, cabinet and an elected unicameral congress.	quetzal	Spanish Maya-Quiché dialects	Roman Catholicism
GUINEA	One party republic with a president, cabinet, premier and unicameral national assembly.	syli	French Sudanese languages	Islam Tribal religions Roman Catholicism
GUINEA-BISSAU	Independent republic, with a state council under the president, and a one-party unicameral assembly.	Guinea-Bissau escudo	Portuguese Sudanese languages	Tribal religions Islam Roman Catholicism
GUYANA	Republic within the British Commonwealth, with president, prime minister, cabinet, and unicameral assembly.	Guyana dollar	English	Christianity Hinduism Islam
HAITI	Nominal republic with president (for life), cabinet, and a unicameral legislature.	gourde	French Creole	Roman Catholicism
HONDURAS	Republic, at present with a president, advisory cabinet and military council.	lempira	Spanish	Roman Catholicism
HONG KONG	British colony ruled by a governor assisted by executive and legislative councils.	Hong Kong dollar	English Chinese (Cantonese)	Confucianism Buddhism Taoism Christianity
HUNGARY	Soviet-type republic with a president, council, premier and unicameral assembly. Actual power is in the hands of the politburo of the Communist party.	forint	Hungarian	Roman Catholicism Protestantism
ICELAND	A republic with a president, premier, an elective bicameral parliament, and an appointive cabinet.	króna	Icelandic	Protestantism
INDIA	An independent republic within the British Commonwealth with a president, vice-president, prime minister, cabinet and a bicameral parliament.	Indian rupee	Hindi; English Assamese, Bengali, Gujarati, Kannada, Kashmiri, Malayalam, Marathi, Oriya, Panjabi, Sanskrit, Tamil, Telugu, Urdu	Hinduism; Islam Buddhism Animism Christianity Sikhism Jainism Zoroastrianism Lamaism
INDONESIA	Republic headed by a president, appointed cabinet, and consultative assembly (containing a unicameral parliament).	rupiah	Bahasa Indonesia (Indonesian Malay) Papuan	Islam Christianity Hinduism Buddhism Tribal religions
IRAN	Republic, provisionally governed by a premier and a secret revolutionary council.	Iranian rial	Persian (Farsi) Kurdish Arabic Turkic languages	Islam Zoroastrianism Christianity Judaism
IRAQ	Nominal republic headed by a president and a revolutionary council, and an appointed cabinet.	Iraqi dinar	Arabic Kurdish	Islam Christianity Judaism
IRELAND	Republic with a president, prime minister, cabinet, and a partly-elected bicameral parliament.	Irish pound	Irish English	Roman Catholicism Protestantism

MAJOR PRODUCTS

Coffee, bananas, sugarcane, tobacco, rubber, cotton, chicle, abacá; fish; cattle; mahogany; nickel, zinc, lead; textiles, chemicals, essential oils, wood, metal & electric goods, processed meat & foods, sugar, hides & skins, apparel.

Rice, millet, coffee, kola nuts, peanuts, palm oil & kernels, quinine, pineapples, cassava, bananas; livestock; bauxite, iron ore, diamonds, gold; timber; hides & skins, textiles, wood & food products, cigarettes, aluminum.

Rice, palm kernels, palm oil, wax, peanuts, coconuts; hides and skins; fish; timber.

Sugarcane, corn, rice, coconuts, coffee, citrus & tropical fruits, cacao, balata, rubber; timber; livestock; shrimp; bauxite, diamonds, manganese, gemstones, gold; textiles, milled rice, beer, rum, lime oil, sugar, wood & pulp, molasses, aluminum.

Coffee, sugarcane, sisal, cotton, fruits, rice, corn, cocoa; livestock; shellfish; bauxite; fiber, cement, essential oils, handicrafts, molasses, textiles, cement, sugar, soap, rum.

Bananas, coffee, coconuts, tobacco, corn, beans, sugarcane, cotton, rice, henequén; mahogany; cattle; lead, zinc, gold, silver; meat & food products, sugar, lumber, vegetable oils.

Rice, sugarcane, vegetables; fish; poultry, pigs; iron ore, wolfram, graphite; iron & steel, ships, enamel ware, apparel, textiles, cotton & plastic goods, toys, cameras, radios, electric & electronic goods.

Cereal grains, sugar beets, tobacco, grapes, fruits, potatoes; livestock, poultry; fish; timber; coal, petroleum, natural gas, iron ore, bauxite; flour, sugar, iron & steel, wines, textiles, chemicals, cotton & woolen goods, dairy, food, wood & paper products, machinery, tools & metal products, transportation equipment, drugs, aluminum, bicycles, cement.

Hay, potatoes, turnips, fruits, vegetables; livestock; fish; diatomite; dairy products, processed fish & fish products, meat, hides & skins, textiles, apparel, chemicals, cement, motors, vegetable oils.

Cereal grains, peanuts, seeds, tea, tobacco, opium, jute, cotton, rubber, coffee, sugarcane; fish; livestock; timber; coal, manganese, iron ore, petroleum, salt, mica, chromite, ilmenite, clay, copper, bauxite, gypsum; textiles, silk, cotton & jute fabrics, carpets, wood & metalwork, leather, cement, ships, refined petroleum, sugar, iron & steel, machinery, typewriters, aluminum, autos, transportation equipment, aircraft, chemicals.

Rice, sugarcane, corn, coconuts, cassava, sweet potatoes, spices, tea, coffee, fruits, rubber, tobacco, cotton, kapok; livestock; fish; timber; tin, petroleum, iron ore, natural gas, salt, bauxite, nickel, copper; refined petroleum & products, sugar, cement, copra, textiles, paper, ships, chemicals, palm oil, food products, glass, rubber goods, autos.

Cereal grains, cotton, dates, raisins, fruits, opium, sugar beets, nuts, tea, tobacco; livestock; fish; timber; petroleum, natural gas, copper, lead, coal, iron ore, salt; hides, wool, textiles, carpets, leather & tobacco products, caviar, sugar, glass, tools, vehicles, iron & steel, cement, aluminum, refined petroleum, metal products, chemicals & petrochemicals, vehicles, flour, processed foods.

Dates, fruits, barley, wheat, rice, tobacco, cotton, vegetables, sorghum; livestock; petroleum, sulphur, salt; refined petroleum, cement, chemicals, drugs, hides & skins, wool, glass, textiles, processed foods, electrical equipment.

Hay, potatoes, turnips, sugar beets, cereal grains; fish; livestock; lead, zinc, silver; tobacco, textiles, apparel, wood, clay, paper & metal products, machinery, dairy products, meat, processed foods, beer, malt, chemicals, vehicles.

INDIA: A typical scene in one of the busy streets of the native section in Bombay.

TWA–Trans World Airlines

INDONESIA: Educational progress—a mother and daughter attending school together.

Indonesian Info. Office

Social and Economic Tables

POLITICAL DIVISION	GOVERNMENT	MONETARY UNIT	LANGUAGE	RELIGION
ISRAEL	Republic with a president, prime minister, cabinet and elected unicameral parliament.	Israeli pound	Hebrew Arabic English	Judaism Islam Christianity
ITALY	Constitutional republic with a president, premier, a bicameral elective parliament and an appointive cabinet.	lira	Italian	Roman Catholicism
IVORY COAST	One-party republic with a president, cabinet, and a unicameral legislature.	CFA franc	French Sudanese languages	Tribal religions Islam Christianity
JAMAICA	Independent member of the British Commonwealth, with a governor-general, prime minister, cabinet, and bicameral parliament.	Jamaican dollar	English Jamaican Creole	Protestantism Roman Catholicism
JAPAN	Constitutional monarchy, with a prime minister, cabinet, and a bicameral diet. The duties of the emperor are merely ceremonial.	yen	Japanese	Buddhism Shintoism Christianity
JORDAN	Constitutional monarchy, with a king, prime minister and cabinet.	Jordanian dinar	Arabic English	Islam
KENYA	One-party republic of the British Commonwealth, with a president, vice-president, cabinet, and unicameral national assembly.	Kenyan shilling	English; Kiswahili Bantu, Hamitic and Sudanese languages	Christianity Tribal religions Islam
KOREA	Divided country with two governments. South Korea is a republic with a president, prime minister, cabinet & unicameral assembly. North Korea is ruled by the politburo of the Communist party, and has a president, prime minister & unicameral assembly.	won	Korean	Buddhism Confucianism Christianity
KUWAIT	Constitutional state with an emir, prime minister and cabinet, at present ruled by decree.	Kuwaiti dinar	Arabic	Islam
LAOS	Communist republic with a president, premier and appointed assembly, controlled by the party.	kip	Lao French	Buddhism Tribal religions
LEBANON	Republic with a president, an appointed premier and cabinet, and an elected unicameral assembly.	Lebanese pound	Arabic French	Islam Christianity
LESOTHO	Monarchy presently ruled by a prime minister (by decree), cabinet and assembly.	South African rand	Sesotho English	Christianity Tribal religions
LIBERIA	One-party republic, with a president, cabinet, and an elective bicameral Congress.	U.S. (Liberian) dollar	English Sudanese languages	Tribal religions Christianity Islam
LIBYA	Arab republic ruled by a council under its president, with an appointed premier and cabinet.	Libyan dinar	Arabic; Berber English Italian	Islam

MAJOR PRODUCTS

Wheat, cotton, tobacco, vegetables, fruits; livestock, poultry; fish; potash, salt, petroleum; textiles, apparel, processed foods, dairy products, glass, drugs, instruments, paper, metal, wood, rubber & leather products, polished diamonds, electric & electronic products, chemicals, wine, vehicles, refined petroleum, transportation equipment.

Cereal grains, sugar beets, potatoes, tomatoes, olives, grapes, citrus fruits, tobacco; timber; fish; livestock; natural gas, sulphur iron ore, coal, zinc, bauxite, mercury, marble; textiles, chemicals, wine, autos, machinery, electrical goods, sugar, olive oil, apparel, processed foods, petrochemicals, typewriters, iron & steel, aluminum, shoes, transportation equipment.

Coffee, cocoa, sugarcane, bananas, pineapples, nuts, rubber, cotton; tropical woods; livestock; fish; diamonds, iron ore; textiles, processed foods, lumber & wood products, refined petroleum, metal products, palm oil.

Sugarcane, bananas, tobacco, coconuts, coffee, citrus fruits, pimento, spices; fish; timber; bauxite, gypsum; rum, molasses, textiles, aluminum, copra, apparel, chemicals, processed foods, sugar, cement, metal, paper & rubber products.

Rice, wheat, barley, potatoes, fruits, vegetables, sugarcane, hemp, tobacco, soybeans, tea; livestock; fish; timber; petroleum, iron ore, manganese, gold, silver, copper, coal, natural gas; textiles, silk, iron & steel, machinery, autos, ships, instruments, electric & electronic goods, paper, pulp, porcelain & earthenware, toys, sugar, chemicals, apparel, aluminum, fish products, metal products.

Wheat, barley, grapes, vegetables, fruits, olives; livestock; phosphates, potash, marble; wool, tobacco & leather products, cement, soap, olive oil, beverages, refined petroleum.

Sisal, wheat, tea, coffee, pyrethrum, cotton, sugarcane, corn, peanuts, coconuts, wattle bark; livestock; timber; gold, silver, fluorspar, salt; sisal, meat & dairy products, sugar, cement, soda ash, hides & skins, petroleum products.

Rice, barley, wheat, soybeans, tobacco, corn, cotton, fruits; timber; livestock; fish; tungsten, gold, silver, iron ore, copper, coal, petroleum, lead, graphite, kaolin; textiles, silk, apparel, electric & electronic goods, metal, rubber, paper, wood & petroleum products, chemicals, cement, machinery, iron & steel.

Fruits, vegetables; pearls; fish; petroleum, natural gas; refined petroleum & petroleum products, ammonia, chemicals, fertilizer, cement, fish products, wool.

Rice, coffee, tea, citrus fruits, corn, cinchona, opium, potatoes, tobacco, cardamon, stick-lac; livestock; timber; tin; textiles, cigarettes, beverages, lumber, milled rice.

Wheat, barley, corn, potatoes, fruits, onions, vegetables, olives, tobacco; livestock; iron ore; textiles, metal & tobacco products, refined petroleum, chemicals, processed foods, cement, olive oil.

Cereal grains, beans, peas; livestock; diamonds; wool, mohair, hides & skins, carpets, textiles, shoes, candles, chemicals, jewelry, processed foods.

Rubber, rice, coffee, sugarcane, cocoa, palm oil & kernels, piassava; timber; fish, shrimp; iron ore, diamonds; petroleum products, cement, processed foods & rubber, lumber.

Barley, wheat, olives, grapes, dates, vegetables, figs, peanuts, citrus fruits, almonds, esparto; livestock; sponge & tuna fishing; hides & skins; petroleum, natural gas; textiles, crude petroleum, processed foods, leather, olive oil.

ITALY: A gondolier and his craft on one of the many waterways in Venice.

TWA–Trans World Airlines

LUXEMBOURG: La Place Guillaume, in the heart of the grand duchy's picturesque capital city.

Office Nat'l du Tourisme

Social and Economic Tables

POLITICAL DIVISION	GOVERNMENT	MONETARY UNIT	LANGUAGE	RELIGION
LIECHTENSTEIN	Constitutional hereditary monarchy, with a prince, prime minister, and unicameral parliament.	Swiss franc	German Alemannic dialect	Roman Catholicism
LUXEMBOURG	Constitutional monarchy with a grand duke, premier, cabinet, and a bicameral parliament.	Luxembourg franc	Letzeburgisch (German dialect) French; German	Roman Catholicism
MACAO	Partly autonomous Portuguese overseas province, under a governor, cabinet, and a legislative assembly.	pataca	Chinese (Cantonese) Portuguese	Buddhism; Taoism Confucianism Christianity
MADAGASCAR	Republic of the French Community with a head of government, premier and legislature. Rule is by a military council.	Malagasy franc	Malagasy French Bantu languages	Tribal religions Christianity Islam
MALAWI	One-party republic of the British Commonwealth, with president (for life), cabinet, and unicameral assembly.	Malawi kwacha	Chichewa English Bantu languages	Christianity Islam Tribal religions
MALAYSIA	Constitutional monarchy of the British Commonwealth, with a paramount ruler, prime minister, cabinet and bicameral parliament.	ringgit	Malay English Chinese Hindi, Tamil	Islam; Buddhism Confucianism Hinduism; Taoism Christianity
MALDIVES	Republic with a president and unicameral legislature.	Maldivian rupee	Divehi	Islam
MALI	Republic ruled by a president and a military committee.	Malian franc	French Sudanese and Hamitic languages	Islam Tribal religions
MALTA	An independent member of the British Commonwealth, with a president, prime minister, a cabinet and a unicameral parliament.	Maltese pound	Maltese English	Roman Catholicism
MARTINIQUE	Overseas department of France, with a prefect and an elected general council.	French franc	French Creole	Roman Catholicism
MAURITANIA	One-party republic, with a president, premier, appointed cabinet, and a unicameral assembly.	ouguiya	French; Arabic Sudanese and Hamitic languages	Islam
MAURITIUS	Independent member of the British Commonwealth, with a governor-general, prime minister, cabinet, and unicameral parliament.	Mauritian rupee	English; French Creole; Tamil Hindi; Urdu Chinese	Hinduism Christianity Islam Buddhism
MAYOTTE	French territorial collectivity.	CFA franc	Arabic; French Kiswahili	Islam
MEXICO	Constitutional federative republic with a president, council of ministers and a bicameral congress.	Mexican peso	Spanish	Roman Catholicism
MONACO	Constitutional hereditary principality, with a prince and a unicameral council.	French franc	French	Roman Catholicism
MONGOLIA	Soviet-type republic, with a president (chairman of Communist party politburo) & unicameral legislature.	tughrik	Mongolian Turkic languages	Lamaism

of the World

MAJOR PRODUCTS

Corn, wheat, potatoes, grapes; livestock; textiles, wine, leather, dairy products, ceramics, precision instruments, drugs, canned foods, postage stamps.

Oats, potatoes, wheat, rye, grapes; livestock; timber; iron ore, slate, salt, gypsum; iron & steel, metal products, chemicals, tobacco, leather, wine, dairy products, rubber products, fertilizers, plastic goods.

Rice, vegetables; fish; cement, metal work, lumber, processed tobacco, matches, wine, textiles, fireworks.

Cassava, rice, corn, sweet potatoes, vanilla, cloves, sugarcane, coffee, bananas, beans, manioc, sisal, tobacco, raffia; timber; livestock; fish; graphite, mica, chromite; textiles, processed meat & foods, refined petroleum & petroleum products, cement, paper, sugar, beer, leather.

Tobacco, tea, cotton, sugarcane, tung nuts, pulses, sisal, corn, fruits, sorghum, rice, millet, peanuts, rubber; timber; livestock; bauxite, stone, gold; hides & skins, tung oil, meat, transportation equipment, machinery, ghee, sugar.

Rubber, rice, coconuts, sugarcane, coffee, cocoa, pineapples, pepper, tea, tobacco, vegetables; livestock; fish; timber; tin, petroleum, copper, gold, antimony, bauxite, iron ore, manganese; rubber & wood products, steel, autos, refined petroleum, textiles, electric goods, sugar, fibers.

Coconuts, corn, millet, pumpkins, sweet potatoes, fruits, nuts; fish, cowries; mats, boats, dried fish & fish products, handicrafts, copra, coir, ambergris, lace.

Millet, rice, sorghum, peanuts, corn, cotton, tobacco, nuts, sisal; livestock; fish; salt, gold, bauxite, iron ore, uranium; hides & skins, ceramics, jewelry, leather, rice mills, soap, processed fish & foods, textiles, sugar, cement, meat, fibers.

Wheat, barley, potatoes, onions, grapes, vegetables, fruits, cumin seed, cotton; livestock; fish; lace, wine, beer, cigarettes, buttons, pipes, gloves, textiles & yarn, flowers, ceramics, rubber & electronic goods, apparel.

Sugarcane, cocoa, mangoes, avocados, pineapples, bananas, coffee; fish; rum, sugar.

Cereal grains, beans, peanuts, melons, dates, gum arabic, henna, sweet potatoes; livestock; lobsters, fish; manganese, gypsum, iron ore, copper, salt; hides & skins, fish products.

Sugarcane, aloe fiber, corn, coffee, vanilla beans, hemp, potatoes, sisal, peanuts, tea, yams, manioc, pineapples, tobacco, coconuts; molasses, rum, copra, sugar, dairy, tea & tobacco products, processed foods, textiles, fibers.

Vanilla, sisal, sugarcane, essential oils, rum; fish.

Grains, coffee, cotton, tomatoes, sugarcane, bananas, chicle, beans, oranges, henequén; timber; fish; shrimp; livestock; silver, gold, lead, zinc, petroleum, coal, sulphur, manganese, natural gas, iron ore, copper; sugar, hides, textiles, fibers, chemicals, aluminum, machinery, autos, refined petroleum, petrochemicals, cement, paper, drugs, metal products.

Principal revenue from gambling casino and tourism. Postage stamps, perfume, liqueurs, olive oil, oranges, chemicals, instruments, glass, processed foods, ceramics.

Grains; livestock; coal, petroleum, lead, gold; dairy products, wool, hides & skins, processed foods, machinery, furs, meat & dairy products, textiles, leather, cement.

MEXICO: The Pyramid of the Sun at San Juan Teotihuacan, not far from Mexico City.

J. Walter Thompson

MOROCCO: Downtown Casablanca, the chief port, with the Place Lyautey in the foreground.

French Gov't Tourist Office

Social and Economic Tables

POLITICAL DIVISION	GOVERNMENT	MONETARY UNIT	LANGUAGE	RELIGION
MOROCCO	Constitutional monarchy, with a king, an appointed prime minister, cabinet, and a unicameral parliament.	dirham	Arabic Berber French Spanish	Islam Judaism Christianity
MOZAMBIQUE	One-party republic with a president, cabinet and a unicameral assembly.	Mozambique escudo	Portuguese Bantu languages	Tribal religions Islam Roman Catholicism
NAURU	Republic with a president, cabinet, and unicameral assembly.	Australian dollar	English Nauruan	Protestantism
NEPAL	Constitutional monarchy, with king, prime minister, cabinet, and a unicameral parliament.	Nepalese rupee	Nepali; Newari Hindi English	Hinduism Buddhism Christianity
NETHERLANDS	A constitutional, hereditary monarchy governed by the queen, a premier and cabinet, and a bicameral partly elected states general.	guilder (florin)	Dutch	Roman Catholicism Protestantism
NETHERLANDS ANTILLES	Self-governing part of Netherlands Union with governor, minister-president, cabinet & unicameral legislature (staten).	Dutch guilder	Dutch Papiamento Spanish	Roman Catholicism Protestantism

NEW CALEDONIA	French overseas territory with a governor, government council & an elected territorial assembly.	CFP franc	Melanesian and
			  Polynesian
			  dialects
			French
				Roman Catholicism
				Tribal religions

NEW HEBRIDES	British and French condominium administered by British and French high commissioners, with a partly elected assembly.	Australian dollar New Hebrides franc	Melanesian dialects Pidgin English English; French	Tribal religions Protestantism Roman Catholicism
NEW ZEALAND	An independent member of the British Commonwealth governed by a governor-general, a prime minister, a cabinet and a unicameral parliament.	New Zealand dollar	English Maori	Protestantism Roman Catholicism
NICARAGUA	Constitutional republic with a president, cabinet, and elective bicameral congress.	córdoba	Spanish	Roman Catholicism
NIGER	One-party republic, with a president, the head of a military government.	CFA franc	French Sudanese and Hamitic languages Arabic; Berber	Islam Tribal religions
NIGERIA	Federal republic of the British Commonwealth, now under the chairman of a supreme military council, with an advisory federal executive council.	naira	English Sudanese languages	Islam Tribal religions Christianity

NIUE	Self-governing New Zealand dependency, with a prime minister and an assembly.	New Zealand dollar	Melanesian
			  and Polynesian
			  dialects; English
				Protestantism

NORTHERN IRELAND	Integral part of the United Kingdom with local government presently being reorganized.	pound sterling	English	Protestantism Roman Catholicism

228

of the World

MAJOR PRODUCTS

Wheat, barley, legumes, olives, nuts, citrus fruits, sugar beets, grapes; vegetables; cork, timber; livestock; fish; phosphates, iron ore, fluorite, coal, lead, zinc, manganese, petroleum, cobalt; textiles, carpets, pulp, wine, essential oils, olive oil, food & fish products, perfumes, wool.

Sugarcane, cereal grains, coconuts, cotton, cashew nuts, peanuts, sisal, beans, tea, tobacco; timber; livestock; fish, shellfish; gold, coal, iron ore, bauxite; sugar, textiles, milled rice, cement, vegetable oils, processed foods & fish, copra.

Phosphates.

Rice, wheat, corn, millet, jute, sugarcane, potatoes, tea, oilseeds, medicinal herbs; timber, livestock; iron ore, copper; processed rice, tobacco, leather & wood products, textiles, sugar, chemicals, ghee, hides & skins.

Potatoes, sugar beets, cereal grains, flax, legumes, flower bulbs, seeds, vegetables, fruits; livestock; fish; coal, petroleum, natural gas, salt; metal products, textiles, paper, chemicals, processed foods, apparel, ships, ceramics, cement, dairy, wood & tobacco products, petroleum products, machinery, electric & electronic products, transportation equipment, flowers, glass, processed diamonds.

Fish; salt, phosphates; refined petroleum, petrochemicals, electronic equipment, textiles, beer.

Coconuts, coffee, cotton, corn, tobacco, bananas, pineapples, vegetables, rice; timber; livestock; nickel, chrome, manganese, iron ore, cobalt, copper, lead, silver, gold; canned meat, nickel & coffee processing, copra.

Coconuts, cocoa, coffee, bananas, yams, taro, manioc, fruits; timber; cattle; fish, trochus shell; manganese; meat and fish products, copra, lumber.

Cereal grains; livestock; timber; fish; gold, coal, mineral sands, limestone, petroleum, natural gas; meat, wool, hides & skins, apparel, timber & wood products, dairy products, food & tobacco products, autos, chemicals, fertilizers, beer, bricks, cement, electrical goods, machinery, paper, rubber & petroleum products.

Coffee, sugarcane, sesame, corn, bananas, rice, cocoa, tobacco, cotton, beans; cattle; fish; hardwoods; gold, copper, silver; sugar, wood products, meat products, textiles, cottonseed, chemicals, petroleum products, paper, food products.

Millet, rice, manioc, peanuts, cotton, gum arabic, beans, sorghum; livestock; uranium, cassiterite, limesetone, salt, natron; hides & skins, meat, food & leather products, textiles, cement, peanut oil.

Palm oil and kernels, cocoa, spices, tobacco, peanuts, cotton, rubber, soybeans, corn, rice, millet, coffee; livestock; fish, shrimp; timber; tin, coal, limestone, natural gas, petroleum, marble; metal products, cement, timber & wood products, textiles, beer, refined petroleum, hides & skins, processed foods & oils.

Limes, kumaras, passion fruit, bananas; copra, woven handicrafts.

Potatoes, oats, fruits, vegetables, barley, hay; poultry, livestock; limestone, basalt & igneous rocks, sand & gravel; linen, apparel, wool textiles, dairy products, meat & meat products, aircraft, machinery, tobacco, whiskey, electronic & transportation equipment, ships.

NEW ZEALAND: Mt. Cook, the country's highest peak, and the Southern Alps are seen across Lake Matheson, on the South Island.

Nat'l Publicity Studios

NORWAY: The popular resort of Balestrand, on the Sogne Fjord in western Norway.

Scandinavian Travel Comm'n

Social and Economic Tables

POLITICAL DIVISION	GOVERNMENT	MONETARY UNIT	LANGUAGE	RELIGION
NORWAY	Constitutional hereditary monarchy, with a king, premier, cabinet, and unicamerally elected but bicamerally operating parliament.	Norwegian krone	Norwegian	Protestantism
OMAN	An independent sultanate and an absolute monarchy, with an advisory cabinet.	Omani rial	Arabic Hindi; English	Islam Hinduism
PACIFIC ISLANDS, TRUST TERR.	United States U. N. trusteeship, with a high commissioner. Northern Marianas are to become a U.S. commonwealth.	U.S. dollar	English Micronesian dialects	Roman Catholicism Protestantism
PAKISTAN	Federal republic with a president, presently ruled by a military council and an administrator.	Pakistani rupee	Urdu English Punjabi, Pushtu Sindhi, Baluchi	Islam
PANAMA	Nominal republic with a president and unicameral legislature.	balboa	Spanish	Roman Catholicism
PAPUA NEW GUINEA	Independent British Commonwealth member, with a governor-general, prime minister, cabinet, and unicameral parliament.	kina	English Pidgin English Hiri Motu	Tribal religions Protestantism Roman Catholicism
PARAGUAY	Centralized republic with a president, an appointed cabinet and a bicameral congress.	guaraní	Spanish Indian (Guaraní)	Roman Catholicism
PERU	Nominal republic, presently ruled by a military junta, with a president, prime minister and cabinet.	sol	Spanish Indian (Quechua, Aymará)	Roman Catholicism
PHILIPPINES	Republic governed by a president and an assembly.	piso	Pilipino (Tagalog) English; Spanish	Roman Catholicism Protestantism Islam Tribal religions
PITCAIRN ISLANDS	British colony, with a governor, an island magistrate & council.	New Zealand dollar	English	Seventh Day Adventist
POLAND	Soviet-type republic with a chief of (council of) state, premier, & unicameral parliament; actual power lies with the politburo of the Communist party.	zloty	Polish	Roman Catholicism
PORTUGAL	Constitutional republic with a president, premier, cabinet and unicameral parliament.	escudo	Portuguese	Roman Catholicism
PUERTO RICO	Self-governing commonwealth associated with the United States, with a governor, advisory council, and bicameral congress.	U.S. dollar	Spanish English	Roman Catholicism
QATAR	Independent state with an emir and advisory council.	Qatari riyal	Arabic	Islam
RÉUNION	French overseas department, with a prefect and general council.	French franc	French	Roman Catholicism

MAJOR PRODUCTS

Hay, oats, barley, wheat, rye, potatoes, fruits; livestock; fish; timber; iron ore, petroleum, nickel, zinc, natural gas, coal; pulp, paper, cellulose, ships, aluminum, machinery, chemicals, metal & electro-chemical products, transportation equipment, iron & steel, processed & canned fish & foods, textiles, wool, dairy products, leather, furs.

Wheat, alfalfa, dates, limes, frankincense, coconuts, tobacco; livestock; fish; petroleum; dried fish & limes, ghee.

Vegetables, tropical fruits, coconuts; fish, trochus shell; poultry, livestock; copra, meat, handicrafts.

Cereal grains, cotton, sugarcane, citrus fruits, dates, tobacco; livestock; fish; petroleum, salt, chromite, natural gas, gypsum, limestone; textiles, rugs, apparel, leather, wool, hides & skins, handicrafts, surgical instruments, sporting goods, sugar, chemicals, cement, iron & steel, refined petroleum, electric goods, tires.

Bananas, cocoa, abacá, coconuts, rice, sugarcane, coffee, fruits; fish, shrimp; livestock; timber; beer, sugar, wood & leather products, textiles, refined petroleum, processed foods, cement, apparel, drugs, fishmeal.

Coconuts, coffee, copra, cocoa, rubber, sago, rice, kapok, sisal, bamboo, bananas; dairying, livestock, poultry, fish; timber; gold, silver, copper; tobacco products, boats, brewing.

Cotton, tobacco, sugarcane, cereal grains, yerba maté, soybeans, coffee, citrus fruits; livestock; timber, quebracho; beef, meat products, flour, refined petroleum products, oilcake & essential oils, hides, textiles, cement.

Cotton, sugarcane, potatoes, cereal grains, beans, potatoes, vegetables, fruits, coffee, guano; fish; livestock; petroleum, lead, zinc, copper, silver, gold, salt, iron ore; textiles, foodstuffs, fishmeal, sugar, cement, apparel, chemicals, refined metals, iron & steel, tires, hides & skins.

Rice, sugarcane, abacá, corn, tobacco, cocoa, coffee, nuts, kapok, peanuts, vegetables, maguey, rubber, fruits; livestock; fish; timber, gum resins; gold, iron ore, copper, chromite, silver, manganese, salt, coal, petroleum; sugar, textiles, rubber & tobacco products; lumber & wood products, autos, handicrafts, milled coconut oil & rice, fruit canning, copra, steel, cement, glass, chemicals, paper.

Fruits, vegetables; goats, poultry; handicrafts, postage stamps.

Potatoes, cereal grains, sugar beets; livestock; fish; timber; coal, lead, zinc, sulphur, iron ore, petroleum, copper, natural gas; iron & steel, chemicals & petrochemicals, coke, electric & electronic equipment, autos, ships, aluminum, metal, food & dairy products, sugar, glass, transportation equipment, cement, machinery, paper.

Cereal grains, potatoes, tomatoes, citrus fruits, grapes, olives; livestock; fish; timber; coal, wolfram, iron ore, sulphur, tungsten; wine, olive oil, cork, canned fish, food products, pulp, refined petroleum, ships, autos, textiles, electronic equipment, machinery, cement, steel.

Sugarcane, tobacco, fruits, coconuts, coffee, cotton, vegetables; livestock; stone, sand & gravel; rum, molasses, sugar, canned fish & fruit, tobacco products, cement, leather, textiles, apparel, petrochemicals, metal & electronic products.

Dates, fruit, vegetables; shrimp, fish; livestock; natural gas, limestone, petroleum; fish products, cement, refined petroleum, petrochemicals.

Sugarcane, tea, tobacco, vanilla, corn, manioc; livestock; essential oils, fruit & vegetable products, rum, sugar, molasses.

PERU: The beginning of festivities in the bull ring in Lima, the capital city.
Pan American World Airways

PORTUGAL: The Praça dos Restauradores in Lisbon, with the monument dedicated to the seventeenth century restorers of Portuguese independence.
Photo "Sni-Yan"

Social and Economic Tables

POLITICAL DIVISION	GOVERNMENT	MONETARY UNIT	LANGUAGE	RELIGION
RUMANIA	A Soviet-type republic with a president, a state council, a cabinet, and a unicameral assembly; actual power resides in Communist party politburo.	leu	Rumanian Hungarian	Rumanian Orthodoxy Roman Catholicism
RWANDA	Nominal republic, at present under military rule by a president and advisory committee.	Rwanda franc	Kinyarwanda French Kiswahili	Roman Catholicism Tribal religions Islam
ST. CHRISTOPHER-NEVIS-ANGUILLA	Associated British state with a governor, prime minister, cabinet & unicameral assembly.	East Caribbean dollar	English	Protestantism
ST. HELENA	British colony with a governor, legislative and executive councils.	pound sterling	English	Protestantism
ST. LUCIA	Independent British Commonwealth state with a governor, prime minister, cabinet & unicameral assembly.	East Caribbean dollar	English French patois	Roman Catholicism Protestantism
ST. PIERRE AND MIQUELON	French overseas department, with a prefect and general council.	CFA franc	French	Roman Catholicism
ST. VINCENT	Associated British state with a governor, prime minister, cabinet & unicameral assembly.	East Caribbean dollar	English	Protestantism Roman Catholicism
SAN MARINO	Republic with two regents, a cabinet, and unicameral council.	Italian lira	Italian	Roman Catholicism
SÃO TOMÉ AND PRÍNCIPE	One-party republic with a president, appointed premier and cabinet, and a unicameral assembly.	São Tomean escudo	Bantu languages Portuguese	Tribal religions Roman Catholicism
SAUDI ARABIA	Absolute monarchy under a king and advisory council of ministers; the king exercises all authority.	Saudi riyal	Arabic	Islam
SCOTLAND	Integral part of United Kingdom, with secretary of state for Scotland in the U.K. cabinet, controlling local agriculture & fisheries, home & health, education, development, & economic planning.	pound sterling	English Gaelic	Protestantism Roman Catholicism
SENEGAL	One-party republic of the French Community, with a president, a prime minister, cabinet and unicameral assembly.	CFA franc	French Sudanese languages	Islam Tribal religions Roman Catholicism
SEYCHELLES	British Commonwealth republic with a president, appointed cabinet and unicameral assembly.	Seychellois rupee	French Creole English; French	Roman Catholicism
SIERRA LEONE	One-party republic of the British Commonwealth, with a president, cabinet and unicameral parliament.	leone	English Sudanese languages Pidgin (Krio)	Tribal religions Islam Christianity
SINGAPORE	Republic of the British Commonwealth, with a president, prime minister, cabinet & unicameral parliament.	Singapore dollar	Chinese (Mandarin) Malay Tamil; Hindi English	Confucianism Buddhism Taoism; Hinduism Islam Christianity
SOLOMON ISLANDS	Independent member of the British Commonwealth with a governor-general, prime minister, cabinet and a unicameral parliament.	Solomon Islands dollar	English Pidgin English Melanesian dialects	Tribal religions Protestantism Roman Catholicism
SOMALIA	One-party republic with a president and advisory cabinet, all power being held by the party's central committee.	Somali shilling	Somali; Arabic English Italian	Islam

of the World

MAJOR PRODUCTS

Wheat, barley, corn, potatoes, sugar beets, tobacco, fruits; livestock; timber; petroleum, natural gas, coal, lignite, salt, iron ore, copper, bauxite, manganese, uranium; iron & steel, machinery, chemicals, lumber, wood & paper products, electric goods, refined petroleum, ships, cement, sugar, food products, textiles, metal products.

Coffee, cotton, rice, tea, corn, peanuts, pyrethrum, vegetables; livestock; cassiterite, tungsten, tantalite, beryl, wolfram; textiles, handicrafts, processed foods, beer, hides.

Sugarcane, cotton, rice, vegetables, tropical fruits, corn, yams, coconuts, livestock; fish, shellfish; salt; molasses.

Fruit, vegetables, lily bulbs, flax, sweet potatoes, potatoes; livestock, poultry; cordage, fibers, lace.

Bananas, coconuts, cocoa, tropical & citrus fruits, nutmeg, mace; fish; rum, copra, coconut oil, soap, cigarettes.

Codfish; cattle; sienna earth, yellow ocher; fish products, furs.

Bananas, arrowroot, coconuts, rice, tropical fruits, cotton, corn, spices, peanuts, cocoa; fish; livestock; copra, rum, processed foods, cigarettes.

Wheat, fruits, grapes, vegetables; stone; livestock; textiles, postage stamps, wine, pottery, hides, cement, paper, leather.

Cacao, coffee, coconuts, cinchona, bananas; livestock; palm oil, copra.

Dates, corn, wheat, coffee, fruits, henna, vegetables; fish; livestock; petroleum, gold, silver, gypsum, lead, copper; refined petroleum, petrochemicals, fertilizers, iron & steel, cement, meat & dairy products, hides, wool.

Potatoes, sugar beets, wheat, barley, vegetables, fruits; livestock; fish, shellfish; petroleum, coal, iron ore, lead, stone; iron & steel, machinery, metal, dairy, tobacco & food products, textiles & yarn, watches, transportation equipment, electric & electronic goods, autos, ships, paper, whiskey, refined petroleum, aluminum, chemicals.

Millet, sorghum, rice, corn, peanuts, cotton, fruits, vegetables, sweet potatoes; livestock; fish; phosphates, titanium, limestone; textiles, processed fish & foods, cement, peanut oil & cakes, refined petroleum, chemicals.

Coconuts, cinnamon, patchouli, vanilla, tea; fish, tortoise shell, guano; copra, coconut oil, dried fish, coir, essential oils.

Palm oil & kernels, rice, coffee, kola nuts, ginger, vegetables, cassava, piassava, peanuts, cocoa; livestock; fish, shrimp; diamonds, iron ore, bauxite, rutile; palm products, rice & oil milling.

Rubber, coconuts, fruits, vegetables, rice, coffee, tapioca, tobacco; livestock; fish; tin, rubber & petroleum processing, rice & coconut milling, steel, chemicals, cement, lumber & wood products, textiles, bricks, palm & food products, paper, refined petroleum, drugs, ships, electric goods.

Copra; livestock; fish; timber; copper, bauxite, nickel.

Sugarcane, cotton, cereal grains, peanuts, sesame, tobacco, bananas, beans; livestock; fish, shellfish; salt; fish, food & meat products, sugar, textiles, hides & skins.

PUERTO RICO: One of the island's chief products, pineapples, on their way to the cannery.

Hamilton Wright

SCOTLAND: Loch Garten, a highland lake in the eastern part of Inverness.

British Travel Ass'n

Social and Economic Tables

POLITICAL DIVISION	GOVERNMENT	MONETARY UNIT	LANGUAGE	RELIGION
SOUTH AFRICA	Constitutional republic, with a state president, prime minister, cabinet & bicameral parliament. Transkei was granted independence in 1976; Bophuthatswana in 1977.	rand	Afrikaans English Bantu languages Bushman Tamil; Hindi	Protestantism Roman Catholicism Islam Hinduism Buddhism Judaism
SOUTH-WEST AFRICA (NAMIBIA)	South African controlled territory with an administrator-general.	South African rand	Afrikaans English; German Bantu languages Bushman	Tribal religions Protestantism
SPAIN	Monarchy with a king, premier and cabinet, and a bicameral parliament.	peseta	Spanish (Castilian) Catalan; Valencian Basque Galician	Roman Catholicism
SRI LANKA (CEYLON)	Independent republic of the British Commonwealth, with a president, a prime minister, a cabinet and a unicameral assembly.	Sri Lanka rupee	Sinhala Tamil English	Buddhism Hinduism Christianity Islam
SUDAN	Republic with a president, cabinet and unicameral assembly. Local autonomy has been granted the southern provinces.	Sudanese pound	Arabic English Sudanese and Hamitic languages	Islam Tribal religions Christianity
SURINAME	Independent republic with a president, premier, cabinet, and elective unicameral parliament.	Suriname guilder	Dutch Creole English	Christianity Hinduism Islam
SWAZILAND	British Commonwealth monarchy, with a titular king, prime minister (who rules by decree) and cabinet.	lilangeni	English siSwati Afrikaans	Tribal religions Christianity
SWEDEN	A constitutional hereditary monarchy with a titular king, prime minister, cabinet and a unicameral parliament.	krona	Swedish	Protestantism
SWITZERLAND	Federal republic with a president, vice-president & executive federal council, & a bicameral elected federal assembly.	Swiss franc	German French Italian Romansch	Protestantism Roman Catholicism
SYRIA	Arab republic with a president, premier, and unicameral legislative people's council, appointed by presidential decree.	Syrian pound	Arabic; Armenian Turkish; Kurdish French; English	Islam Christianity
TANZANIA	One-party united republic of the British Commonwealth, with a president, vice-president, prime minister, cabinet and unicameral parlament proportionately representing Tanganyika and Zanzibar.	Tanzanian shilling	Kiswahili English Bantu languages Arabic Gujarati	Tribal religions Islam Christianity Hinduism
THAILAND (SIAM)	Constitutional monarchy, at present under a prime minister and a bicameral assembly.	baht	Thai Khmer; Malay Chinese; Lao	Buddhism Islam Confucianism

MAJOR PRODUCTS

Cereal grains, tobacco, sugarcane; fruits, peanuts; livestock; fish, lobsters; gold, coal, diamonds, copper, asbestos, manganese, limestone, platinum, chromite, iron ore, vanadium, tin, antimony, uranium; timber; chemicals, wool, iron & steel, machinery, apparel, textiles, fish & food products, sugar, aluminum, metal products, hides, autos, cement, transportation equipment, dairy products.

Livestock; fish, shellfish; diamonds, copper, lead, zinc, salt, tin, manganese, vanadium, iron ore, cadmium, silver, fluorspar, tantalite, phosphate, sulfur, germanium; karakul wool & hides, fish processing, dairy products.

Cereal grains, potatoes, legumes, citrus fruits, vegetables, olives, grapes, sugar beets, esparto, flax, hemp, pulses, nuts, sugarcane; livestock, poultry; fish; timber; coal, lignite, iron ore & pyrites, lead, zinc, mercury, copper, uranium, gypsum; textiles, paper, cement, hides, wine, olive oil, processed foods, cork, machinery, chemicals, leather, autos, refined petroleum, apparel, silk, shoes, processed foods & fruit, iron & steel.

Tea, coconuts, rubber, rice, cotton, spices, cocoa, nuts, sugarcane, fruits; fish; livestock; graphite, mineral sands, ilmenite, gem stones, limestone, salt, pearls; copra, plywood, leather, shoes, glass, steel, acetic acid, ceramics, quinine, strychnine, chemicals, drugs, textiles, cement, beer, refined petroleum, coconut & tobacco products, paper, apparel.

Cotton, cereal grains, gum arabic, oilseeds, senna, castor beans, resins, peanuts, sesame, dom & shea nuts, dates; livestock; ivory, trochus shell, mother-of-pearl; iron ore, manganese, chromite, salt, gold; textiles, cement, hides & skins, cottonseed, oilcake, sugar, leather, paint, soap.

Rice, citrus fruits, coconuts, coffee, bananas, sugarcane, cacao, balata, corn, tobacco; livestock; shrimp; timber, balata; gold, bauxite; sugar, rum, lumber & plywood, molasses, aluminum, food & dairy products.

Tobacco, corn, peanuts, sugarcane, sorghum, cotton, rice, pineapples, citrus fruits; livestock; timber; asbestos, iron ore, coal; meat & dairy products, sugar, pulp, canned fruits, textiles, hides & skins, wood & tobacco products.

Hay, sugar beets, potatoes, oilseeds, oats, wheat, rye, barley; timber; livestock; fish; iron ore, zinc, copper, lead; lumber, paper & wood products, machinery, textiles, iron & steel, metal & electric goods, chemicals, dairy, food & tobacco products, porcelain, glass, ships, furs, transportation equipment, matches, autos, munitions, liquor, instruments.

Cereal grains, sugar beets, potatoes, vegetables, fruits, tobacco; livestock; timber; salt, iron ore, manganese; dairy & tobacco products, watches & clocks, electric & glass products, instruments, jewelry, machinery, metal products, chocolate, wine, drugs, textiles & yarn, chemicals, aluminum, iron & steel, cement, sugar, meat, apparel, dyes, foods.

Cereal grains, cotton, vegetables, olives, grapes, sugar beets, tobacco; livestock; petroleum, natural gas, phosphates, gypsum; leather, textiles, cement, refined petroleum, wool, hides & skins, sugar, processed foods & oils, apparel, glass, tobacco goods.

Sisal, fruits, cocoa, coconuts, cotton, cloves, pyrethrum, spices, coffee, tobacco, nuts, tea, oilseeds, sugarcane; livestock; hides & skins; diamonds, gold, phosphates, mica, salt, tin, gem stones; processed foods, cement, textiles, refined petroleum, copra, hides & skins, sugar, dairy & wood products, cordage, rolled iron & aluminum.

Rice, coconuts, sugarcane, rubber, peanuts, tobacco, tapioca, jute, kenaf, cotton, corn; teak & other timber; livestock; fish; tin, wolfram, lead; lac, sugar, cement, textiles, tobacco & petroleum products, paper.

SOUTH AFRICA: Commissioner Street, in the downtown part of Johannesburg, the country's largest city.

South African Gov't Info. Office

SWITZERLAND: Milk still being delivered by dog cart in a rural section of the republic.

TWA–Trans World Airlines

Social and Economic Tables

POLITICAL DIVISION	GOVERNMENT	MONETARY UNIT	LANGUAGE	RELIGION
TOGO	One-party republic with a president and an appointed civilian-military cabinet.	CFA franc	French Sudanese languages	Tribal religions Roman Catholicism Islam
TOKELAU	An island territory of New Zealand governed by an administrator.	New Zealand dollar	Samoan	Protestantism Roman Catholicism
TONGA	Constitutional British Commonwealth monarchy, with a king, appointed prime minister, and unicameral assembly.	pa'anga	Tongan English	Protestantism Roman Catholicism
TRINIDAD AND TOBAGO	Independent British Commonwealth republic with a president, prime minister, cabinet and bicameral parliament.	Trinidad and Tobago dollar	English Hindi	Protestantism Roman Catholicism Hinduism; Islam
TUNISIA	Republic with a president (for life), an appointed premier and cabinet, and an elective unicameral assembly.	Tunisian dinar	Arabic French Berber	Islam
TURKEY	Constitutional republic with a president, premier, cabinet, and a bicameral parliament.	Turkish lira	Turkish Kurdish Arabic	Islam
TUVALU	Independent member of the British Commonwealth with a governor-general, prime minister and a unicameral parliament.	Australian dollar	English Samoan	Protestantism
UGANDA	Republic of the British Commonwealth with a provisional government, president and cabinet.	Ugandan shilling	English; Kiswahili Sudanese, Bantu, and Hamitic languages	Christianity Tribal religions Islam
U.S.S.R.	Federation of 15 union republics with a bicameral Supreme Soviet, which elects the presidium & council of ministers. Real power is largely exercised by the politburo & secretariat (under its general secretary) of the central committee of the Communist party.	ruble	Russian, Ukrainian, White Russian, Uzbek, Tatar, Azerbaidzhani, Georgian, Lithuanian, Latvian, Mordvinian, Chuvash, Tadzhik, Estonian, Kazakh, etc.	Russian Orthodoxy Islam Roman Catholicism Judaism
UNITED ARAB EMIRATES	Constitutional Arab federation of seven sheikhdoms, with a president, vice-president, premier and cabinet and a unicameral assembly.	U.A.E. dirham	Arabic	Islam
UNITED KINGDOM	See: England and Wales, Northern Ireland, Scotland.			
UNITED STATES	Federal republic with a president, vice-president, an appointed cabinet, and a bicameral congress (senate and house of representatives). It consists of 50 states, each with a governor and a state legislature (all except Nebraska being bicameral).	U.S. dollar	English	Protestantism Roman Catholicism Judaism
UPPER VOLTA	Republic with a president, premier and a unicameral assembly.	CFA franc	French Sudanese languages	Tribal religions Islam Roman Catholicism

of the World

MAJOR PRODUCTS

Palm oil & kernels, manioc, kapok, cocoa, coconuts, yams, cereal grains, coffee, cotton, peanuts, nuts, cassava; livestock; timber; phosphates, limestone; textiles, copra, cement.

Coconuts, fiber, taro; pigs, chickens; fish; hats, mats, copra.

Coconuts, bananas, yams, breadfruit, taro, cassava, papayas, pineapples, melons, tobacco, corn, peanuts, candlenuts; fish; livestock, poultry; copra, processed fruits.

Coffee, cocoa, coconuts, sugarcane, citrus fruits; cattle; timber; petroleum, natural gas, asphalt, coal, clay; rum, textiles, sugar, chemicals, plastic, glass, clay, wood & food products, cement, electric goods, refined petroleum.

Cereal grains, grapes, esparto, olives, vegetables, nuts, fruits, dates; cork, timber; livestock; fish; phosphates, petroleum, iron ore, lead, zinc; flour, wine, olive oil, sugar, wool, pottery, leather, textiles, food processing, chemicals, iron & steel, paper, refined petroleum, metal & electric goods.

Tobacco, cereal grains, cotton, fruits, opium, seeds, olives, nuts, sugar beets; livestock; fish; timber; chromite, iron ore, petroleum, copper, coal, lignite; textiles, iron & steel, chemicals, refined petroleum, rugs, paper, olive oil, wool, furs, sugar, mohair, silk, cement, skins.

Copra, fish, handicrafts, postage stamps.

Cotton, coffee, tea, plaintains, sisal, peanuts, millet, corn, tobacco, sugarcane; livestock; salt, copper, gold, phosphates, tin; cement, beverages, sugar, chemicals, smelted copper, processed foods, textiles, hides & skins, steel.

Cereal grains, sugar beets, cotton, flax, potatoes, seeds, vegetables, tobacco; livestock; fish; timber; petroleum, natural gas, bauxite, uranium, platinum, iron ore, lead, zinc, copper, phosphates, mercury, gold, manganese, nickel, chromite, asbestos, potash; iron & steel, machinery, chemicals, refined petroleum, petrochemicals, ships, autos, aircraft, lumber & wood products, meat & dairy products, textiles, wool, sugar, tools & metal products, aluminum, furs, cement, paper, electric goods, instruments, transportation equipment, foods & beverages.

Dates, cereal grains, vegetables; livestock; fish, pearl fishing; petroleum; cement, refined petroleum, petrochemicals, postage stamps, dried fish.

Cereal grains, hay, soybeans, potatoes, peanuts, sugar beets, sugarcane, vegetables, nuts, fruits, cotton, tobacco, flax; livestock, poultry; fish, shellfish; timber; petroleum, natural gas, coal, iron ore, copper, lead, zinc, gold, silver, molybdenum, bauxite, gypsum, phosphates, sulphur, stone, sand & gravel; iron & steel, machinery, transportation equipment, metal products, electric & electronic goods, autos, ships, aircraft, munitions, chemicals, tobacco, leather, rubber & plastic products, glass, wool, textiles, cement, food & dairy products, lumber & wood products, paper, refined petroleum, petrochemicals.

Cereal grains, sweet potatoes, peanuts, cassava, karite (shea nuts), vegetables, cotton, sisal, sesame, tea; livestock; gold, manganese, copper; hides & skins, meat products, sugar, flour, textiles, processed foods & oils, soap, cigarettes.

THAILAND: The heroine and hero in costume for a classical dance in the Asian kingdom.

Gov't of Thailand

TURKEY: The Galata Bridge, spanning the Golden Horn in Istanbul, one of the most heavily traveled bridges in the world.

Turkish Info. Office

Social and Economic Tables

POLITICAL DIVISION	GOVERNMENT	MONETARY UNIT	LANGUAGE	RELIGION
URUGUAY	A republic governed by a president, cabinet and a council of state.	Uruguayan peso	Spanish	Roman Catholicism
VATICAN CITY	The Pope exercises absolute legislative, executive & judicial power.	Italian lira	Italian Latin	Roman Catholicism
VENEZUELA	Constitutional federal republic with a president, appointive cabinet, and an elected bicameral congress.	bolívar	Spanish	Roman Catholicism
VIETNAM	Communist republic with a president, premier and unicameral assembly; actual rule is by the party's central committee and politburo.	dong	Vietnamese Khmer; Cham Lao French; Chinese Montagnard	Buddhism Taoism Confucianism Roman Catholicism Tribal religions
VIRGIN ISLANDS (BR.)	British colony with an administrator, chief minister and councils.	B. W. I. dollar; U.S. dollar	English Creole	Protestantism
VIRGIN ISLANDS (U.S.)	Unincorporated U.S. territory with an elected governor & unicameral legislature.	U.S. dollar	English Creole	Roman Catholicism Protestantism
WALLIS & FUTUNA	French overseas territory with an administrator, & a local council and assembly.	CFP franc	French Polynesian dialects	Roman Catholicism
WESTERN SAMOA	Independent member of the British Commonwealth, with a head of state, prime minister, cabinet and unicameral legislative assembly.	tala	Samoan English	Protestantism Roman Catholicism
YEMEN ARAB REP.	Arab republic with a president, premier and cabinet, and an advisory military council.	Yemeni riyal	Arabic	Islam ·
YEMEN, PEOPLES DEM. REP. OF	One-party Arab republic with a presidential council.	South Yemeni dinar	Arabic	Islam
YUGOSLAVIA	A Soviet-type federal republic with a president (for life), premier and federal executive council, and a bicameral assembly. Actually ruled by the Communist party.	Yugoslav dinar	Serbian-Croatian Slovenian Macedonian Montenegrin	Eastern Orthodoxy Roman Catholicism Islam
ZAIRE	One-party republic with a president, premier, executive council and unicameral legislative council; rule is by decree.	zaire	Bantu languages French	Tribal religions Roman Catholicism
ZAMBIA	One-party republic of the British Commonwealth, with a president, prime minister, cabinet, and a unicameral assembly.	Zambian kwacha	Bantu languages English	Tribal religions Christianity Hinduism Islam
ZIMBABWE RHODESIA	Self-proclaimed independent state with a president, premier, council of state, cabinet and parliament.	Zimbabwe Rhodesian dollar	English Bantu languages	Tribal religions Protestantism Islam

of the World

MAJOR PRODUCTS

Cereal grains, seeds, peanuts, fruits, hops, sugar beets, grapes, tobacco; livestock, meat & meat products, hides, wool, textiles, leather, wines, chemicals, refined petroleum, aluminum, steel, cement, sugar, metal products.

Postage stamps, religious articles.

Coffee, cotton, cocoa, sugarcane, cereal grains, tobacco, beans, sisal, balata, rubber, bananas; livestock; fish, shrimp; petroleum, natural gas, iron ore, gold, coal, phosphates, nickel, salt, diamonds; leather, rubber, metal & wood products, sugar, food, dairy & meat products, vehicles, chemicals, refined petroleum, petrochemicals, paper, steel, transportation equipment, apparel.

Rice, corn, sugarcane, coffee, fruits, nuts, vegetables, tea, manioc, peanuts, sweet potatoes, tobacco, cotton, rubber, silk; livestock, poultry; fish, shellfish; timber; coal, iron ore, chromite, uranium, phosphates, gold, tin; paper, textiles, chemicals, machinery, tobacco, lumber & wood products, sugar, processed foods, glass, beer, handicrafts, steel.

Bananas, tropical fruits, coconuts, vegetables; livestock, poultry; fish, turtles; handicrafts, rum, petroleum refining.

Vegetables, sugarcane, citrus fruits, coconuts; cattle; fish; rum, bay rum & oil, molasses, handicrafts, sugar, lime juice, hides, bitters.

Coconuts, bananas, taro, yams, cassava, arrowroot, vegetables; livestock, poultry; fish, trochus shell; copra, handicrafts.

Breadfruit, coconuts, coffee, fruits, seeds, yams, pawpaws, cocoa, bananas, taro; fish; timber; livestock; copra, handicrafts, hides, lumber, processed foods, apparel, beverages, soap.

Coffee, cereal grains, cotton, grapes, fruits, qat, sesame; cattle; fish; rock salt; textiles, hides, leather, handicrafts.

Dates, cereal grains; coffee, qat, gums, tobacco, cotton, fruit, sesame; livestock; fish; salt; ship bunkering, refined petroleum, hides & skins, textiles, fish products.

Cereal grains, sugar beets, tobacco, potatoes, seeds, hemp, nuts, fruits; livestock; fish; timber; coal, gold, iron ore, manganese, petroleum, bauxite, chromite, mercury, antimony, copper, lead, zinc, salt; textiles, lumber & wood products, cement, sugar, food & metal products, machinery, chemicals, iron & steel, ships, wine.

Palm oil & kernels, cotton, coffee, tea, cocoa, rice, sugarcane, rubber; livestock; ivory; timber; copper, diamonds, gold, cobalt, tantalite, petroleum, zinc, manganese, bauxite, cassiterite; textiles, processed foods, sugar, rubber products.

Cereal grains, tobacco, peanuts, cassava, sugarcane, fruits, cotton; timber; fish; livestock; copper, lead, coal, manganese, zinc, cobalt; iron & steel, metal & tobacco products, textiles, chemicals, refined petroleum & copper, processed foods & beverages, sugar, drugs, tires.

Corn, tobacco, peanuts, wheat, cotton, tea, sugarcane, citrus fruits; livestock; fish; copper, gold, asbestos, chromite, coal; textiles, apparel, cigarettes, wood, food, dairy & rubber products, meat & meat products, sugar, iron & steel, vehicles, electrical goods, metal products, chemicals, hides.

UNITED STATES: The American Falls at Niagara Falls, New York, a major tourist attraction.

N.Y. State Dep't of Commerce

VENEZUELA: Avenida Bolívar and the thirty story office buildings of downtown Caracas.

Hamilton Wright

ECUADOR: Independence Plaza in Quito, with the Cathedral, the center of tourist activity in the country.

Hamilton Wright

ENGLAND: Trafalgar Square and the famous pillar dedicated to Lord Nelson, in London.

British Info. Services

AUSTRALIA: A view of Sydney Harbour, with the botanical gardens at Farm Cove in the foreground.

Qantas

INDIA: The Hawa Mahal at Jaipur, in the state of Rajasthan, with old and new forms of transportation.

Gov't of India Info. Bur.

TRINIDAD & TOBAGO: A typical mosque in Port of Spain.

Trinidad & Tobago Tourist Board

This alphabetical list of cities and towns gives statistics of population based on the latest official census reports or most recent reliable estimates. Each line begins with the name of a place, followed by the name of the country or state, the population, the index reference and plate number. This index reference gives the location of the city or town name on ,the accompanying map plates. The name is found within the square formed by the two lines of latitude or longitude which enclose each of the coordinates—i.e. the marginal letters and numbers. In the case of maps consisting entirely of insets, the name is found near the intersection point of imaginary lines'connecting the co-ordinates.

Where space on the map has not permitted giving the complete form of a name, the extended form is shown in the index. Where a place may be known under different names or by various spellings of the same name, the different forms have been included, to a large extent, in the index. Where an alternative spelling in parentheses is shown on the map itself, the first name gives the local official form, the conventional form following in parentheses.

* Capitals of countries, states and provinces.   † Population figure includes suburbs or subdivision.

Aachen, Germany, 177,642 ....A 3 23	Alençon, France, 30,368 ....D 3 24	Ann Arbor, Mich., 99,797 ....F 6 143
Aalst, Belgium, 45,900 ....C 6 20	Aleppo, Syria, 566,770 ....G 4 46	An Nasiriya, Iraq, 60,405 ....E 3 44
Abadan, Iran, 262,962 ....E 3 44	Alessandria, Italy, 65,908 ....B 2 28	Annecy, France, 53,361 ....G 5 25
Abbeville, France, 23,770 ....D 2 24	Alexandretta (Iskenderun),	Anniston, Ala., 31,533 ....G 3 104
Abécher, Chad, 19,650 ....L 9 63	Turkey, 69,382 ....G 4 46	Annonay, France, 19,591 ....F 5 25
Abenrå, Denmark, 15,101 ....F 9 19	Alexandria, Egypt, 1,803,900 ....M 5 63	Anshan, China, 833,000 ....K 3 51
Abeokuta, Nigeria, 217,201 ......G10 62	Alexandria, La., 41,557 ....A 4 134	Antâkya, Turkey, 57,855 ....G 4 46
Aberdare, Wales, 38,210 ....E 5 17	Alexandria, Va., 110,938 ....L 3 185	Antalya, Turkey, 71,833 ....D 4 46
Aberdeen, Scotland, 181,089 ......E 2 16	Al Falluja, Iraq, 38,072 ....D 3 44	Antananarivo,* Madagascar,
Abidjan,* Ivory Coast, 180,000 ...E10 62	Algeciras, Spain, 51,096 ....D 4 26	332,885 ....R15 65
Abilene, Tex., 89,653 ....E 5 180	Algiers,* Algeria, 943,142 ....G 4 62	Antibes, France, 47,393 ....G 6 25
Abo (Turku), Finland, 155,000 ...N 6 19	Alhambra, Calif., 62,125 ....C10 113	Antofagasta, Chile, †126,252 ...F 8 70
Abu Dhabi,* United Arab	Alicante, Spain, 103,289 ....F 3 27	Antsirabe, Madagascar, 29,914 ...R16 65
Emirates, 22,000 ....F 5 45	Aligarh, India, 254,008 ....D 3 48	Antung, China, 370,000 ....K 3 51
Acámbaro, Mexico, †80,259 ....J 7 81	Aliquippa, Pa., 22,277 ....B 4 172	Antwerp (Antwerpen), Belgium,
Acapulco, Mexico, †234,866 ....J 8 81	Alkmaar, Netherlands, †52,091 ....E 2 20	234,099 ....D 5 20
Accra,* Ghana, 337,828 ....G10 62	Al Kuwait,* Kuwait, 80,008 ....E 4 44	Anyang, China, 153,000 ....H 4 51
Accrington, England, 36,340 ......G 1 16	Allahabad, India, 493,524 ....E 3 48	Anzhero-Sudzhensk, U.S.S.R.,
Acre, Israel, 28,100 ....C 2 47	Allentown, Pa., 109,527 ....L 4 173	106,000 ....J 4 38
Adana, Turkey, 289,919 ....F 4 46	Alleppey, India, 160,064 ....D 7 49	Aomori, Japan, 252,000 ....F 2 52
Adapazarı, Turkey, 86,124 ....D 2 46	Alma-Ata, U.S.S.R., 730,000 .....L 5 42	Apeldoorn, Netherlands, 123,628 ...G 3 20
Addis Ababa,* Ethiopia, 644,120 ...O10 63	Almelo, Netherlands, †58,941 ......J 3 20	Apia,* Western Samoa, 27,000 ...J 7 56
Adelaide,* South Australia,	Almería, Spain, 76,643 ....E 4 27	Apolda, Germany, 29,735 ....D 3 23
†727,916 ....D 7 58	Alor Star, Malaysia, 52,915 ....B 6 53	Appleton, Wis., 57,143 ....J 7 187
Aden,* Peoples Dem. Rep. of	Altenburg, Germany, 47,462 ....E 3 23	'Aqaba, Jordan, 8,908 ....D 5 47
Yemen, 150,000 ....E 7 44	Alton, Ill., 39,700 ....A 6 125	Aracaju, Brazil, 179,512 ....N 6 69
Adwa, Ethiopia ....O 9 63	Altoona, Pa., 63,115 ....F 4 172	Araçatuba, Brazil, 85,660 ....K 8 69
Afyon, Turkey, 44,026 ....D 3 46	Altrincham, England, 41,000 ....G 2 16	Arad, Rumania, 132,757 ....E 2 34
Agaña,* Guam, 2,131 ....E 4 56	Amadora, Portugal, 36,331 ....A 1 26	Aragua de Barcelona, Ven.,
Agen, France, 34,592 ....D 5 25	Amagasaki, Japan, 532,000 ....E 4 52	8,241 ....H 2 68
Agra, India, 594,858 ....C 3 48	'Amara, Iraq, 64,847 ....E 3 44	Arak, Iran, 71,925 ....E 3 44
Agrigento, Sicily, Italy, 46,947 ...D 6 29	Amarillo, Tex., 127,010 ....C 2 180	Araraquara, Brazil, 82,607 ....L 8 69
Agrínion, Greece, 24,763 ....E 6 35	Ambala, India, 83,649 ....D 2 48	Archangel, U.S.S.R., 343,000 .....F 2 36
Aquascalientes, Mexico, †222,105..H 6 80	Ambato, Ecuador, 53,372 ....E 4 68	Ardebil, Iran, 83,596 ....E 2 44
Ahlen, Germany, 50,411 ....B 3 22	Amboina (Ambon), Indon.,	Arequipa, Peru, 194,700 ....F 7 68
Ahmadabad, India, 1,588,378 ......C 4 48	†70,000 ....H 6 55	Argentan, France, 14,418 ....D 3 24
Ahmadnagar, India, 117,215 ....C 5 49	Amecameca, Mexico, †21,753 ......M 1 81	Argenteuil, France, 87,106 ....A 1 24
Ahwaz, Iran, 206,375 ....E 3 44	Amersfoort, Netherlands,	Århus, Denmark, 117,266 ....F 8 19
Aix, France, 74,948 ....F 6 25	†78,189 ....F 3 20	Arica, Chile, †92,394 ....F 7 68
Aix-les-Bains, France, 20,594 ......G 5 25	Amiens, France, 116,107 ....E 3 24	Arles, France, 33,575 ....F 6 25
Aizuwakamatsu, Japan, 104,000...F 2 57	Amman,* Jordan, 330,220 ....D 4 47	Arlington, Texas, 89,723 ....F 2 180
Ajaccio, Corsica, France,	Amoy, China, 308,000 ....J 7 51	Arlington, Va., 174,284 ....L 3 185
38,776 ....B 7 25	Amravati, India, 193,636 ....D 4 49	Armavir, U.S.S.R., 146,000 ....F 5 37
'Ajman, U.A.E., 3,725 ....G 4 45	Amritsar, India, 432,663 ....C 2 48	Armentières, France, 24,460 ....E 2 24
Ajmer, India, 262,480 ....C 3 48	Amsterdam,* Neth., 831,463 ....E 3 20	Arnhem, Netherlands,
Akashi, Japan, 187,000 ....E 4 52	Amsterdam, N.Y., 25,524 ....M 5 161	132,531 ....H 4 20
Akhisar, Turkey, 46,167 ....C 3 46	Anaheim, Calif., 166,408 ....D11 113	Arras, France, 48,494 ....E 2 24
Akita, Japan, 233,000 ....E 3 52	Ancona, Italy, 77,748 ....D 3 28	Artigas, Uruguay, 23,429 ....J10 71
Akola, India, 168,454 ....D 4 49	Anchorage, Alaska, 48,081 ....J 2 107	Aš, Czechoslovakia, 10,000 ....B 1 32
Akron, Ohio, 275,425 ....G 3 166	Anderlecht, Belgium, 103,832 ....D 6 20	Asahikawa, Japan, 293,000 ....F 2 52
Aktyubinsk, U.S.S.R., 150,000 .....F 6 38	Anderson, Ind., 70,787 ....F 4 126	Asansol, India, 157,388 ....F 4 48
Alajuela, Costa Rica, 25,196 ....E 6 78	Andizhan, U.S.S.R., 188,000 ....H 5 38	Aschaffenburg, Germany,
Alameda, Calif., 70,968 ....J 2 112	Andorra la Vella,* Andorra,	56,236 ....C 4 23
Albacete, Spain, 61,635 ....F 3 27	2,250 ....G 1 27	Aschersleben, Germany,
Albany, Ga., 72,623 ....D 7 121	Andria, Italy, 69,499 ....F 4 29	36,777 ....D 3 22
Albany,* N.Y., 115,781 ....N 5 161	Angarsk, U.S.S.R., 204,000 ....L 4 39	Asheville, N.C., 57,681 ....E 8 162
Albany, Western Australia,	Angers, France, 127,415 ....C 4 24	Ashkhabad, U.S.S.R.,
11,419 ....B 6 58	Angmagssalik, Greenland, 721 .....C11 10	253,000 ....F 6 38
Albi, France, 38,867 ....E 6 25	Angora (Ankara),* Turkey,	Ashland, Ky., 29,245 ....M 4 133
Ålborg, Denmark, 82,871 ....G 8 19	905,660 ....E 3 46	Ashqelon, Israel, 28,400 ....B 4 47
Albuquerque, N. Mex.,	Angoulême, France, 46,584 ....D 5 25	Ashton, England, 48,180 ....G 2 16
243,751 ....C 3 158	Ankara,* Turkey,	Asmara, Ethiopia,
Alcoy, Spain, 48,712 ....F 3 27	905,660 ....E 3 46	190,500 ....O 9 63
Aldershot, England, 38,120 ....F 5 17	Anking, China, 129,000 ....J 5 51	Asnières, France, 79,942 ....A 1 24
Aldridge-Brownhills, England,	Annaba, Algeria, 152,006 ....H 4 62	Asti, Italy, 44,455 ....B 2 28
87,530 ....G 3 16	An Najaf, Iraq, 128,096 ....D 3 44	Astrakhan', U.S.S.R.,
Alegrete, Brazil, 45,522 ....J 9 71	Annapolis,* Md., 30,095 ....H 5 139	411,000 ....G 5 37

Khíos, Greece, 24,053 ....G 6 35
Khorramshahr, Iran, 88,536 ....E 3 44
Kiamusze, China, 232,000 ....L 2 51
Kidderminster, England, 46,740 ....E 4 17
Kiel, Germany, 276,600 ....D 1 22
Kielce, Poland, 113,200 ....E 3 21
Kiev, U.S.S.R., 1,632,000 ....D 4 37
Kigali,* Rwanda, 24,000 ....N12 65
Kilmarnock, Scotland, 47,631 ......D 3 16
Kimberley, Cape of Good Hope,
  95,200 ....L17 65
Kingston,* Jamaica, 117,900 ....C 3 76
Kingston, N.Y., 25,544 ....M 7 161
Kingston, Ontario, 56,032 ....H 3 91
Kingston upon Thames,
  England, 143,670 ....B 6 17
Kingstown,* St. Vincent, †23,482..G 4 77
Kingtehchen, China, 266,000 ......J 6 51
Kinshasa,* Zaire, 431,296 ....K12 64
Kirin, China, 583,000 ....L 3 51
Kirkby, England, 65,260 ....F 2 16
Kirkcaldy, Scotland, 52,097 ....C 1 16
Kirkuk, Iraq, 167,413 ....D 2 44
Kirov, U.S.S.R., 332,000 ....G 3 36
Kirovabad, U.S.S.R., 190,000 ......G 6 37
Kirovograd, U.S.S.R., 189,000 .....D 5 37
Kiruna, Sweden, 29,210 ....L 3 18
Kisangani, Zaire, 229,596 ....M11 65
Kiselevsk, U.S.S.R., 126,000 ....J 4 38
Kishinev, U.S.S.R., 357,000 ....C 5 37
Kisi, China, 253,000 ....M 2 51
Kispest, Hungary, 66,547 ....E 3 33
Kitakyushu, Japan, 1,042,319 .....C 4 52
Kitchener, Ontario, 131,870 ....D 4 90
Kiukiang, China, 64,600 ....J 6 51
Kladno, Czechoslovakia, 55,000 ..B 1 32
Klagenfurt, Austria, 69,218 ....C 3 32
Klaipėda, U.S.S.R., 140,000 ....B 3 36
Klang, Malaysia, 75,649 ....C 7 53
Knoxville, Tenn., 174,587 ....O 3 179
Kobdo, Mongolia, 11,000 ....D 2 50
Kobe, Japan, 1,288,754 ....E 4 52
Koblenz, Germany, 106,189 ....B 3 23
Kochi, Japan, 242,000 ....D 4 52
Kofu, Japan, 185,000 ....E 4 52
Kokiu, China, 180,000 ....F 7 50
Kokkola, Finland, 20,715 ....N 5 18
Kokomo, Ind., 44,042 ....E 4 126
Kolar Gold Fields, India, 76,143...D 6 49
Kolarovgrad, Bulgaria, 59,362 ...H 4 34
Kolding, Denmark, 39,656 ....F 9 19
Kolhapur, India, 259,068 ....C 5 49
Kolín, Czechoslovakia, 25,000 ...C 1 32
Köln (Cologne), Ger., 866.308 ...B 3 23
Kolomna, U.S.S.R., 136,000 ......E 4 37
Komárno, Czechoslovakia, 26.000..D 3 33
Kommunarsk, U.S.S.R., 123,000...E 5 37
Komotiní, Greece, 28,355 ....G 5 35
Komsomol'sk, U.S.S.R., 218,000...O 4 39
Kongmoon, China, 110,000 ....H 7 51
Königsberg (Kaliningrad),
  U.S.S.R., 297,000 ....B 4 36
Köniz, Switzerland, 30,600 ....D 3 30
Konstanz, Germany, 61,617 ......C 5 23
Konya, Turkey, 157,934 ....E 4 46
Köpenick, Germany, 52,294 ......F 4 23
Kopeysk, U.S.S.R., 156,000 ......G 4 38
Korçe, Albania, 43,700 ....E 5 35
Koriyama, Japan, 240,000 ....F 3 52
Kotrijk (Courtrai), Belg.,
  45,310 ....B 6 20
Košice, Czechoslovakia, 115,332 ..F 2 33
Kostroma, U.S.S.R., 223,000 .....F 3 36
Koszalin, Poland, 56,800 ....C 1 21
Kota, India, 213.005 ....D 3 48
Kota Bharu, Malaysia, 38,103 ....C 6 53
Kota Kinabalu,* Sabah,
  Malaysia, 21,704 ....F 4 54
Kotka, Finland, 33,953 ....P 6 19
Kouvola, Finland, 25.275 ....P 6 19
Kovrov, U.S.S.R., 123,000 ....F 3 36

Kowloon, Hong Kong, 692,800......J 7 51
Kozhikode, India, 333,980 ....D 6 49
Kragujevac, Yugoslavia, 56,000....E 3 34
Kramatorsk, U.S.S.R., 151,000 ...E 5 37
Krasnodar, U.S.S.R., 465,000 ......E 6 37
Krasnoyarsk, U.S.S.R.,
  648,000 ....K 4 39
Krefeld, Germany, 228,726 ....B 3 23
Kremenchug, U.S.S.R., 148,000 ...D 5 37
Krems, Austria, 21,046 ....C 2 32
Kristiansand, Norway, 52,542 ....F 8 19
Kristianstad, Sweden, 27,527 .....J 9 19
Krivoy Rog, U.S.S.R.,
  573,000 ....D 5 37
Kroonstad, O.F.S., 50,700 ....M17 65
Krung Thep (Bangkok),*
  Thailand, 1,299,528 ....C 4 53
Kuala Lumpur,* Malaysia,
  325,000 ....C 5 54
Kuching,* Sarawak, Malaysia,
  56,000 ....E 5 54
Kudus, Indon., 62,130 ....J 2 55
Kumagaya, Japan, 119,000 ....E 3 52
Kumamoto, Japan, 432,000 ...... C 4 52
Kumasi, Ghana, 281,600 ....F10 62
Kumbakonam, India, 112,971 ....D 6 49
Kunming, China, 900,000 ....F 6 50
Kuopio, Finland, 63,800 ....Q 5 18
Kure, Japan, 237,000 ....D 4 52
Kurgan, U.S.S.R., 244,000 ....G 4 38
Kurnool, India, 136,682 ....D 5 49
Kursk, U.S.S.R., 284,000 ....E 4 37
Kushiro, Japan, 195,000 ....G 2 52
Kustanay, U.S.S.R., 123,000 ......G 4 38
Kut, Iraq, 42,116 ....E 3 44
Kütahya, Turkey, 49,301 ....C 3 44
Kutaisi, U.S.S.R., 161,000 ....F 6 37
Kuybyshev, U.S.S.R., 1.047,000...H 4 37
Kwangju, S. Korea, 403,737 ....B 4 52
Kweilin, China, 170,000 ....G 6 51
Kweisui (Huhehot), China,
  320,000 ....H 3 51
Kweiyang, China, 530,000 ....G 6 50
Kyoto, Japan, 1,418,933 ....E 4 52
La Asunción, Venezuela,
  5,517 ....H 1 68
La Ceiba, Honduras, 33,934 ......D 3 78
La Chaux-de-Fonds, Switzerland,
  42,800 ....C 2 30
Lachine, Quebec, 41,503 ....H 4 89
La Coruña, Spain, 161,260 ....B 1 26
La Crosse, Wis., 51,153 ....D 8 191
Lae, Papua New Guinea, 12,392...B 7 54
Lafayette, Ind., 44,955 ....D 4 126
Lagos,* Nigeria, 841,749 ....G10 62
La Guaira, Venezuela, 20,497 ......G 1 68
Lahore, Pakistan, 1,296,477 ......C 2 48
Lahti, Finland, 87,237 ....O 6 19
Lake Charles, La., 77,998 ....D 6 134
Lakewood, Calif., 82,973 ....C11 113
Lakewood, Colo., 92,787 ....J 3 115
Lakewood, Ohio, 70,173 ....G 9 167
La Línea, Spain, 58,169 ....D 4 26
Lalitpur, Nepal, 47,713 ....E 3 48
La Louvière, Belgium, 23,447 .....D 7 20
Lampang, Thailand, 36,488 ....B 3 53
Lancaster, England, 48,170 ....E 3 17
Lancaster, Pa., 57,690 ....K 5 173
Lanchow, China, 732,000 ....F 4 50
Landshut, Germany, 51,393 ......E 4 23
Landskrona, Sweden, 32,079 .....H 9 19
Lansing,* Mich., 131.546 ....E 6 143
Lanús, Argentina, 381,561 ....O12 71
Laon, France, 25,623 ....E 3 24
La Oroya, Peru, 32.600 ....E 6 68
La Paz,* Bolivia, 525,000 ....G 7 68
La Plata, Argentina, †330.310 ...O12 71
Lappeenranta, Fin., 50,543 ....P 6 19
Laredo, Tex., 69,024 ....E10 181
La Rioja, Argentina, 35,431 ....G 9 70

Lárisa, Greece, 55,391 ....F 6 35
La Rochelle, France, 72,075 ....C 4 25
La Serena, Chile, †71,898 ....F 9 70
Las Palmas,* Canary Islands,
  Spain, 166,236 ....B 4 26
La Spezia, Italy, 111,768 ....B 2 28
Las Vegas, Nev., 125,787 ....C 3 154
Latakia, Syria, 72,378 ....F 5 46
La Tuque, Quebec, 12,067 ....E 2 88
Launceston, Tasmania, 37,217 ...H 8 59
Lausanne, Switzerland, 138,300....C 3 30
Laval, France, 45,051 ....C 3 24
Laval, Quebec, 246,243 ....H 4 89
Lawrence, Mass., 66,915 ....K 2 141
Lawton, Okla., 74,470 ....F 5 168
Leamington, Eng., 45,090 ....F 4 17
Lebanon, Pa., 28,572 ....K 5 173
Lecce, Italy, 68,385 ....G 4 29
Lecco, Italy, 47,468 ....B 2 28
Le Creusot, France, 33,581 ....F 4 25
Leeds, England, 503,720 ....F 4 17
Leeuwarden, Netherlands,
  100,006 ....G 1 20
Legaspi, Philippines, 69,000 ......G 3 55
Leghorn, Italy, 152,517 ....C 3 28
Legnica, Poland, 73,400 ....C 3 21
Le Havre, France, 198,021 ....C 3 24
Leicester, England, 278,470 ......F 4 17
Leiden, Netherlands, 101,221 ....E 3 20
Leigh, England, 46,200 ....G 2 16
Leipzig, Germany, 590,291 ....E 3 23
Le Mans, France, 140,521 ....C 3 24
Leninakan, U.S.S.R., 164,000 ....F 6 37
Leningrad, U.S.S.R., 3,513,000 ...C 3 36
Leninsk-Kuznetskiy, U.S.S.R.,
  128,000 ....J 4 38
Lens, France, 41,800 ....E 2 24
Leoben, Austria, 36,257 ....C 3 32
León, Mexico, †453,976 ....J 6 80
León, Nicaragua, 44,053 ....D 4 78
León, Spain, 73,483 ....D 1 26
Le Puy, France, 24,816 ....F 5 25
Lérida, Spain, 50,047 ....G 2 27
Les Cayes, Haiti, †95,446 ....C 3 76
Lethbridge, Alberta, 46,752 ....D 5 97
Leuven (Louvain), Belgium,
  32,125 ....E 6 20
Levallois-Perret, France, 58,810...A 1 24
Leverkusen, Ger., 111,588 ....B 3 23
Lévis, Quebec, 17,819 ....J 3 89
Lewisham, Eng., 282,080 ....B 5 17
Lewiston, Me., 41,779 ....C 7 137
Lexington, Ky., 108,137 ....J 4 133
Lhasa,* Tibet, China, 70,000 .....D 6 50
Liaoyang, China, 169,000 ....K 3 51
Liaoyüan, China, 177,000 ....L 3 51
Liberec, Czechoslovakia,
  71,000 ....C 1 32
Libourne, France, 19,981 ....C 5 25
Libreville,* Gabon, †57,000 ....H11 64
Licata, Sicily, Italy, 38,222 ....D 6 29
Lichtenberg, Ger., 62,841 ....F 4 23
Lidingö, Sweden, 35,400 ....H 1 18
Liège, Belgium, 150,127 ....G 6 20
Lierre (Lier), Belgium, 28,557 .....E 5 20
Lille, France, 189,697 ....E 2 24
Lilongwe,* Malawi, 19,425 ....N14 65
Lima, Ohio, 53,734 ....B 4 166
Lima,* Peru, 2,541,300 ....E 6 68
Limassol, Cyprus, 46,500 ....E 5 46
Limerick, Ireland, 50,786 ....B 4 17
Limoges, France, 127.605 ....D 5 25
Limón, Costa Rica, 30,676 ....F 6 79
Linares, Chile, †61,011 ....F11 70
Linares, Spain, 50,527 ....E 3 26
Lincoln, England, 75,570 ....F 4 17
Lincoln,* Neb., 149,518 ....H 4 153
Lindsay, Ontario, 12,834 ....F 3 91
Linköping, Sweden, 77,881 ....K 7 19
Linz, Austria, 205,762 ....C 2 32
Lipetsk, U.S.S.R., 290,000 ....E 4 37